PALESTINIAN WOMEN'S ACTIVISM

Gender, Culture, and Politics in the Middle East
miriam cooke, Simona Sharoni, and Suad Joseph, *Series Editors*

Palestinian Women's Activism

NATIONALISM, SECULARISM, ISLAMISM

ISLAH JAD

Syracuse University Press

For a listing of books published and distributed by Syracuse University Press,
visit www.SyracuseUniversityPress.syr.edu.

ISBN: 978-0-8156-3608-3 (hardcover) 978-0-8156-3614-4 (paperback)
978-0-8156-5459-9 (e-book)

Library of Congress Cataloging-in-Publication Data
Names: Jād, Iṣlāḥ, author.
Title: Palestinian women's activism : nationalism, secularism, Islamism / Islah Jad.
Other titles: Gender, culture, and politics in the Middle East.
Description: First edition. | Syracuse, New York : Syracuse University Press, 2018. |
    Series: Gender, culture, and politics in the Middle East | Includes bibliographical
    references and index.
Identifiers: LCCN 2018051492 (print) | LCCN 2018046834 (ebook) | ISBN
    9780815636083 (hardcover : alk. paper) | ISBN 9780815636144 (pbk. : alk.
    paper) | ISBN 9780815654599 (ebook) | ISBN 9780815654599 (E-book)
Subjects: LCSH: Women, Palestinian Arab—Political activity—West Bank. |
    Women, Palestinian Arab—Political activity—Gaza Strip. | Feminism—West
    Bank. | Feminism—Gaza Strip. | Non-governmental organizations—West Bank.
    | Non-governmental organizations—Gaza Strip. | Islam and politics—West
    Bank. | Islam and politics—Gaza Strip. | Palestinian Federation of Women's
    Action Committees. | Women's Center for Legal Aid and Counselling. |Ḥizb
    al-Khalāṣ al-Waṭanī al-Islāmī. |Ittiḥād Jamʻīyāt al-Marʻah al-Filasṭīnīyah.
Classification: LCC HQ1236.5.W45 J34 2018 (ebook) | LCC HQ1236.5.W45
    (print) | DDC 305.42095694/2—dc23
LC record available at https://lccn.loc.gov/2018051492

Contents

Contents

Illustrations

Preface

THE ESTABLISHMENT of the Palestinian Authority (PA) in 1994 pursuant to the Oslo Agreement heralded major transformations not only in Palestinians' governance, but in the society as a whole. My original aim in this research was to explore the implications of the PA's establishment for the Palestinian women's movement from a gender perspective, and to examine the changes occurring within the women's movement during a new era of "state building." I viewed my research as involving a novel subject in its exploration of the incongruity of a state—or, more precisely, a quasi-state—born after long years of colonization but that could not be called postcolonial as colonization was still flagrantly manifest in all aspects of Palestinian life. I was particularly intrigued by the ways in which this quasi-state would handle issues related to the control of its resources and development planning and how those issues would influence gender relations and the women's movement. I was also curious to probe the difficult connections between a national liberation movement, geared to mobilizing its constituencies for a long struggle, and a new state bureaucracy in need of different types of structures, constituencies, and discourses. The study of the Palestinian women's movement would be no less intriguing. It is concurrently faced with three major tasks: continuing the national struggle and participating in state building while at the same time pressing for women's rights. Like women's movements worldwide, the Palestinian women's movement has grappled with both "old" agendas of mobilization and liberation as well as new ones involving women's equality and empowerment. Under normal circumstances, it is difficult to straddle these two agendas—all the more so when there is an extraordinary situation in which the Israeli Occupation threatens the very physical existence of both state and society.

The extremity of the situation became shockingly apparent in March 2002, when women leaders examined the possibility of pouring into the streets to stop the advance of Israeli tanks reoccupying Palestinian cities. The conclusion was simple but very revealing: "We are not organized," they said. The capacity of not only women, but of many other social groups, to be mobilized had evidently *diminished* during the era of supposed state building. I realized that I might have been pursuing a passing moment, a vanishing project that was being overtaken by history.

The various conflicts I was tracing among different women's groups that were trying to position themselves and articulate new feminist interests and discourse all assumed the existence of a state apparatus to which they could direct their demands, protests, or opposition. But the nascent state structures were clearly ill equipped to respond. The physical destruction of most official buildings, including the headquarters of the PA's chief executive, along with many other institutions and resources, forced me to shift my focus to the arena of civil society and the opportunities there for women to continue resisting the Occupation while working toward a more equitable gender order. The new Palestinian civil society that had emerged, though it provided a forum to discuss democratization, human rights, and women's rights, was largely depoliticized and had effectively lost its own previous capacity to organize and mobilize different groups, and in particular, women's groups aiming to combat the Occupation.

A central contributing factor to these developments was a shift in the role of the NGO sector that led to pressure on women's groups to alter their shared agenda from one that combined the national struggle with women's emancipation into one targeting the state to claim women's rights. Many successful women's grassroots organizations increasingly came under the influence of NGO practices or were outright transformed into NGOs. One of my main arguments is that the transformation from organizations of mass mobilization into NGOs was ultimately disempowering in that it weakened the mobilizing potential of secular feminist women's organizations and depoliticized their activism. I aim to contribute a critical perspective to the growing trend in Middle East studies in which secular, feminist NGOs are depicted as the "modern" and democratic "agents of civil society" (Moghadam 1997, 25; Kandil 1995), by problematizing the unqualified and interchangeable use of the terms "NGO" and "social movement" in the Palestinian case, in particular, and in the Middle East, in general (Kandil 1995; Moghadam 1997; Bishara 1996; Beydoun 2002; Barghouti 1994; Chatty and Rabo 1997; Shalabi 2001). Many scholars view the proliferation of NGOs in the Middle East as evidence of a vibrant civil society and paradoxically as counterhegemonic to Islamist discourse (Norton 1993, 1995; Ibrahim 1993, 1995; al-Sayyid 1993; Moghadam 1997). However, little is done to evaluate the impact of the proliferation of NGOs on the empowerment of the different social groups they claim to represent and in their capacity to present a viable alternative to Islamist groups. Specifically, there has been little attempt to verify whether they succeed in mobilizing or organizing different groups in pursuit of their rights. In addition, few studies on the Middle East focus on how NGOs affect and interact with other forms of social organization such as unions, political parties, or social movements involving students, women, or workers (Hanafi and Tabar 2002; Beinin and Vairel 2011).

In an attempt to critically read the history and evolution of the Palestinian women's movement from its inception, I reviewed the literature on Palestinian society in general and Palestinian women's activism in particular starting from the turn of the twentieth century, focusing on the span from the 1930s through the 1980s. I undertook new field research to cover the period from the beginning of the 1990s, with a special focus on the political and social processes that the Oslo Agreement triggered, leaving deep imprints on all forms of social organization in the Occupied Territories. The initial phase of this research, which took place between 2000 and 2004—encompassing most of the period of the second intifada—examined the diminishing space for the Palestinian women's movement that used to be linked to political parties under the umbrella of the PLO. It also examined the rising power, since 1987, of the Islamists of Hamas and their politically and socially engaged female cohort, newcomers to the scene of women's activism in Palestine. As a consequence of this diversification, amplified by the establishment in 1995 of Hamas's Islamic National Salvation Party and its influential Women's Action Department, I speak of Palestinian women's *movements* in the plural from the mid-1990s forward. The legislative elections of 2006 and subsequent political schism of 2007 inspired me to renew my research to trace developments under the two parallel governments that resulted, the secular-nationalist one in the West Bank and the Islamist one in Gaza. This stage of research, which figures in the epilogue, reinforced the focal argument that the NGO-ization of feminist organizations has undermined their mobilizing potential and led to their depoliticization, leaving a vacuum that was filled by the Islamists.

As my research illuminated the relevance of the growing power of the Islamists, now taking on the mantle of national struggle despite their being widely seen as undemocratic, fundamentalist, and not part of "true" civil society, I took aim at another mark: to reconceive the juxtaposition of the image of the secular, feminist "modern" agent of civil society with that of the Islamist woman, seen by many Palestinian feminists as the "traditional," "backward," and anti-feminist "moving tent."[1] This juxtaposition is portrayed in Islamist discourse as a conflict between the Islamist woman "giver" to her nation under Occupation and the secular feminist woman "taker," who makes claims for her nation while ignoring its plight. These are caricatures, I argue, that do nothing to elucidate the growing power of the Islamists in civil society in Palestine and the broader Middle East. Most crucially, they hinder the recognition of possible common ground between women's groups.

1. The "tent" metaphor refers to their long, usually dark-colored robes and veils.

By studying, for the first time, women activists in the National Islamic Salvation Party—a component of Hamas—against the background of the gender ideology and daily practice of the party and women's activism, I aim to problematize the relationship between feminism, secularism, and Islam (seen as intrinsically anti-secular and consequently anti-modern) (Bill and Springborg 1990; Lewis 1964, 1988; Kedourie 1992; Crone 1980). Many scholars have portrayed Islam as a threat to secularism, which is understood as the total separation of the realm of politics from the realm of religion (al-Azmeh 1996; Roy 1999; Tibi 1987). I concur with Asad's (2003) approach of not separating the two realms but rather of examining the historical circumstances in which the secular political project or the Islamist vision prevails (189).

Debates on Islam and feminism have centered on the compatibility of Islam with women's rights, and some have suggested that Islamist movements might be empowering in certain circumstances (White 2002; Haeri 1993; Mir-Hosseini 1996, 2003; Moghadam 1988; Najmabadi 1998; Hoodfar 1995a, 1995b; Afshar 1994; Afkhami 1994; Göçek and Balaghi 1994; Mahmood 2005). *Shari'a* law has been a terrain of contestation and power struggle between Islamists and secularist feminists, not only in Palestine but in the Middle East at large. The Islamists seek to preserve *shari'a* law as one step toward the Islamization of all laws in their quest for an Islamic state, while secularist feminists want to replace it with secular laws based on individual rights and driven by the principle of total equality. Recent works by feminists (Karam 1998; Mir-Hosseini 1996, 2003, 1999; Badran 1994, 1995; Anwar 2009) appear more keen to accommodate the Islamists and present Islam and feminism as compatible through the flexibility of the religious text and through *ijtihad* (independent intellectual investigation of religious texts). This hermeneutic approach contrasts with an approach that focuses on the actual lived experience of women under Islamist rule or secular nationalism (Hale 1994; White 2002; Kandiyoti 1991b, 1996; Mahmood 2009).

Based on my empirical findings, I argue that gender roles and relations and women's rights are not immutable under Islam but rather are evolving in the context of the activism of its women's movement and its changing identity. The articulation of women's rights depends on many internal and external factors. Internal factors include the dynamics of the Islamist movement itself, women's place within the hierarchy of the Islamist movement, and women's ability to establish an autonomous agenda. External factors include the discourses and activism of secular feminist movements that strongly influence the debate on women's rights in the Islamist movement. The brand of "feminism" created by Islamists, I argue, is contingent upon and reactive to a secular backdrop. It has proven difficult, with the data at hand, to categorize any form of Islamist "feminism" without first scrutinizing the rejoinders it offers to modernist, secularist principles. Thus, the notion of Islam's inner logic might be better conceived of not as fixed, but as a "reactive" position that is in tension and dialogue with contending ideologies.

In sum, the relative positions of and interrelationship between secular and Islamist women's activism in the post-Oslo Palestinian sphere have been broadly misunderstood in two fundamental ways. First, it has been widely assumed that Western development institutions and donors' ever-growing connections with and influence over the women's groups that developed out of the PLO and their successors in the PA have "of course" benefitted the latter; I show, in fact, that those connections and that influence have weakened secular women's groups both conceptually and practically, greatly strengthening the hand of their Islamist counterparts. Second, Islamist women's activism is routinely described as if it takes place in an ideological bubble, in which all the significant influences are largely unchanging religious ones; I show, in fact, that even as the Islamists have gained in relative efficacy, they have developed their concepts and strategies in a process that involves constant engagement, both oppositional and appropriative, with those of their secular counterparts.

My attempt to problematize the perception of Hamas's ideology and practices as immutable and "frozen" on the part of some women's groups, and in particular the feminist NGO sector, is specifically prompted by the ongoing debate on proposed reforms of *shari'a* law, the implications of which extend well beyond Palestinian society. I am searching for a common ground for better understanding, recognition, and the encouragement of a spirit of "dialogic engagement" (Beinin and Stork 1997, 22) between different women's groups and activisms. The critical pursuit of "dialogic engagement" might help women pay more attention to historical specificity, as well as clarify the nuances of difference and similarity between and within Islamist movements across the Muslim world. It might also assist in the effort to put forward aspirations for social change, whether those of Islamist or secular groups, in more workable ways that take into consideration a broad range of factors related to history, society, politics, economics, and culture.

Acronyms

DFLP Democratic Front for the Liberation of Palestine. Founded as the Popular Democratic Front for the Liberation of Palestine (PDFLP) in 1969, following a split from the PFLP.

Fateh Largest faction of the PLO, founded and commenced military activity in 1965. Fateh is a reverse acronym derived from the Arabic for the group's original name, the Palestinian National Liberation Movement.

GUPW General Union of Palestinian Women, PLO-affiliated women's organization, formed in 1965.

Hamas The Islamic Resistance Movement, formed in Gaza in 1987 (Hamas is an acronym from the group's Arabic name). Offshoot of the Muslim Brothers group in Palestine, founded in 1946. An integrated political/military organization until the formation of the Izz al-Din al-Qassam military wing in 1991.

IMCAW Inter-Ministerial Committee for the Advancement of Women's Status, formed by the Palestinian Authority in 1994 as a quasi-governmental agency with the tasks of "developing" women and gender mainstreaming.

JCW Jerusalem Center for Women, founded in 1993. As a result of Jerusalem Link, a Palestinian-Israeli women's joint venture, two independent women's centers were founded: the Palestinian JCW and the Israeli Bat Shalom.

PA Palestinian Authority, formally established in 1993, after the signing of the Oslo Agreement between the PLO and Israel. Active originally in Gaza and Jericho as of 1994. Also commonly referred to as the Palestinian National Authority (PNA).

PCP   Palestinian Communist Party. Now the Palestine Popular Party (PPP).

PFLP   Popular Front for the Liberation of Palestine, founded in 1967.

PFWAC   Palestinian Federation of Women's Action Committees, DFLP-affiliated. Outgrowth of the Women's Work Committee, founded in 1978.

PLO   Palestine Liberation Organization, created in 1964 as the umbrella group for most major Palestinian military organizations. The Palestinian Communist Party was allowed to join at a later stage. Currently, Hamas and Islamic Jihad refuse to join unless general elections at all levels are organized.

PWC   Palestinian Women's Committees. Affiliated with the PFLP, they were founded in 1982. Now collectively known as the Union of Palestinian Women's Committees (UPWC).

WAC   Women's Affairs Center. Independent women's study center, established in Nablus in 1988, then in Gaza in 1989.

WAD   Women's Action Department, a division of Hamas's legal political arm, the Islamic National Salvation Party.

WATC   Women's Affairs Technical Committee, formed in 1992. Coalition involving most of the Palestinian women's organizations affiliated with political parties, as well as some independent women's centers and groups.

WCLAC   Women's Center for Legal Aid and Counseling, established by the PFWAC in 1991. Later became independent.

WSC   Women's Study Center, established by the PFWAC in 1989. Later became independent.

WSWC   Women's Social Work Committees, Fateh-affiliated. Created in 1983.

PALESTINIAN WOMEN'S ACTIVISM

1

Uprooted Nation, Stateless Nationalism

Palestinian Women's Activism in Context

THE AIM OF THIS CHAPTER is to place Palestinian women's activism in the context of Palestine's political history of nationalist struggle. Women had to forge a space for themselves in the national struggle, since the construction of Palestinian nationalism centered on the image of the male fighter as liberator of the nation, and on struggle and sacrifice as hallmarks of patriotism. Women's activism introduced some changes to the gender imagery of Palestinian nationalism but did not reach the point of changing the prevailing gender order. The Palestinian women's movement was, and continues to be, led by a middle-class urban elite. The discourse of the "modern" versus the "traditional" employed by this elite resulted, historically speaking, in the marginalization of the important role played by rural and, more recently, refugee women. The moment in the 1940s that this movement was able to transcend class and regional divides (urban versus rural and later refugees), it managed to mobilize and organize women on a large scale, incorporating them into the national struggle. A mirror image of the urban elite's discourse was later used by the Islamists to undermine that elite's leadership role. Gender was thus flexible, yielding different images and different sorts of women's participation in each phase of nationalism, but central to all of them.

1

The establishment of the Palestinian Authority (PA) in 1994 marked a turning point in the history of the Palestinian national movement and the Palestinian women's movement. Israeli harassment and land confiscation discredited the PA and gave power to the Islamists as the bearers of the flag of "true" national liberation. The PA was the impetus for major changes in all Palestinian political movements. In the Palestinian women's movement, power was granted to new feminist elites working from within civil society in NGOs or from within the PA apparatuses, leading to the emergence of "femocrats."[1] This changed the composition and the strategies of what must now be categorized as the secular women's movement at the expense of women cadres of rural or refugee background. Islamists are the main contesters of this hegemony.

The Trouble with Nationalism(s)

Palestinian nationalism projected a contradictory image of Palestinian women and their movement during the Mandate period. On one hand, women were seen as the "modernizers" and civilizing agents of the long-awaited independent nation. This enabled the women's movement to develop and become visible. On the other hand, women were also seen as the emblem of their nation's "authenticity" and of historic social patterns. In this role, women were confined to "private" space as

1. "Femocrat" appears to have been an Australian neologism for a feminist bureaucrat; it is equivalent to the term "state feminist" as used in Scandinavia. The term originally referred to women who are employed within state bureaucratic positions to work on advancing the position of women in the wider society through the development of equal opportunity and anti-discrimination strategies of change. This professionalization of feminism and its incorporation into the state have been significant points of tension for feminists who identify with grassroots women's movements, and who were able to regard their ideological commitment as uncompromised either by motives of career advancement or incorporation into the agenda of a state still under the control of men. Femocrats are distinguished from women career public servants in non-femocrat positions, the former occupying career positions that feminism has legitimized (Yeatman 1990, 65). See chapter 2 for more on the femocrat in the Palestinian context.

the wards of their male relatives. Due to what Chatterjee (1993) calls the "inherent contradictoriness" in nationalist thinking (38), "modernity" claims to "advance" and "progress" the nation while at the same time preserving its distinctiveness and particular traditions.

These troubled links between Palestinian women and their national movement were comparable to experiences in other third world countries in which nationalist vanguards were acting as the "modernizers" of their nation and their women. As Jayawardena (1986) notes in her analysis of women's roles in nationalist movements throughout the third world, "the status of women in society was the popular barometer of 'civilization'" (8). Education, freedom of movement, and monogamy became hallmarks of "civilized" modernity. British, Arab, and Zionist leaders all gave their attention to the process of "modernizing" women as a measure of the legitimacy of their power in Palestine (Katz 1996, 93; 2003; Fleischmann 2003; Chatterjee 1993).

I would propose an alternative model of investigating the histories of the struggles of different social groups. Nationalist projects often articulate different interests, from political autonomy to liberation from economic oppression that may concern different social groups to very different degrees. This was the case in Mandate Palestine, where the interests of the national elite, men and women, differed from those of peasants in many ways. The first tended to be conciliatory toward the colonial power, while the latter saw in the presence of this power their utter demise and destruction.

Dominant accounts generally define the *fellaheen* (peasants) as "traditional, backward, and conservative," as "activated by tribal and religious loyalties" (Budeiri 1979, 46–47), and as "too isolated, ignorant and poor" to play a significant role in the national movement (Lesch 1979, 17). In the same vein, rural women have been portrayed as victims of ignorance and poverty and the object of middle-class women's charity (Mogannam 1937; Khartabil 1995; Shahid 1999). These views consider peasants, and especially women peasants, as incapable of political initiative or collective action. Swedenburg (1988) showed that while subordinate to the rule of the notables, the peasantry nonetheless possessed a significant tradition of opposition to the hegemony of the British and Palestinian elite, as reflected in the Great Revolt of 1936–39. As Gramsci noted, the hegemony of a dominant class is never "total or exclusive"; it is, rather, a process, a relation of dominance that has "continually to be renewed, recreated, defended and modified" (Williams 1977, 112–13).

Thus, instead of ascribing particular developments to "tradition" or to "Islam," I shall seek to understand the ways specific cultural and religious currents influenced the behavior of particular groups in particular circumstances, and how the social and political settings in which movements occurred helped shape the choice of strategies and thus the outcomes as well. By situating the movements discussed in this chapter in a broad context, it is possible to see more clearly the connections between changes within groups and their effects on society, the economy, and the ruling power (whether colonial or national).

Nationalism and Women's Activism under the British Mandate (1918–1948)

This section focuses on the relationship between national liberation and women's emancipation during the successive waves of national struggle. Palestinian national movements, whether during the British Mandate or in their reinvigoration in the mid-1960s, are evaluated by many feminist scholars as, at best, unable to articulate a coherent vision or platform on gender (Sayigh 1988; Peteet 1991; Jad 1991), and at worst, as conservative, traditional, and chauvinist (Massad 1995; Parker 1999; Budeiri 1995; Rubenberg 2001). I argue here that while the successive Palestinian national movements were unable to articulate a coherent platform on gender, their fragmented gender views came about as a reaction to women's activism. Women's activism, in turn, was, to a great extent, the product of the national movement and its various factions. In this chapter and the next, I examine the gender agenda of the secularist national movements. In chapters 3 and 4, I examine the ideology of the Palestinian Islamists, who, like the nationalists, were also reactive to women's activism.

The link between nationalist and gender discourses has been analyzed in different historical and cultural contexts. Kandiyoti (1991a) argues, for example, that the integration of women into modern "nationhood" follows a different trajectory from that of men. For instance, the protection of women's "sexuality" constitutes a "crucial distinction between the nation and its 'others'" (430). Common to the various analyses is the centrality given to the role of women in nationalist projects. Anthias and Yuval-Davis identify "five major . . . ways in which women have tended to participate in ethnic and national processes and in relation to state practices":

(a) as biological reproducers of members of ethnic collectivities;

(b) as reproducers of the boundaries of ethnic/national groups;

(c) as participating centrally in the ideological reproduction of the collectivity and as transmitters of its culture;

(d) as signifiers of ethnic/national differences—as a focus and symbol in ideological discourses used in the construction, reproduction and transformation of ethnic/national categories;

(e) as participants in national, economic, political and military struggles (Anthias and Yuval-Davis 1989, 7).

It is important to bear in mind that there is no unitary category of women that can be unproblematically conceived as the focus of ethnic, national, or state policies and discourses. In the Middle East, nationalist and liberationist movements animated women as actors and as symbols (Badran 1995; Afkhami and Friedle 1997). Women constitute the nation's actual symbolic figuration (Anthias and Yuval-Davis 1989, 10), while distinctions between ethnic groups or nations are constituted centrally by the sexual behavior of women.[2]

During the Mandate period, the Palestinian national movement ascribed a new role to urban elite women as the companions of men to save the nation (Mogannam 1937; Fleischmann 2003). But this

2. Several writers looking at different regions point to the ways in which dress and sexual behavior take on symbolic value in the struggle over cultural and national identity. Whether Sikh or Cypriot (Anthias and Yuval-Davis 1989), Bangladeshi (Kabeer 1989), Iranian or Afghani (Moghadam 1992), women are all expected to behave in sexually appropriate ways. If they do not, then neither they nor their children may be considered part of the community.

new role was contested by peasant men, and women for that matter, who sought to affirm their power through their involvement in the struggle for national liberation. This contestation was not related, I argue, to peasant "traditionalism," but rather was a reflection of class antagonism directed against the cultural hegemony of the urban elite, including the women; it was a way to assert their newly empowered peasant identity through their collective participation in the Great Revolt. The main strategy of the national elite (male and female) was to hold the colonizers accountable to their own value system and to their discourse as "modernizers" promising emancipation (Chatterjee 1993). This recourse to persuading the British of the legitimacy of Palestinian aspirations was largely ignored, during the 1936 revolt, by the peasants, as rural villages became increasingly impoverished. More assertive and ultimately violent resistance was not a strategy developed or planned by the urban elite, as they were not the ones to bear the brunt of the British oppression. The collective act of resistance gave peasants more power as a group distinct from the urban elite.

The tradition of women's activism was, like that of the male elite, more pacific. Women in Palestine, as in other countries, began this tradition by establishing charitable organizations in urban centers (Badran 1995; Baron 1994; Chatty and Rabo 1997; Joseph 1997). Women leaders were drawn from "bourgeois and rich families as well as female relatives of civil servants" in cities like Jerusalem, Jaffa, and Haifa (Khartabil 1995, 57). They were mainly Christians empowered by the emergence of missionary education (al-Tibawi 1956; Shahid 1999; Mogannam 1937; Muslih 1988) and they focused on the education of girls and the relief of the poor and sick (Khartabil 1995; Jammal 1985). From its charitable origins, the Palestinian women's movement was shaped to a great extent by the deterioration of the political situation prompted by British colonial policies and the brutality of the Mandate in suppressing the Palestinian revolts, the rise of the Palestinian resistance to the Zionist project, and the consolidation of the Palestinian national movement in the 1920s and the 1930s.

These events pushed women to try to transcend religious boundaries.[3] Differences between Christians and Muslims, and between rural and urban dwellers, however, hindered the realization that patriarchy was the common enemy to struggle against (Alexandra Aboud in Fleischmann 2003, 274).[4]

The national turmoil also led women's groups to widen the scope of their programs and develop their organizations. The establishment of the Arab Women's Association in 1930 was an important step in pooling women's activism. However, it failed to create a national coalition or a national women's organization (Mogannam 1937; Jad 1990; Peteet 1991; Fleischmann 2003). Nor could the loose coalition of women's charitable organizations act as a unifying national force. As is the case with women's NGOs today, each women's charitable organization had its different bylaws and objectives. These decentralized organizations met in response to the deteriorating political situation or in support of men's delegations that were negotiating with the British government (Mogannam 1937; Khartabil 1995). During

3. Mogannam (1937) states that this was not the first time that a women's society with mixed membership was established in Jerusalem. As early as 1919 an Arab ladies' association was formed for similar purposes. Madame Faiz Bey Haddad, one of the leading promoters and organizers of this society, was delegated to convey to King Feisal in Damascus in 1919 the congratulations of the Arab women of Jerusalem on his accession to the throne, and to seek his aid of the society (56). One might add that any emphasis on mixed membership could be attributed not to religious tolerance but rather to the pursuit of national interests.

4. One might argue also that this difference in religious identity inhibits a unifying women's movement from taking a critical stand vis-à-vis prevailing religious conservatism. Christian women had greater representation in the leadership of the women's movement than in the population (25 percent and 11 percent, respectively). This overrepresentation might not have been helpful in confronting a social order set by the Muslim majority. It is interesting to note the different political demands made of women in the 1930s compared to the 1990s. In the first case, women were called upon to show more Palestinianism, while in the latter, during the first intifada, they were asked to show more "Islamism."

the Great Revolt, the social work of providing charity was politicized when women were asked by the rebels to distribute food and medicine to besieged villages (Khartabil 1995, 76). But it was not until 1944 that that activists formed the Arab Women's Union, in a fledgling attempt to unify their ranks on a national level.

The ability to run or head a women's organization was largely determined by a woman's class background and her exposure to Western education (Mogannam 1937; Khartabil 1995; Zu'aytir 1980).[5] A wide cultural gap separated women peasants from the urban national elite.[6] This was mainly due to the lack of universal education for women, combined with the elite women's political inability to use the press or printed media to reach out to peasant women (Mogannam 1937), as well as the obstacles they faced in moving about freely in the

5. The name of Maimana al-Qassam—daughter of Izz al-Din al-Qassam, the popular leader in Haifa's slums who triggered the 1936 revolt—figured only once in the 1938 Women of the East Conference. Without a suitable class background, her father's renown was insufficient to win her prominence in women's organizations. Khartabil (1995) relates that Maimana moved to Tulkarem after the death of her father and was mentioned as a member of the local charitable association of which Khartabil herself, also a newcomer to the city, was asked by a group of women to assume the presidency. In contrast to Maimana, Khartabil had an upper-class background, a high level of education, and was married to a senior doctor in the British Mandate government (70–71).

6. The Palestinian elite benefited from the great increase in imports during the 1930s and 1940s, changing the upper class lifestyle which increasingly encompassed luxurious receptions, extravagant weddings, and Westernized modes of dress. As described by a member of one of the richest Christian families at the time: "We used to travel to Lebanon to spend the summer and weekly we used to organise receptions in turn in each one of the high families constituting our community. In these receptions, women used to display the best they have, dressed in the latest fashion cloth, they distribute invitation cards to the invited families stating the date and the place of the coming reception. The reception starts at early Sundays noon, by offering fresh juices, light snacks, meals, fruits, desserts all made by women who were competing in regard of organisation, cleanliness, cleverness, elegance and high manners. We used to speak in French and invite Muslim well known families" (Shahid 1999, 32).

urban public space. Female peasants did not suffer the same restrictions (Tucker 1993).

The continuously evolving cultural construction of national identity (Schlesinger 1987, 261) helps explain the backlash against elite women during the late-1930s era of the Great Revolt. Thus, one can see the recourse to tradition, in this case imposing the veil on mainly *urban* women,[7] not as "traditionalism" but rather as a "new" peasant invention to assert their own power, not least since they did not impose the same on their own women.[8] In this crisis, elite women were abandoned by their male national leaders and were called upon to dress modestly like their "sisters, the warriors of the villages" (Swedenburg 1995, 181). This led to the withdrawal of elite women from public space to focus their efforts on "social and development issues" rather than on demonstrations and anti-government denunciations (Fleischmann 2003, 178). This decline in women's political activism could also be attributed to the fact that urban elites and their families fled, mostly to Lebanon and Egypt, during the Great Revolt (Shahid 1999, 68, 113, 117, 123). The pretensions of the nationalist male elite to modernity faltered when confronted by the militancy of the rebellious peasantry, leaving their women in

7. According to Zu'aytir (1980), one of the local leaders disseminated a statement asking all men in cities to wear the peasants' *koffeya* instead of the tarboush (fez). This was not analogous to asking urban women to veil; for men the demand was tactical, to protect peasants when they were in urban areas, as they were the primary targets of the British police (440).

8. In the chant of the popular poet and *zajal* singer Nuh Ibrahim: "And you, the Arab woman march into step with your sisters the warriors [*mujahidat*] of the villages. Stop using your make-up, stop going to the cinema and other kinds of entertainment. Rise to the level of your sisters who carry water jugs on their heads, joining the warriors, singing and cheering them and so easing their death" (Swedenburg 1995, 182). The mockery and contempt of "Westernized" women was reflected in children's songs, such as one that young boys would recite when seeing a woman wearing a hat: *'umm al-burnita al-raqqasa biddha bumba we rasasa* (the woman who wears a hat, the dancer, deserves a bomb and a bullet) (R. Sayigh 1987, 28).

a precarious position. In response to the peasants' claim that elite women were "less authentic," nationalist men politicized the meaning of women's domesticity, elevated it to new heights, and imbued it with nationalist significance (Fleischmann 2003, 10; Chatterjee 1990, 238–40, 248).

The dilemma of Palestinian women of how to combine the national and feminist struggles is one of the markers of the women's movement from its inception to today. The words of Khartabil (1995) at the Cairo Arab Women's Conference in 1944[9] are significant in clarifying the difference between the struggle of women still fighting for the recognition of their nation and their existence and "other women who live in a secure nation and a state" (91). The deterioration of the political situation in Palestine forced both men and women to change course. Men realized their need for women's activism and organization in general, which brought them back to the public space, this time with the support and under the protection of the male-led national movement.

The women's movement under the British Mandate was not born out of a feminist impulse to articulate women's rights per se, but rather out of women's experience within the national movement. Their speech was subtle and indirect, since there was no authority to which their claims could be directed, especially when the nation itself was under threat. The reason why the middle classes united with the peasant fighters was that they shared a common sense of that threat. This phenomenon would be reexperienced throughout the different phases of the Palestinian women's movement—there were successive phases of rapprochement between the professional middle classes and the popular masses in times of crisis and a distancing and divergence of agendas during periods when it looked as though a process of state consolidation might be underway. This pattern can be traced

9. Huda Sha'rawi, who convened the 1938 Conference of Women of the East (*mo'tamar nissa' al-sharq*) to support the Palestinian cause (Zu'aytir 1980, 471), resisted attempts by some Palestinian intellectuals to call it the "Arab Women's Conference."

through the history of the Palestinian women's movement after the *nakba* of 1948.

From "Palestinianness" to "Palestinianism"

Most Palestinian historians agree that the emergence of the Palestinian national movement in the 1960s marked the emergence of the contemporary form of Palestinian nationalism (e.g., Budeiri 1995, 1998; Y. Sayigh 1987; Khalidi 1997). Sayigh, for example, states that "the experience of *al-nakba* made for a distinct Palestinianness, but not necessarily for Palestinianism" (1997, 666). It was the emergence of the PLO and the gradual transformation of its ideology and its institution-building that would develop this Palestinianism (Sayigh 1979; Kimmerling and Migdal 1993, 220). A new image of the Palestinians emerged from the trauma of loss as well as the active creation of identity by Fateh. Struggle now became a core ingredient of Palestinian national identity (Schulz 1999, 37–38). "Revolution" and "armed struggle" were not only political strategies but became crucial principles of nationhood and served as the main discursive touchstones (Y. Sayigh 1987, 26), supporting the formation of a military, revolutionary culture.

If struggle was a core aspect of the new Palestinian identity, it was intertwined with the notion of Palestine as the "land of longing and exile" (Peteet 1998). For Palestinians in the diaspora, this was crucial in formulating sentimental links to the land and the desire to return. For those in the Occupied Territories, "steadfastness" on the actual land was the core of their Palestinian identity.

Whatever form Palestinian nationalism has taken, the stress on sacrifice as "giving" has remained constant. This has clashed with the call for women's rights, perceived as excessively demanding when the suffering of the diasporic exile and the Occupation is ravaging all aspects of Palestinian life, in particular of the poor and refugees. What has also made it difficult for women to claim their rights, either under the PLO or after the PA was established in 1994, has been the lack of a clear position concerning gender relations and ideology in the contemporary construction of Palestinian nationalism.

Gender and Nationalism in the "Revolution" Era (1974–1982)

From its inception, the PLO has never been much concerned with issues of gender or gender relations (Peteet 1991, 205). This lack of vision is apparent in many texts produced by the PLO and its various organs, for example, the "progressive" Palestinian Charter modified after militant elements of the PLO took control of the organization in 1969. Examining the two main ideological and political trends in the PLO in Lebanon, those associated with the Marxist-Leninist PFLP and those associated with the nationalist Fateh, Peteet (1991) concluded that they "display theoretical differences on the question of women in which the PFLP appear to have developed a more coherent analysis recognizing the moral dimension of the issue and the need for consciousness raising. Both, however, insist on the complete integration of the women's movement into the national struggle. Neither accords room for women to define their own priorities and to organize and struggle for these in autonomous organizations" (164). Peteet implies that autonomous women's organizations are necessarily more "feminist" and free from male control, a perspective I question. As I argue throughout this book, autonomous women's organizations are not automatic guarantors of a gender agenda informed by women's "true" interests and needs. While it is uncontestable that the Palestinian national movement did not have a well-articulated gender vision on social change, the Marxist parties did adopt a more nuanced gender vision than Fateh, were more open to women's activism, and were more responsive to their needs, as detailed later.

The absence of a well-considered commitment, however, has shifted the burden to the women's movement itself to articulate and formulate the gender interests of women in their different social positions. Fateh policy has consistently held that struggles other than national liberation are of a secondary order, thus denying an intimate relationship between polity and society (Peteet 1991, 161). One of Fateh's leaders, Mounir Shafiq, saw that "throughout the different phases of the national struggle, women did not separate themselves from the cause of their people" (Shafiq, in al-Ghounimi 1981, 201). Shafiq used an elaborate Marxist class analysis to delegitimize *tali'a* (vanguard) women who sought to liberate themselves at the expense of the masses by prioritizing women's equality which he denounced as elitist, Westernized, and bourgeois, and who, by their acts, were hindering women's mobilization to join the revolution (Shafiq 1977, 215). While Shafiq saw women's role as crucial in the "people's war" and objected to those who sought to spare women the "trouble of taking part in the struggle" (206), he nonetheless maintained that women should not challenge "traditions" reflected in prevailing gender roles, in particular in caring for their families and children (224). Sakher Habash, another leading figure in Fateh, stressed that certain types of oppression were faced by men and women alike, while *salafiya*[10] values (al-Ghounimi 1981, 126) were the main source of oppression for women, thus denying gender hierarchy in the national movement.

The above vision was contested in the mid-1970s by women in Fateh and two other groups: the General Union of Palestinian Women (GUPW), founded in 1965 as women's representative body within the PLO; and Samed ("resistant"), an income-generating project established in 1969 by activist women in Fateh to provide jobs and services for the needy (Mai Sayigh, cited in al-Ghounimi 1981, 125). Arguing that women's oppression would not be solved by greater involvement in the revolution or new economic opportunities, many leaders, women and men, stressed the need to mobilize, raise consciousness, and form cadres in different organizations and in the Palestinian community to address women's issues. They also sought to integrate women's issues in their groups' internal bylaws and regulations, and aimed to change the legal contours of Palestinian citizenship by revising the

---

10. *Salafiya* refers specifically to the Islamic reformers at the beginning of the twentieth century headed by the Egyptian Mohammed Abduh, who wanted to purify Islam of certain folk religious practices seen as un-Islamic (Swedenburg 1988, 189); in the above context, however, Habash was referring more generally to religious beliefs.

Palestinian Charter to make it clearly state the principle of equality and recognize the "social role" of women's responsibilities, motherhood in particular. They also called for expanding the women's union to truly represent women's interests, by including more women on a more democratic representative basis (al-Ghounimi 1981, 127). The atmosphere encouraged criticism of the lack of women's representation in the various decision-making bodies of the PLO and its constituent organizations (al-'Amad 1981, 11).

As women became increasingly active in the different tasks of the resistance, they started to pressure the leadership for a clear position on the gender order. This pressure led to much discussion and debate, fed by books and papers on women's place in the "revolution" (Abu 'Ali 1975; al-Khalili 1977; Shafiq 1977; al-'Amad 1981). Most of the writings stressed the achievement of the "revolution" in bringing more women into active roles, but many shortcomings were identified as well.

In an important study, "Observations on Women's Status in the Palestinian Revolution," Salwa al-'Amad draws on the many debates and workshops on women's status that took place in 1981. She states that the revolution opened a space for women to join, by the thousands, in social activism, working in all types of institutions—economic, cultural, media, medical, and military (al-'Amad 1981, 11). She admits that the "revolution" introduced many social changes in women's lives and encouraged more economic independence and self-reliance, especially for relatives of martyrs or prisoners. However, she also claims that the "revolution" dealt with these social transformations by means of "improvisation" and "reactiveness."

In Zeinab al-Ghounimi's (1981) account of a workshop organized by the journal *Sho'oun Falastineyya* (Palestine Affairs) to discuss women's status in the "revolution," the head of the GUPW, Mai Sayigh, stressed that "women in the revolution and even in the military are still used as a propaganda façade for the political organization; women are still far from playing a real role in the revolution seen as the preserve of different organizations in political competition and rivalry" (125). Influenced by Marxist women in the PFLP such as Naila Ahmed and Samira Salah, Sayigh went on to articulate the three basic forms of female oppression as "the enslavement of women to men, to the society, and to the Occupation" (al-Ghounimi 1981, 123).

With women's increased pressure, a new family law was proposed that would institute equal rights for marriage and divorce, impose restrictions on polygamy, and establish women as independent legal actors, which caused great controversy. The campaign for the law was derailed in 1982 when Israel invaded Lebanon and the PLO, along with its female cadres and institutions, was dispersed. The proposed law was not brought up again until the PLO relocated its headquarters to the Occupied Territories after the Oslo Agreement in 1993. A full discussion of the new context in which the family law issue would be reopened appears in chapter 4.

The "progressive" ideology of the Marxist-Leninist organizations in the PLO—in particular the PFLP and the Democratic Front for the Liberation of Palestine (DFLP)[11]—made them more receptive to women's demands but did not alter their classical Marxist stance on gender: women are oppressed, but the national and class struggle must first rid the people of colonialism and then of capitalist exploitation. They all encouraged women to play an active role equal to that of men in these struggles. All avoided confrontation with the prevailing gender order and worked to change it indirectly through the individual intervention of many leaders, male and female, to solve gender-related concerns among "progressive couples" and their families (Naila Ahmed, interview). Marxists, like most Arab male leftist-nationalists, often strongly distinguished between women's liberation in the public sphere and their sexual/bodily freedom, the latter being viewed as superficial and individualistic (Hasso 1997, 114). Based on her own experiences among fighters and revolutionary cadres, al-'Amad (1981)

---

11. The West Bank branch of the Jordanian Communist Party was never represented in the PLO. In 1982, two small, independent communist parties were founded in the Occupied Territories: the Revolutionary Palestinian Communist Party (RPCP)—members of the PLO between 1982 and 1987—and the Palestinian Communist Party (PCP, now the Palestinian People's Party)—members of the PLO since 1987.

confirms this view, stating that male fighters tended to reduce women's liberation to sexual liberation, yet remained faithful to prevailing gender divisions of labor when it came to marriage.

Nonetheless, as Hasso (1997) shows in her analysis of women's power in one of these Marxist organizations, "the self-consciously modernizing and civilizational ideology of the DFLP men and women created a discursive opening for women's involvement; competent cadres of DFLP women, genuinely committed to both nationalism and feminism, took advantage of this opening and for a period helped redefine the politics of both projects" (116). As Islamists' power grew after the signing of the Oslo Agreement, and both the influence of secular leftist-nationalist ideology and women's power and activism in the national movement waned, that discursive opening closed to no small degree, inhibiting aspirations long held by the pre-1993 women's movement and foreclosing their achievement.

Political Activism under the Israeli Occupation

After the defeat of Jordan, Egypt, and Syria in the 1967 war, Israel, much like Jordan, tried to prevent any form of national mobilization among Palestinians in the Occupied Territories of the West Bank and Gaza (Ma'oz 1984, 63). Responses to Israeli policies came from *al-hay'a al-islamiya* (the Islamic Committee) (Dakkak 1983, 70), while a semi-secret national leadership was simultaneously formed in Jerusalem under the name *lajnet al-tawjih al-watani* (the National Guidance Committee, NGC-I).[12] The two committees worked in harmony, the first comprising clerics, *shari'a* court judges, and some civil representatives, and the latter comprising activists in the Jordanian Communist Party (JCP) and the Arab Nationalist Movement (Dakkak 1983; Ma'oz 1984).

In August 1973, mostly independent and JCP activists organized the Palestinian National Front (PNF), often referred to simply as the

12. The Roman numeral I was added to distinguish this committee from the one formed in 1978 under the same name. The second committee is designated NGC-II.

Front (*Jabha*), which was joined over the following year by members of Fateh, the DFLP, and the PFLP. The Front was successful in mobilizing many groups, youth and women in particular, and in invigorating nationalist sentiment. The municipal elections of 1976, a crucial test in demonstrating the Front's influence, were a turning point in the history of the Palestinian national movement (Ma'oz 1984). While the Israelis intended the elections to marginalize the PLO, the results brought the younger generation of the group's local leadership to the forefront, proving the PLO's power to represent the Palestinian people. Such a success could not have been achieved without the extension of suffrage, which for the first time qualified tens of thousands of West Bank women and teenagers to vote for mayors and town councils (Abdel-Jawad 1986). A new "progressive" culture was taking root, with youth and women at the center.[13] A new distinction between "traditional," "reactionary" leadership and "progressive," "leftist," "nationalist" leadership helped young women identify where and how they could be politically active.

Although the Front advocated a political solution rather than the military one sought by some of its constituents, the Israeli government still viewed the organization as a threat and responded by arresting or deporting its activists (Hasso 1997, 65). The PLO, fearing the rise of alternative leadership in the Occupied Territories, worked to undermine the local secular leadership, in particular in Gaza, which indirectly empowered the Islamists (Dakkak 1983, 79–81). In 1977, the right-wing Likud party took power in Israel. It pursued a policy of integrating the West Bank into Israel rather than containing the Palestinians there, which had been the Labor Party's policy. Particularly

13. It became a common sight to see young men and women holding hands in the volunteer camps organized to "beautify the land" by planting trees and working with peasants in their fields to help them maintain and hold on to their land. Land Day is celebrated on March 30 each year; it became a national occasion when Israeli forces opened fire on Palestinian citizens of the Israeli state during a 1976 protest against land confiscation. Since then, Land Day is celebrated by Palestinians in both Israel and the Occupied Territories.

after the mid-1980s, Likud adopted administrative measures to suppress the national activities of the various Palestinian associations and restrict the mayors' powers, facilitating the expansion of Israeli settlements. Although the overt activities of the Palestinians were disrupted for a long time, national solidarity was strengthened by antagonism toward Israel, which led to the first intifada in 1987 (Ma'oz 1984, 164, 170–76; Hilal 1998, 44–45; Sandler and Frisch 1982, 66–67; Taraki 1990; al-Shu'aibi 1986).

The Era of Women's Power:
New Forms of Mobilization (1978–1993)

The experiences of the Palestinian National Front and the National Guidance Committee had demonstrated the importance of public efforts to organize the masses. The popular organizations that emerged were associated with different PLO factions; each sought to strengthen its following. Labor unions, university students, secondary school students, voluntary work organizations, and women's organizations were all duly factionalized. While it may be argued that a single organization would have sufficed for each, the divisions had the advantage of increasing the number of recruits by appealing to the partisans of every political group. It was also much harder to destroy these new organizations, which had a more diffuse, regionalized structure than the monolithic ones of the past.

In this milieu, and in the aftermath of the intense national resistance of 1976, International Women's Day on March 8, 1978, was pivotal. Female activists held a meeting that resulted in the creation of the Women's Work Committee (*lajnet al-'amal al-nissa'i*). Its membership was largely drawn from participants in political organizations, especially the DFLP, PFLP, Communist Party, and Fateh. These women persistently tried to join the structure of the GUPW, headed at that time by Samiha Khalil,[14] who denied them access, fearing their

14. In 1996, Samiha Khalil was the first woman to run against Yasser Arafat for a top leadership position—the presidency of the Palestinian Authority.

"militant" backgrounds might threaten the powerful charitable Family Rehabilitation (*in'ash al-usra*) organization, used as a façade for the women's union.

The birth of the new Women's Work Committee in 1978, outside the umbrella organization representing "all" Palestinian women, created a power struggle, which lingers to this day, over the leadership, vision, and strategies of the GUPW. The Women's Work Committee included the cadres who had emerged from various voluntary work camps, which proliferated especially after the 1976 municipal elections, and who had Marxist-feminist orientations toward political work. Although the Women's Work Committee was initially made up of active cadres irrespective of political affiliation, in time a partisan power struggle emerged within its ranks, producing a panoply of women's grassroots organizations (Jad 1990, 131) (see appendix A).

The largest organization to emerge from the Women's Work Committee was the DFLP-affiliated Palestinian Federation of Women's Action Committees (PFWAC), which was a significant force through the early 1990s. The PFWAC agenda was to attain equal rights for women in the "public sphere"—wages, job opportunities, education, and political participation (Hasso 1997, 220). As a Marxist group, the PFWAC held that women's oppression stemmed from the linked trio of nation, class, and gender (*qawmi, tabaqi, jensi*). Strategic gender interests (Molyneux 1985) would thus be addressed by organizing and mobilizing women both in the national struggle and to respond to the immediate needs of poor and working-class women in areas such as health care, education, social assistance, and employment, which was seen as the guarantor of their liberation from the constraints of dependence on men (PWWC 1985, 7; PFWAC 1988). From a discursive perspective, the issue of gender oppression was not placed at the forefront of these service campaigns, but rather addressed discreetly within the circle of the PFWAC's and DFLP's members.

The PFWAC succeeded in mobilizing many intellectual, academic, and professional women. It was also one of the first women's organizations to be affected by the influx of foreign funding and professionalism during the first Palestinian intifada. Adversely affected by the split of its institutional base, the DFLP, in 1991, the PFWAC made increasing overtures to women outside the political parties. Ultimately, the PFWAC was a victim of the international donors' shift of focus, after the 1993 Oslo Agreement, to projects promoting Palestinian "civil society," good governance, and "conflict resolution"—i.e., "joint ventures" between Palestinians and Israelis.

One of the most important ingredients in the success of the PFWAC had been its commitment to helping women by focusing on their "practical needs," in Molyneux's (2001) schema, such as the means of generating income and the provision of day care and preschool services. The crucial task was seen not so much as "the satisfaction of needs arising from women's placement within the sexual division of labour" (153), but as paving the way for the pursuit of the more "strategic interests" of national liberation as well as the transformation of social relations to secure a more lasting repositioning of women within the gender order and society at large (Siham, Amal, Zahira, interviews).

This linkage between strategic interests and the practical needs of women was reflected through the formulation of the PFWAC's income-generating projects, which differed from those of the charitable women's organizations in that they had a stated commitment to group decision-making. Moreover, the goals of PFWAC projects were not profitability or "charity" but socialization and mobilization. The organization tried to provide services that women wanted, a measure of economic independence through paid work, and a politicized social space shared with other women. In addition, the PFWAC sought to increase its mass support and that of its parent party, the DFLP. The creation of income-generating projects for women and girls was also shaped by the group's knowledge that in order to recruit working-class and peasant women it would have to provide a safe work environment that families and communities would find acceptable (Hasso 1997, 223; Siham, interview). During the first intifada, the popular demand for these income-generating projects increased as the economic situation deteriorated.

By the mid-1980s, the organization had established an extensive network of preschools and nurseries, mostly in villages and refugee camps, that served communities for free or at a nominal cost. By 1987, it employed forty-eight teachers and five directors serving 1,504 children (PUWWC 1987a, 15, cited in Hasso 1997, 224). The PFWAC philosophy was that child care was a social and not a strictly individual responsibility. Its leaders had found that such care was also a prerequisite for mobilizing women: "[W]hen we asked the members what their problems were, they replied: children. [I]f we want to become active, either by going to work or becoming involved in the committees, we need kindergartens and nurseries for our children" (al-Labadi 1992, cited in Hasso 1997, 224).

Hasso concludes that the narratives of women members and activists in the PFWAC had significant feminist content and that most of the women had a strong feminist consciousness, although this did not necessarily translate into feminist action. That is, despite having some very radical ideas, they did not always believe that they could effect significant changes in their lives. However, the PFWAC managed, to a great extent, to construct a group identity according to which they referred to themselves as *banat al-ʿamal al-nissaʾi*—Daughters of Women's Action. As a group, they manifested their identity through cultural festivals, bazaars, demonstrations, and publications. They were empowered by their role in the national struggle (Jayawardena 1986) and by a gender system in which the left, secular parties prevailed over mass organizations and Palestinian culture generally, with all its artistic and symbolic manifestations. Empowered by massive networks and webs of relations, they managed to establish links with women in cities, villages, and refugee camps through their eloquent, well-respected leaders and collective action (Tarrow 1994). The PFWAC asserted that no liberation for the homeland would be possible without women's liberation, that women would work side by side with men for the liberation, and that they should receive equal pay for equal work. This was the moment, in the mid- to late 1980s, when the women associated with the organization were most assertive and gained the reputation of being *qaweyyat* (powerful).

This change in women's day-to-day experience was captured in Hasso's work. One of her respondents, a twenty-eight-year-old villager, stressed the importance of PFWAC affiliation, rather than PFWAC employment per se, as she discussed a number of improvements in her life:

> It's not right to say that things changed when I began working. It's more accurate to say that things changed when I joined the PFWAC. Now, if I want to leave, I don't give them [family] reports or have to tell them. They never allowed me to leave the house before. Now I can go on visits, trips to the PFWAC offices, wherever I want to go. I used to expect that my parents would say "no" to everything. I recently asked my father if I could travel to Jordan and he just said "yes." (Respondent #47 [1989] in Hasso 1997, 244)

The growing influence of the PFWAC among women could be partly attributed to the fact that it was working at the level in which people have face-to-face relationships and are likely to have complex multiple connections that provide a solid basis for "collective action" (Uphoff 1993, 609; Tarrow 1994). At the same time, it was acting on another level as a national coordinating body, strengthened through that web of direct personal relations based on trust and "knowing each other." This type of "sustained" (Tarrow 1994) relationship was important in the PFWAC's generation of a group identity and the collective action that drew strength from it.

In the PFWAC/DFLP case, nationalist participation combined with a feminist agenda was often empowering for women, transforming their sense of themselves as citizens and as gendered beings (Hasso 1997, 310). As I will argue throughout, national identity, like any other social identity, is always evolving. It is through organized, collective, and sustained acts of resistance that oppressed and marginalized social groups gain more power. In a situation in which a whole society is constantly under external threat, there is a vital need for collectivity and a sense of "togetherness" (Harris 2000). Nationalism, with its leftist associations in the Palestinian context, acted as the social glue for this "togetherness." This is not to say that left-leaning nationalism was a haven for gender equality (Jad 1990; Sayigh 1993; Peteet 1991; Massad 1995). However, women activists were, through their collective actions, carving out a space for different understandings of gender and gender roles; they were shaping an alternative empowering structure separate from family and kinship ties and they were "opening up new areas of struggle and renegotiation of the relations between genders" in society and in the national movement (Kandiyoti 1988, 275).

The permanent splintering of the women's movement does not reflect differences in the agenda and goals of the different groups. Rather, the common goal of involving the greatest possible number of women in the national movement demanded flexibility. In contrast, for instance, to the membership conditions of the charitable organizations, this enabled women from different social classes to participate; thus, the women's movement was not restricted to middle-class women as in the past (Taraki 1989, 62). The first concern of all these organizations was the national struggle, yet "emancipating Palestinian women" was an item on the agenda of all the groups, especially the left-oriented ones. The visible power of women in the public arena was opening a wider field for their activism. Projects undertaken by the women's committees provided a permanent pool of recruits for various activities, whether in the cities, villages, or refugee camps. The process in itself helped many women cadres to develop an understanding of the needs and demands of the women they worked with. While the number of organized women was limited, they nonetheless represented an influential bloc that challenged the discourse of more conservative social groups. The latter half of the 1980s was the golden era for women's activism in the West Bank and Gaza.

At the time, women in groups such as the PFWAC strongly believed that the rising generation of Palestinian leaders could not ignore the role of women in the resistance; women were going to be liberated through legal reforms and a long-term process of social change. This promise is still unfulfilled, but the hope remains that the leadership of an independent Palestinian state will someday see it through.

The Palestinian Women's Movement and the First Intifada

From the start of the first intifada, which broke out on December 9, 1987, women of all ages and social classes, in particular women from poor neighborhoods and refugee camps, took part in the demonstrations. They were an integral part of every significant form of resistance. Their actions were sometimes violent, and they were often involved in serious confrontations with the Israeli army (Jad 1990, 133). Most importantly, women were crucial in sustaining the intifada through the networks connecting the Unified National Leadership of the Uprising (UNLU) with the masses. Networking was built on traditional jail and home visits by women, providing support for prisoners, their families, martyrs' families, and others affected by Israeli oppression. Women in the Occupied Territories, like female activists in the PLO in Lebanon, were empowered by their important roles in the intifada, and began to contest for leadership positions in their respective parties. And as the underground male leadership was imprisoned on a massive scale, women activists replaced them (Rabiha Diab, interview).

The massive success of the UNLU in organizing and mobilizing hundreds of thousands of people into peaceful and popular resistance was met with an Israeli policy of brutal suppression. Sweeping arrests, killings, home demolitions, school and university shutdowns, curfews, and road closures were some of the means employed by the Israeli army. The intifada also witnessed the emergence of the Islamists as a political movement that strongly contested the space thus far controlled by the secular nationalist forces. The first intifada, like the Great Revolt, was accompanied by economic deterioration and the spread of poverty. This led to contradictory gender effects: an expansion of venues for women in the political public sphere and, at the same time, an expansion of venues for the imposition of sexual control. The Israeli authority frequently used social conservatism, especially with regard to female sexuality, to repress the Palestinian population. This was implemented in two ways: girls and women detained and accused of nationalist activities were sexually assaulted or threatened with such violence, especially during interrogations; and Israeli interrogators frequently threatened sexual violence against daughters, sisters, or wives as a method of extracting information or "confessions" from male detainees (Al-Haq 1990, 208, 511–12, cited in Hasso 1997, 175).

These tactics, accompanied by the school closures, restrictions on movement, and mounting impoverishment, led many girls to drop out of school and marry at an early age. It also led to the enforcement of the dress code (veiling) advocated by the Islamists and seen by many young activists as an act of national solidarity on the part of women (Hammami 1990). The first intifada ended with the signing of the Oslo Agreement in 1993. (The first intifada and its contradictory effects will be discussed in greater detail in chapters 3 and 4.) In the new phase that followed, Palestinians became, for the first time in their history, citizens governed by a Palestinian authority.

2

The Conundrums of Post-Oslo Palestine

From Militants to Citizens without Citizenship

THE SIGNING OF THE OSLO AGREEMENT led to the formation of the Palestinian Authority, which started to function as a quasi-state. The formation of the new PA entailed the reconstruction of the "imagined" Palestinian community (Anderson 1983), within which approaches to gender policies have been reformulated to suit a new era. However, women are not passive subjects of the PA. I will examine the impact of women's activism on PA policies and how it expands the boundaries of their rights as equal citizens. I will demonstrate that women's activism is not a movement representing all women's interests, but rather a site of conflicting interests, power relations, and variable positionings. And I will argue that the Palestinian women's movement, in the process of claiming citizenship rights, assumed the "normality" of the newly established PA and that a period of political stability would lead to a fulfillment of their national, political, and social rights. However, the feminist use of the concept of citizenship itself is in question in the context of the prolonged Occupation of Palestine. In particular, the shift by secular woman's groups toward making claims on behalf of citizens of an institutionally impaired "state" led them to abandon their historically successful focus on grassroots mobilization and activism. At the same time, the PA's failure to achieve the promised social benefits of (quasi-) statehood, let alone

26

national independence, lent increasing popular credence to the discourse of Islamists, amplified by the PA's brazen attempts to sideline them, which served only to compromise the nascent legal framework in the Occupied Territories.

The emergence of the notion of citizenship in the Middle East was related to the quest for equality for women in the public sphere and the attempt to theorize women's status in relation to both the state and the community (Joseph 1986, 3–8; 2000, Joseph and Sylomovics 2001; Molyneux 1985; Kandiyoti 1991b, 2001, 2002). This in turn was associated with a theorization of democracy and a heated debate over the relationship between the state and civil society (Bishara 1996; Norton 1993, 1995). In some quarters, the debate revived a dominant understanding of the Middle East based on an ahistorical notion of regional exceptionalism. Some neo-Orientalist scholars cast the Middle East as blighted by a failure to modernize due to its essentialized nature (Pipes 1983, 187–88, cited in Sadowski 1993, 18; Bill and Springborg 1990; Lewis 1964, 1988; Kedourie 1992; Crone 1980).

Feminist evaluations of citizenship in the Middle East suggest that the question of women's rights exposes severe "fault lines in modern concepts of citizenship" (Kandiyoti 2000, xv). The feminist critique focuses on the continuing role of kin-based communal entities and their incorporation into different systems of governance, either as recognized parts of the political system, or as the source of various forms of nepotism and clientelism. Some feminists have argued that citizenship concepts do not apply and call for a more culture-specific approach (Joseph 1994, 2000; al-Torki 2000; Charrad 2000). Al-Torki, for example, has argued for working through kinship and communal structures that may act to empower and disempower women simultaneously. Others, arguing in favor of citizenship concepts, call for the expansion of women's rights as individuals and "condemn the stranglehold that communal and religious forces exercise over them" (Kandiyoti 2000, xv; see also Hatem 2000; Hale 2000; Jad, Johnson, and Giacamann 2000; Amawi 2000).

In the above views, it is assumed that the state exists as a sovereign entity within a well-defined territory, which is not the case in

Palestine. While citizenship concepts may be applicable to states with recognized sovereignty, women's strategies to expand their citizenship rights must be viewed in light of the social, economic, and political structures affecting these rights. As I detail later, the call for rights in a situation where the state does not exist in legal or political terms may lead women to limit themselves to a narrowly defined notion of rights, while their societies and communities are falling apart. This may, in turn, lead to a greater marginalization of women's rights and demands.

In the Arab world, the issue of women's rights was tackled by postcolonial national elites in their modernization and development initiatives. Following different models such as Arab socialism (Egypt, Syria, Iraq, and Algeria) and Marxist socialism (Yemen), states introduced important changes in women's status through the wide-scale provision of basic social services such as education, health care, and family planning. A salient feature of these states' developmental policies was the inclusion of women in the labor force, with all the legal reforms needed to facilitate this task (Kandiyoti 1991b; Molyneux 1991; Hatem 1994). While introducing these top-down reforms and promoting the "new, modern woman," these states tended to restrict and ban all forms of autonomous organizations (Kandiyoti 1991a). In short, they expanded the notion of social rights through the provision of important social services, but simultaneously restricted political and civil rights, which contradicted the evolutionary path of citizenship as charted by Thomas Marshall (1950).

The modernizing projects of postcolonial states in the Arab world were gendered: policies to increase women's employment and education, exert control over women's fertility, and provide essential social services were central to modernization and led to changes in gender relations. However, women's introduction into the labor market did not produce a substantive change in the sexual division of labor. Women were perceived by the elites in these countries as both modern citizens and bearers of cultural authenticity (Anthias and Yuval-Davis 1989). This contradiction figured in most of their national constitutions, in which women were defined as equal citizens but with fewer rights than men because the realm of the family remained governed by *shariʿa*, which primarily defines women as dependents. This dependent image is not related to the *shariʿa* interpretation alone, but also to many cultural, social, economic, and political factors that are not conducive to the prioritization of equal gender relations (Welchman 1999; al-Botmeh 2012). After the September 11, 2001, terrorist attack on the United States, women's rights and *shariʿa* law became central to . Western discourse about the "problems" of the Middle East, including Palestine.

With the United States' assumption of the mantle of sole superpower, and its invasion of Iraq in March 2003, the inability of the Arab despotic states to change became a dominant theme in American foreign policy. Their recalcitrance "necessitated" external intervention to bring about democracy and other desired transformations that would presumably flow from it. The American-led intervention, which dismantled one of the most important postcolonial Arab states, jeopardized not only the notion of citizenship but also the notion of sovereignty on which it depends.

While most postcolonial Arab states are faced with economic, political, and social crises, the PA confronts more immediately threatening circumstances. First among these is the practical limitations of local resources, which restrict the PA's capacity to deliver or promote social transformation. Most of these resources were and remain hostage to Israeli control and punitive actions (Hilal and Khan 2004; Haddad 2018). The second concerns the very existence of the PA, which faces the ongoing and systematic destruction of its infrastructure and most of its development projects. The third concerns the political opposition, which is empowered by the ongoing confrontation and the lack of a peace agreement. The fourth concerns the nature of PA policies themselves. As Molyneux (2001) has stated, government policies and a commitment to women's emancipation have had a crucial impact on the substance of women's citizenship. Each of these circumstances hinders the process of women's emancipation and their claim for their rights. In the Palestinian case, in particular, there is a tendency by critics to ignore how external factors such as Israeli security measures and related sanctions have affected both the normal functioning of the PA and, as a consequence, gender relations in the Occupied Territories.

I now proceed to an overview of how the PA delineated the legal contours of citizenship and gender relations through its legislation, policies, and cultural constructions of Palestinian nationalism. Based on the historical trajectory of the Palestinian national movement, I argue that the Authority has neither a gender vision nor a political project for social change. However, despite being weak, fragmented, and donor dependent, the Authority has had some positive responses to the well-organized women's pressure.

Gender and the PA: The Legal Contours of Palestinian Citizenship

The legal contours of Palestinian citizenship are drawn by gender as well as the specific circumstances of history. As explained above, before the uprooting of the Palestinian people in 1948, citizenship, as defined by the British Mandate, was tied to the land. Palestinians were "those who lived in Palestine" (Massad 1995, 468–69) and had blood ties to it through their fathers.

With the establishment of the Palestinian Authority, the definition of Palestinian citizenship became a quandary. Early drafts of the quasi-constitutional Basic Law, which the PA was granted the right to draft under the Oslo Agreement, reflected the fact that the Authority could not define Palestinian identity according to the tenets of Palestinian nationalism. Rather than formalizing a distinction between Palestinian nationality/identity and Palestinian citizenship, those early drafts postponed the definition of citizenship to some future period of legislation (Hammami and Johnson 1999).

The latest version of Article 12 of the Palestinian Basic Law, dating from March 2003, specifies the ways in which Palestinian nationality is transmitted. Under the pressure of the women's movement, the requirement of blood ties through the father, the basis for the transmission of citizenship prior to 1948, was changed to include blood ties through either parent. Thus, for the first time in an Arab state, women were given the right to pass their citizenship on to their children (Jad et al. 2003, 9; al-Botmeh 2012).

From its earliest drafts, the Basic Law has stated that Palestine recognizes and respects a significant array of international agreements and declarations, including the United Nations Convention on the Elimination of All Forms of Discrimination against Women (CEDAW), which provide a basis for the adoption of universal conventions as sources of legislation. In the first four drafts, which were subject to popular discussion, *shari'a* was not mentioned as a source of legislation, nor was Islam as the state religion. However, both were later added under Islamist pressure by the Palestinian Legislative Council, though its membership was largely secular. It is worth noting that the Legislative Council did not include any Islamists, as the Islamist political groups had boycotted the elections which they saw as an outcome of Oslo, a process they opposed.

It is not my intention to review the Palestinian Basic Law in its entirety, but there are some revealing passages concerning work and motherhood that denote a lip-service approach to changing gender relations. Article 23, for example, declares that women have "the right to participate actively in the social, political, cultural and economic life, and the Law will work to eliminate constraints that forbid women from fully participating in the construction of their families and society" (Jad et al. 2003, 10). The major problem of female unemployment is not explicitly addressed, and it is not at all clear what the "constraints" are that the Law will work to eliminate. Article 23 also states that "women's constitutional and *shari'a* rights (*hoqoq shar'eyya*) are protected and the Law will punish any violations" (10). Thus, the proposed Law employs obscure language that suits any and all ideological inclinations, whether secular or religious. Motherhood, child care, and the family, central to Palestinian nationalism, are dealt with in most PA legal documents as a duty of society but without any commitment on the part of the Authority to realizing that duty (Jad, Johnson, and Giacamann 2000). Child care and maternity service, traditionally the task of women's organizations, were not supported by the PA to keep them functioning. In many laws, such as the Civil Law and Civil Service Law, women are depicted as dependent on men.

In parallel to the opaque definition of citizenship, the PA lacks a coherent set of policies to enforce the rule of law as a guarantor of citizens' rights. The most conspicuous policy is related to the security task assigned to the Authority by the Oslo Agreement (Haddad 2018). Certain aspects of citizenship are thereby severely undermined, especially in terms of the PA's relationship with opposition in general and with the Islamic political movement in particular. Detention without charge, torture, maltreatment, and harassment are methods frequently used against the Islamic political opposition. A higher security court was established by presidential decree as a parallel body to the civil courts. Different security forces are creating their own courts exempt from civil control.

Physical attacks on members of the Legislative Council, raids on the universities, the closure of privately owned media stations, and the arrests of journalists all demonstrated nonadherence to the rule of law and disrespect for civil rights. The Authority has displayed hostility to different social groups attempting to claim their civil or social rights. Student leaders have been arrested, beaten, and imprisoned when they protested against the harassment of their universities by the security forces (as detailed later), and participants in the government teachers' strike in April 2000 received similar treatment. These repressive measures placed (and still place) women's activists in a bind. In order to increase their power, women required alliances with other social groups. Such alliances would require the women's movement to adopt a critical political position vis-à-vis the PA's practices, which might have led to similarly repressive responses to their activism. But failure to adopt a critical position would tend to discredit their demands and decrease their legitimacy in civil society. The grassroots women's organizations linked to Fateh, now the ruling party in the West Bank and Gaza, did, in fact, suffer that sort of loss of legitimacy.

In postcolonial Arab states, the top-down attempt at modernization combined with the violation of civil and political rights was attenuated by the extensive provision of social services which gave those states, however authoritarian, a measure of legitimacy. But with the shift to structural adjustment and other neo-liberal policies, their legitimacy was eroded as their capacity to deliver social services was impaired (Kandiyoti 1991b). This created unrest and dissatisfaction that pushed them to resort to political liberalization as a strategy to pacify / ease discontent (al-Taher 1992, 95; Ayubi 1995). In the case of the PA, it is now unable to provide even the most basic rights— to employment, to basic utilities, to health care—because these are being privatized. There is a pressing question as to whether different groups will be able to achieve their social rights without simultaneously struggling for their civil and national rights.

The above-mentioned deficiencies contrast with the gender friendly language frequently employed by Palestinian officials, supposedly demonstrating their commitment to women's emancipation and gender equality. This tendency can be attributed to the PA's dependence upon donor funding and the requirements of United Nations agencies. After its establishment, the PA encountered numerous demands from donors and UN agencies to "mainstream gender" and to "take gender into account" in all its projects, as explored later in more detail.

The New "Nation" and Its "New" Woman: Cultural Articulations of Palestinian Citizenship

The "ideal woman" varies according to the national project for modernization of each new state. Veiled/unveiled, working woman/ housewife, fighter/caretaker—each of these dichotomies represents different national visions in which women's role and image are essential. Feminists have discussed the concept of the national ideal critically with reference to the public/private distinction, the deprivation of women's rights, and discrimination against women in general. It is in the name of the "nation" that the position of women has often suffered. National unity is used to rationalize postponement of the resolution of women's problems. "Priority is thus given again and again to other problems and excludes both popular demands and women's claim for a better status in their society. . . . The time for women's demands is never now" (Hélie-Lucas 1994, 6, 9).

In the historic discourse of the Palestinian national movement, women were constructed either as the struggling militant or as the self-sacrificing mother (Peteet 1991; Jad 1990). In the face of death, uprooting, rejection, and annihilation, many Palestinian poets glorified the woman with a large number of children, especially male children.[1] However, national slogans like "the right of return" and "struggle" required a different model for women. The image of the woman "freedom fighter" with a gun in her hand was promoted by various Palestinian factions, especially on the left. What happened to these images of women under the PA? And what happened to the core idioms of "struggle," "sacrifice," and "suffering" that constitute Palestinian national identity in the diaspora?

In her study of Palestinian nationalism, Helena Schulz (1999) underlined the "ambiguity of Palestinian nationalism and national identity. Even within one and the same political faction and within the official leadership, concepts of identity and nationalism are unevenly distributed" (156). The sometimes ambiguous national narratives should also be seen against the background of the fluctuating intensity of the Palestinian-Israeli conflict. During the national struggle, Israel, the United States, or even Arab "brothers" used to be referred to as "the other," the external enemy. In the new era, "the other" came to denote the Islamists as the internal enemy. When the Islamists refused to be controlled by the PA and insisted on continuing the "resistance" until the liberation of Palestine (thus threatening the role assigned to the PA to help ensure Israeli security), they became the greatest threat to the PA (Schulz 1999). Opposition to the Palestinian Authority was also branded as being supported by Syrians, Jordanians, or "others" whose acts did not stem from "loyalty" to the nation.

1. For example, the poem "Ahmed al-Za'tar," by Mahmoud Darwish, written after the 1976 attacks by the Syrian army on the Palestinian refugee camp Tel al-Zaatar during the Lebanese civil war.

In the new, post-Oslo era of unachieved national independence, "belonging," "loyalty," and "commitment" are the *mots d'ordre* for the new political regime around which the reconstruction of Palestinian nationalism has taken place. Belonging to Palestine is the main slogan, without specifying which Palestine or whose Palestine. Belonging to Palestine is extended to mean belonging to Fateh, the main political party. As for commitment, it is represented by four main pillars: belief in the "cause" (of Palestine), the will to organically integrate with the "organization" (i.e., Fateh), readiness to assume the duties and responsibilities of this commitment, and finally, full acceptance of the political positions, program, internal platform, and decisions taken by the organization (PNGD 1988, 14).[2] One might argue that this ideological indoctrination is solely directed at Fateh candidates and members, but this process is actually taking place throughout the PA and under its auspices.

Accompanying this process, one sees media and overt propaganda indicating the PA's sovereignty through two key symbols: the flag and the president.[3] Throughout Arafat's incumbency, life-size pictures of the president in his military uniform as a symbol of the continuation of the struggle were ubiquitous, not least in every PA office. After his death in 2004, these images were largely replaced by photos showing Arafat with his successor, Mahmoud Abbas. "Struggle" was replaced with "symbolic militarism,"[4] reflected in the frequent sight of youngsters marching in military formation. Summer military camps

2. From an internal document of the PA's Political and National Guidance Directorate, delivered as a lecture to Fateh cadres at the Majid Abu Sharar School for Cadre Formation in September 1988.

3. General Tawfiq al-Tirawi, head of the Intelligence Service office in Jericho, declared in a local television interview on December 18, 1999, "We have two majesties, the president and the flag."

4. I use the term "symbolic militarism" because when Israeli troops invaded the PA-administered area in September 2002, there was apparently no national strategy for resistance, either military or civil, and the political leadership denounced many local groups' or individuals' actions as acts of "terror."

for youth were organized as a new symbol of the continuing struggle, to simultaneously teach about peace and about the importance of following the decisions of the leadership. This symbolic militaristic orientation is enforced through the Authority's mushrooming security apparatus, each service sporting its own military-style uniform. This culture of symbolic militarism has returned to glorify the male fighter and overshadow the old image of the woman militant developed during the PLO years in Lebanon.

Gender and Militarism: The Plight of the Woman Militant

One of the roles for women during the national struggle was that of guerrilla combatant. With the establishment of the Authority, militancy was transformed into militarism with a male countenance and women were obliged to retreat. They were not allowed to join the war veterans' association until they successfully brought political pressure to bear ('Etaf, interview). Female guerrilla combatants were for many years not granted military status by the president. In the Jordanian army, by contrast, even women who serve in clerical positions have military status. In the Preventive Security Force, women police and clerical officers were ultimately "added" to the rolls later on (Brand 1998).

Feminists have paid close attention to militarism and its negative impact on women and gender relations (Cock 1989; Enloe 1988; Alvarez 1990; Waylen 1996). Militarism excludes women from war on the grounds of their physical inferiority and their presumed peaceful, nurturing qualities. Cock (1989) argues that "dividing the protector from the protected, defender from the defended, is the linchpin of masculinist as well as military ideology" (52). In militarism, women are categorized as peripheral, as serving safely at the "rear," on the "home front." Women as women must be denied access to the "front," to "combat"; the military has to constantly redefine the "front" and "combat" as wherever women are not (Enloe 1988, 15). Waylen (1996) observes that "until recent exceptions, women soldiers have remained in 'feminine' servicing roles rather than undertaking 'masculine' combat roles" (99). These authors' observations find resonance in the Palestinian context.

Their observations are of particular importance in assessing the role of the security forces in the PA from a gender perspective. The fact that the security apparatus absorbs over 45 percent of all employees in the public sector (Hilal 1999, 54) and consumes over one-third of the total public budget means that women are excluded from the largest sector of potential jobs. They have been awarded military titles and monthly allowances but are not permitted to enter active service, with the exception of the police force.[5] As has happened time and again in the history of the Palestinian national struggle, however, women more recently claimed the fighter's mantle during the second intifada, when a number compelled militant groups to recruit them for military actions.

As the Israeli-Palestinian conflict intensified and Israel enforced the policy of separating Palestinian communities from one another by hundreds of checkpoints and separation walls, the goal of a unitary Palestinian national identity was superseded by the reality of localized identities connected with the ruling Fateh party, Islamists, or kin loyalties. These localized identities introduced variations in women's citizenship. For instance, proximity to the ruling party, exemplified by those active in the PA apparatus, now often determines the type or extent of privileges one may obtain. Similarly, adherence to Hamas, for instance, improves access to important services and financial aid.

The Sacrificing Woman

The PA has promoted the ideal woman as fertile, self-sacrificing, and steadfast, giving rise to contradictory public discourses. In the national struggle, the fertile woman was deemed essential because the conflict partly rested on the demographic balance between Jews and Arabs. In 1995, in a public meeting at a refugee camp, President Arafat addressed women using the old formula—as "mothers of the nation" needing incentives and protection to fulfill that role—and granted them three

5. The poet Mahmoud Darwish (2002) highlights the contradiction between the nationalist romanticization of women fighters and the PA's actual policy and discourse: "We differ on the duties of women / (we would have done well to choose a woman to run the security services)."

months' maternity leave (in contrast to the previous leave of six weeks). Yet the following year, the head of the Palestinian Central Bureau of Statistics publicly warned of a demographic catastrophe unless concerted efforts were made to reduce population growth. Palestinian women's fertility rate is among the highest in the region (PCBS 1997a). Nonetheless, the dominant discourse on the subject of women continues to revolve around the glorification of mothers of martyrs, as exemplified by the poetry of the Palestinian icon Mahmoud Darwish.

Glorifying the passive role of the grieving mother, the giving mother, the maternal figure who always provides for the resistance, may help to obscure the fact that decades of Israeli violence and oppression have to a considerable extent rendered men passive and helpless. The sisters and daughters of martyrs have also been subject to conflicting messages. A national discourse glorified mourning women, elevating their personal suffering into national defiance and resistance; a feminist discourse urged them to be themselves, to express their "true" feelings and suffer the pain;[6] an Israeli discourse depicted them as "abnormal" mothers willing to sacrifice their own children, countering glorification with demonization—of them, their dead children, and Palestinians in general.

Amid these conflicting discourses, how may one characterize the "new woman" in the PA national project? Images of the "new woman" emerged not from the formal policies of the PA but from different forms of activism. The Islamist groups portrayed the "model woman" as the veil-wearing caretaker of her husband and children, modest, patient, and pious, as in the past. Most importantly, she was the bearer of male children to be sacrificed in order to continue the resistance; in short, the woman as "giver."[7] In contrast, feminist activism presented a new image of the woman as urban, professional, elegant, claiming

6. During the second intifada, many women's NGOs ran counseling programs for mothers and children to assist them in coping with the immense psychological stress of the Israeli violence.

7. Hamas issued many statements forbidding women from military activities, since there were "enough men to continue the struggle" (see chapter 4).

her individual rights from the PA, society, and her family; in short, the woman as "taker." These images all co-exist.

The character and conduct of the PA influence the articulation of gender equality, with consequences for political culture as a whole, and particularly for the politicization of inequalities in relations between men and women. Goetz (1997) has argued that the importance of the state stems from its capacity to generate social legitimacy for gender equality. The state is an arena for bargaining between interest groups, hence women's interests must be articulated within that space. While women's NGOs and grassroots organizations have an important role to play in creating space for women to politicize their demands, there are serious limits to what civil society institutions can achieve. The state is still responsible for regulating macro level forces in a more gender-equitable manner (Razavi and Miller 1995, 4). Goetz (2003) has shown that the success of "the gender equity interest in policy making and policy implementation will depend upon the interaction of three major factors: the strength of the gender equity lobby in civil society, the credibility of feminist politicians and policies in political competitions, and the capacity of the state to enforce commitments to gender equity" (30). What then can femocrats and their gender units do in a situation with no unified women's front, no political stability, and a questionable commitment to equality by the quasi-state?

The state has significant power to improve women's access to productive resources, employment, information, education, and health; to provide protection from gender violence in the family and community; and to counteract the force of tradition by influencing the discourse on gender relations through the media and educational institutions. These are all potential areas of co-operation between the state and women's groups. However, the state can also use its resources and coercive apparatus to reinforce existing gender-retrogressive biases within the family and community, introducing points of conflict (Rai and Lievesley 1996; Agarwal 1994; Goetz 1997; Kandiyoti 1991b).

Some feminist approaches to the state cast it as a male-dominated apparatus against which women have to fight (Wilson 1977; Eisenstein 1988; Pateman 1988; MacKinnon 1989). There has been less resistance to dealing with the state in countries with a strong tradition of government welfare. There the question of interest articulation has been seen in a positive light, and so has that of participation in state functioning. The femocrat is the creature of this strategy of infiltrating the state in order to influence it in the interests of women (see Franzway, Court, and Connell 1989). Pringle and Watson (1992) thoroughly analyze the trajectory of feminist approaches to the state and reject, from a poststructuralist vantage point, theorizing the state as structurally given, suggesting instead that "it denotes a series of arenas or a plurality of discursive forums" (63; see also Rai and Lievesley 1996; Agarwal 1994; Kandiyoti 1991b; Goetz 1997).

In the Middle East, many feminist scholars consider historical transformations of states, contestations over state power, nation-building, and changing state projects as all crucial factors in the analysis and understanding of women's position and of changes in gender relations. Increasingly, the notion of the state as constituting one homogeneous entity against which social forces, such as feminists and Islamists, struggle, has been replaced with a conceptualization of the state as heterogeneous institutional arenas with different power relations offering different possibilities of contestation. Kandiyoti (2000) has drawn attention, for instance, to how most postcolonial Arab states have reinforced kin-based and communal entities in their quest for legitimacy. The PA was no different, in the sense that in its quest for legitimacy it sought the consent of often opposing social groups, such as the upper middle class, refugees, kin-based tribes, and feminists. As I detail later, women in the PA apparatus were seen as a source of legitimacy, with their gender units—stipulated and supported by foreign funding—presenting a secular, liberal image for the new government.

In the following section, I focus on the PA as the main recruiter for women in the public sector. Gender-mainstreaming units within the government bureaucracy are mandated to pursue their agenda across other government departments (Goetz 1995, 5–6). For this purpose they have devised a range of policy instruments (e.g., gender guidelines, gender training) intended to bring about gender-sensitive institutional, policy, and operational changes across the public sector in order to incorporate responsiveness to women's interests in virtually all governmental activities (6).

The PA is depicted by many scholars as neo-patrimonial. I question this, given the Authority's origins. Also, this perspective does not allow for the externally imposed lack of political stability and the PA's lack of control over national resources, both of which hinder gender mainstreaming. Finally, it takes no account of the conflicts created within and between bureaucracies by the merging of the old PLO with the new PA and the emergence of the new NGOs.

The PA between Neo-Patrimonialism and Realpolitik

The PA has also been extensively theorized as neo-patrimonial[8] based on personal patronage and corruption with inherently patriarchal tendencies that systematically disadvantage women. Parker (1999), for example, concludes that "PA elites might feel compelled to build a

---

8. As described by Bratton and van de Walle, "This term is derived from the concept of patrimonial authority, which Max Weber used to designate the principle of authority in the smallest and most traditional polities. In patrimonial political systems, an individual rules by dint of personal prestige and power; ordinary people are treated as extensions of the 'big man's' household, with no rights or privileges other than those bestowed by the ruler. Authority is entirely personalized, shaped by the ruler's preferences rather than any codified system of laws. The ruler ensures the political stability of the regime and personal political survival by providing a zone of security in an uncertain environment and by selectively distributing favors and material benefits to loyal followers who are not citizens of the polity so much as the ruler's clients" (1997, 61).

As there are few states today without written laws and sophisticated security structures, the definition has evolved. Those hybrid political systems in which the customs and patterns of patrimonialism co-exist with, and suffuse, rational-legal institutions now tend to be characterized as neo-patrimonial (Eisenstadt 1972; Clapham 1985). While some claim that neo-patrimonialism is unable to develop formal structures with formal rules, Bratton and van de Walle claim that although "neopatrimonialism does undermine formal rules and institutions . . . nonetheless patrimonial logic is internalized in the formal institutions of neopatrimonial regimes, it provides essential operating codes for politics that are valued, recurring, and reproduced over time" (1997, 63).

nationalist consensus by giving in to more conservative demands, while feminist demands might be viewed by nationalist leaders as destabilizing and radicalising in a situation where they no longer benefit from 'radical' activities" (182). Hilal (1999) views the PA's neo-patrimonialism as a three-tier system. The ruler personalizes critical decision-making; he is supported by a hegemonic organization (Fateh); and he ensures that the political arena remains plural and diffuse. The neo-patrimonial qualities of the regime have been seen as the main reason for the failure of the Oslo Agreement (Sayigh 1999).

Hilal and Khan's (2004) work on the nature of the Palestinian quasi-state has revealed the simultaneous existence of contradictory features. They observe, for example, that some of the activities of the PA could be described as *predatory*, with rents being created or resources expropriated by PA employees for their personal enrichment at the cost of social development. Other rent-allocation schemes fit better with a description of the PA as a *client state* of Israel and the donor community, receiving and distributing externally generated rents in exchange for delivering the political order desired by external powers. Yet other aspects of rent distribution under the PA suggest that it is a *clientelist* state allocating rents to powerful internal factions in order to maintain stability, even at the cost of considerable economic inefficiency. But most interestingly, some of the rent allocation by the PA, intended to attract investment and generate growth, is also consistent with an emerging *developmental state*.

The problem with the neo-patrimonial approach to analyzing the PA is that it leads to a dead end. It ascribes ultimate power to one man, without taking into account the other external factors influencing the formation of the new regime. But most importantly, the analysis does not account for the space in which opposition groups have emerged, nor does it shed sufficient light on the successive realignments of the PLO as its structure changed and it turned into the PA.[9]

9. Analyzing a similar situation in Uganda, Anne Marie Goetz (2003) states that the assigning of people from across the spectrum of sectarian and other affiliations to political and administrative positions might not necessarily mean "traditionality"

Three major works on the emerging Palestinian political regime by Hillel (1998), Parker (1999), and Hilal (1999)[10] have one point in common, namely the lack of analysis of the impact of the character of the Palestinian regime on gender relations and its commitment to women's rights. In Hillel, the gender issue is not mentioned at all and the assumption is that the ruler fully controls "his hegemonic organization," seen as one bloc of men awaiting the orders of their boss without any internal conflict based on class, gender, or region (1998, 10). In Parker, gender is added as an afterthought in the form of a prediction that the PA elites *might* feel compelled to build a nationalist consensus by giving in to more conservative demands and rejecting feminist demands as destabilizing and radicalizing in a situation where they no longer benefit from "radical" activities. Here the assumption that all women's activism is radical or destabilizing negates the possibility that women's activism may sometimes conform to state policies (see also Alvarez 1990; Caldeira 1998; Haddad 2018). In other words, politics done by women is not necessarily feminist politics. In Hilal, an elaborate socioeconomic class analysis is developed, but gender is not a component of this analysis. This lack of awareness of the PA's role in gender relations and social change leaves a heavy burden on women to examine for themselves the role and impact of the PA on women's rights.

From "Self-Help" to "Self-Government":
Femocrats between Patronage and Feminism

One group of players that came into its own with the formation of the PA is that of the femocrats. Palestinian femocrats are not necessarily feminist, nor are they "employed within state bureaucratic positions to work on advancing the position of women in the wider society

---

and neo-patrimonialism but may rather be "a strategy for palliating the ambitions of other parties to have access to power and economic resources." However, she shows that this path to building legitimacy is "not a way of building accountability" (115).

10. The same lacuna is noticeable in Khan, Giacaman, and Amundsen (2004).

through the development of equal opportunity and anti-discrimination" (Yeatman 1990, 65). Most Palestinian femocrats, in particular those in high-ranking positions, are nominated through patronage relations and not necessarily on the basis of their feminist credentials.[11] However, these women are neither simply co-opted subjects waiting for the president's directives to act on his behalf, nor are they innovators; they are somewhere in between. In other words, some of them may try to develop a gender agenda within the numerous constraints facing the PA and their positioning within it, while others may use the gender agenda and their political access to promote their own interests. Thus, patronage is not necessarily anti-feminist or prejudicial to women's representation. As Goetz (2003) observes in her study of Uganda, patronage might lead to a situation in which "high-profile appointments of women to senior civil service positions . . . significantly enhance[] women's presence in the administration" (110). It is thus reasonable to denote these women as femocrats since they support women's interests and rights, whether they "truly" believe in them or not, in order to make a space for themselves within the PA and society. I depend in this section on my empirical data as well as on publications produced by the different gender units in most Palestinian ministries.

IMCAW, the Inter-Ministerial Committee for the Advancement of Women's Status (*lajnet al-tansiq al-wizariya le-raf'a makanat al-mar'a*) was the locus of femocrats within the Palestinian "state" apparatus from the mid-1990s until its dissolution and the establishment

11. In a study of the situation in Nigeria, Amina Mama (1995) juxtaposes "femocracy" and "feminism." In her view, feminism is the popular struggle of African women for their liberation from various forms of oppression, while femocracy is "an anti-democratic female power structure which claims to exist for the advancement of ordinary women, but is unable to do so because it is dominated by a small clique of women whose authority derives from their being married to powerful men, rather than from any actions or ideas of their own" (41). She questions whether "femocracy" can result in improvement of the status of ordinary women, whether it can be democratized, and whether state structures act as vehicles for ordinary women's struggles or serve only the elite.

of the Ministry of Women's Affairs in 2003. It consisted of women in key positions in their respective ministries, mostly nominated by the president to mainstream gender in their structures.

In 1994, female activists in the Occupied Territories had collectively developed a proposal to establish a Ministry of Women's Affairs in the PA. That November, a delegation from the Women's Affairs Technical Committee (WATC), a coalition of most of the women's groups affiliated with political parties as well as various independent ones, presented the proposal to President Arafat. He rejected the proposal, not because he was a "patriarch" or did not believe in women's rights, but because of the clashing interests of its sponsors. The proposal triggered a conflict between the Minister of Social Affairs, the head of the GUPW (both expatriates), and the head of WATC (a local from the OT). Anticipating the conflict, Arafat suggested to the delegation that such a body should include women in both the government and the GUPW (Arafat, interview); i.e., combining structural elements of both the PA and the PLO. Thus IMCAW was created instead of a ministry.

Women in IMCAW saw success in fund-raising and capacity-building as vital to proving themselves as professionals; it seems they tried to imitate professional women in NGOs at the expense of their former image as militants. As the UNIFEM[12] coordinator for Palestine put it: "The members of IMCAW feel that they need lots of training in capacity-building, they feel they lag behind in the skills of those in the women's NGOs who all know how to fund-raise, how to formulate a strategy, how to manage and communicate. They used to be *mere* freedom fighters, they did not need to fund-raise, they used to get funds through money collections and donations from the Arabs or the Palestinians in the diaspora" (Laila, interview; emphasis added).

Thus, NGO-ization set the model for the "old" militants and became their path to professionalization. In the Palestinian Development Plan for 1996–98, IMCAW was assigned the tasks of

12. United Nations Development Fund for Women (now part of UN Women).

"developing" women and mainstreaming gender but was provided with few resources. It is not surprising that the committee was heavily dependent on donor aid and effectively operated as an NGO: in this case, a GONGO (a governmental nongovernmental organization). As a consequence, women were lumped together in their gender units, into which many activists were co-opted, while gender equity was not integrated into the economic and political agendas of the new "secular" PA. The lack of an overall development goal led the femocrats in IMCAW to focus on technicalities, such as how many workshops were needed to draw up a mainstreaming plan, and thus they fell into the trap Goetz (1997) warns about. She criticizes the notion of mainstreaming as it often focuses on processes and means rather than ends, leading to a preoccupation with the minutiae of procedures at all levels, rather than clarity and direction regarding goals.

The confusions and conflicts within IMCAW reflect similar problems in every ministry and agency of the PA, which seriously hinder not only gender mainstreaming but also any concerted effort at sustaining development. One can hardly speak of a clearly orchestrated national project for change. Incoherent and contradictory policies and interventions are the rule. An observation of Goetz's (1997) has great resonance here: "[U]nderstanding institutions as historically constructed frameworks for behavioural rules and as generators of experience contributes to understanding why it is that when new agents (such as women) and orientations (such as concerns with gender equity) are introduced to institutions, outcomes can seem so little changed" (6).

The Ministry of Youth and Sports provides an illuminating example of the slight outcomes of gender mainstreaming. In 1997, the ministry pursued a national social agenda for children and teenagers, as seen in its publications and its summer camps, whose programs—aside from sports—focused on civic culture, gender equality, participatory democracy, and the promotion of basic rights. However, the ministry was shadowed by another structure linked directly to the president's office and remnants of the PLO: the Recruitment and National and Political Guidance Directorate, which follows a nationalistic agenda for youth focused on "symbolic" military training and political indoctrination in favor of the ruling party and the political leadership. The ministry and the directorate represent two different policies with two distinct sets of gender subtexts. In the Ministry of Youth and Sports, gender issues are systematically integrated through regulations and programs: equal participation for both sexes in the camps, the highlighting of gender equality through various activities, and efforts at the community level to encourage parents to send their daughters to co-educational camps. The ministry was following the "mainstreaming" agenda as if independence had been achieved, and the new governance structures could incorporate the gender agenda.

In the case of the directorate, gender issues were targeted by including both sexes in the "national agenda" via military training camps. Even in the workshops designed for female cadres, gender issues were not dealt with as a social problem; rather, as in the old PLO formula, the principle that men and women should both participate in liberating Palestine was emphasized. The differences between the ministry and the directorate highlight the confusion between the national and the social agendas. After a few months, the "gender-aware" minister of youth and sports was demoted because of his critical stands on patronage and corruption in the PA. He was replaced by a "religious" figure to accommodate the Islamists.

My empirical data revealed many failures and a few successes. If gender mainstreaming suffered from the conflict and confusion within the PA, women's activism in civil society was in no better shape. The establishment of the PA led to the demobilization of the GUPW as well as of grassroots organizations in general and those associated with Fateh in particular, as explained below.

GUPW: Between Mobilization and NGO-ization

The structure of the GUPW, whether in the homeland or in the diaspora, represents the outcome of the constant political changes that have taken place in the Palestinian political system. This instability led to the cessation of most elections to organs of the PLO. In the case of the GUPW, representatives of the activist women's groups affiliated with all the political parties under the PLO structure used meet in general conference to elect the Executive Committee. After the PLO's expulsion from Lebanon in 1982, women leaders were dispersed and it became difficult to bring them together for such general conferences. The last Executive Committee election was held in Tunisia in 1985. In an attempt to solve the problems posed by geographical dispersion, a new directorate was formed that included the head of the GUPW and PLO party representatives to be the highest decision-making body for the GUPW in the diaspora.

The structure of the GUPW in the Occupied Territories was different from that in the diaspora. The GUPW was banned in the Occupied Territories by the Israeli authority for being part of a "terrorist" organization. This led the leadership to function through the various legal charitable organizations in the main cities of the West Bank. Gaza did not join the network due to the fear that the leader of the Arab Women's Union there, Yussra al-Barbari, would be deported. Thus the GUPW could no longer function as a national organization. Soon, most of the charitable organizations involved in "national" activities were harassed and shut down, and the head of the biggest one, Samiha Khalil (aka Im Khalil), was put under town arrest. These actions paralyzed the power of the union to play a leading role in women's resistance to the Occupation. An older generation of women active in charitable societies was in control of the union, which led to conflict with the younger generation of activists in the new grassroots organizations that started to emerge to fill the vacuum left by the GUPW.

While these new women's committees—which proliferated due to political factionalism—brought new blood to the leadership of the Palestinian women's movement, they were not allowed by the old leadership to join the underground structure of the GUPW. But they were supported by their parties and they started to gain a broad constituency due to their innovative approaches to organizing women. When these committees and their heads became the uncontested leaders of women's activities on the street during the first intifada in 1987, the union and its leaders were marginalized.

Empowered by their success, these committees tried to bypass the structure of the GUPW and create a "Higher Council of Women" in 1988. The effort was quickly thwarted by the union's fierce opposition, as well as the lack of a unified vision of the future role of the Higher Council beyond the intifada. This failed attempt led to the inclusion of representatives of the new committees in the local GUPW's Administrative Committee (AC, *al-hay'a al-idariya*), but their voices were largely drowned out among the large representation of the charitable societies (there were at least fifty-five representatives of charitable societies versus just six from the women's committees) (Jad 1990, 2000).

This was the shape of the local GUPW when the diasporic GUPW and its revived Executive Committee (EC) arrived in the homeland following the establishment of the Palestinian Authority in 1994. As a first step, the head of the West Bank branch asked the diasporic leadership to include the members of the local Administrative Committee in the EC. That request was rejected as "unconstitutional, since the members of the EC were elected by the general conference and not nominated" (Lina, interview). This led to tension between the two bodies, aggravated by the marginalization of the AC in the co-ordination committee of IMCAW, the locus of femocrats within the PA apparatus at the time.

The GUPW's absence from the Gaza Strip left space for the creation of a new, separate branch of the union in the late 1990s, headed by Najla Yassine (aka Im Nasser), treasurer of the GUPW in the diaspora and a member of the EC. She had easy access to the president's office and thus to considerable resources. The Gaza GUPW targeted all women activists in the territory, whether in women's committees, NGOs, or those newly appointed to civil service positions in the public sector. While one of the main issues raised in the West Bank was the independence of the GUPW from the PA, this was not an issue in Gaza, perhaps due to the ways in which new members were recruited there. It seems that as in the PA, patronage links were commonly used for benefits from the distribution of food coupons and exemption from membership fees to the provision of aid and social services. Such links also expedited the distribution of membership forms to women working in government bodies who were urged to join the union (subject interview). The structure of the GUPW in Gaza was mainly built on the persona of its founder. After Yassine fell ill around 2010 (she passed away in December 2015), almost all GUPW activities were frozen and the union proved incapable of competing with the growing power of the Islamists in Gaza.

Meanwhile, attempts to establish a new structure for the GUPW in the West Bank were unsuccessful for multiple reasons: it was already weakened there and, as in the 1930s, it was based on representatives of various charitable societies rather than its own distinct membership. The average age of the charitable society representatives, their middle-class background, and their "do-gooder" approach did not help enlarge the union's constituency. As for the representatives of the women's committees, it is clear that they were too busy with their own committees to invest any real energy in establishing a structure in which they might not gain more power. As Salwa Abu Khadra, the head of the EC, stated in 2001: "I keep urging them to put in more effort, to see themselves in the union's structure. I need to hand the torch to a new generation but they never listen. It is now seven years since the return of the PA and what we have achieved is really very little. We have to set up a new structure, create a new constituency, but where are the other women's organizations?" (interview).

The GUPW's failure to meet its expectations for growth in the West Bank was related not only to the power struggle between the "returnees" and the locals, but also to the facts on the ground created by Oslo. Salwa was faced with persistent criticism about the failure to hold new elections; as she explained it:

> What prevents elections from happening are very real and problematic issues, such as the scope and the location of the elections. The members in the diaspora cannot all come here unless the Israelis grant them permits, and the Israelis don't accept that because of the shaky political situation. We cannot organize [the elections] in the diaspora as a matter of principle: the Occupied Territories are now the location of the headquarters of the leadership. Also, it would be very costly to bring large numbers of women representatives from

the diaspora and the union's coffers are empty. And even if they restrict [participation in] the election to the members living in the homeland in Gaza and the West Bank, the members in Gaza cannot join because of the siege. (interview)

The death in February 1999 of Samiha Khalil, the most powerful figure in the GUPW, mitigated the struggle for control of the union. One of the local committee leaders expressed sorrow over her passing, arguing that the diasporic leadership of the GUPW "did not dare to remove her or object to what she was doing. They could not compete with her popularity, her fame, and the respect she was held in by so many people. She was very strong and aggressive. As for them, the returnees, nobody knows them or knows who they were" (A., interview).

The conflict between the diasporic and the local leadership of the GUPW reflects the conflict over the union's role in relation to women at the grassroots level, as well as in relation to the PA. Upon their arrival in the West Bank, the diasporic leadership announced that the union was a nongovernmental body. Their daily practice gives the lie to that assertion. The leadership and its administrative staff receive monthly salaries and the PA pays the rent on their luxurious villas. These facts were cited by the local leadership to challenge the Executive Committee's claim to be running an NGO. "Here [in the West Bank], we follow our internal administrative culture as spelled out in our constitution for charitable societies, according to which an elected member should not get a salary or any financial grant. We consider that a conflict of interest. Besides, as representatives of a group in the society, how could they claim independence from the PA when they all get salaries from the PA?" (A., interview). Clearly, many local activists see this financial dependence as a sign that the GUPW has become a mere prop for the PA, as another interviewee described:

Every time we want to publish a leaflet or any political document, they always insist that we have to add some glorifying lines about the president, and they ask us to display his photos. We are rebellious here, we are not used to that. Also, they objected to one of our leaders attending a conference in Amman because she was one of the signatories to a leaflet published by an opposition group criticizing the corruption in the PA. Of course we have to criticize the government, that is our right, we are not representing the government, we represent our people, our women. (B., interview)

The new head of the GUPW's Administrative Committee, Rima Tarazi, who came to office in 1999 after Samiha Khalil's death, has been less powerful than her predecessor because her history as a militant is relatively obscure, she is Christian, and she is less political; as a result, the returnees were able to assert more control over the reunified GUPW. This does not mean that women in the local leadership have no power base of their own. They are developing their ties with grassroots women's organizations aligned with political parties and with women's NGOs and they are investing concerted efforts in building a popular base for the union, especially in rural areas. The second intifada also led to the inclusion of the GUPW's top local official in the intifada's joint national and Islamic leadership structure.

In conclusion, the above analysis aims to shed light on the internal dynamics of one of the most important Palestinian women's organizations, the GUPW, which has played a leading role in the Palestinian national movement. The fact that the power of a certain elite derived from their position in the national resistance in the diaspora did not entail a loss of power when both the locale and the political system changed. The women on the EC, as well as some femocrats who were part of the diasporic leadership, are not passive followers of their political superiors. These women recognize the gender inequality practiced by the national leadership, but they choose not to overtly protest against it. To use Agarwal's phrase, they are "compliant but not complicit" with the political hierarchy (1997, 25). In order to secure their own interests while appearing to comply with the leadership and the prevailing patronage norms, they use those same norms to hold their leaders accountable. Compliance with the leadership is a technique that diasporic women leaders use to achieve gains; as Razavi and Miller (1995) show, they don't seek autonomy or independence (as many feminists assume) as a precondition to realize their interests (Peteet 1991; Molyneux 2001).

The case of the GUPW and the gender units demonstrates how international blueprints for women and development may not be the best instruments to overcome the contradictions in a situation such as Palestine in which the Occupation greatly hinders the application of most conventional development mechanisms. All these blueprints assume the existence of a state with functioning structures and a stable and well-defined civil society. Outside "experts" tend to ignore the impact of structural and national instability and to pursue the implementation of previously designed gender mainstreaming "projects" assumed to be universally applicable. However, as I have shown, women in the PA or the GUPW were not mere passive recipients of foreign aid—they worked to direct this aid to increase their gains and strengthen their negotiating power vis-à-vis both the PA and other women's groups in civil society. As I have detailed, the increasing power of femocrats and the diasporic leadership in the GUPW came to be, in Radtke and Stam's term, *power over* other local women's organizations (1994, 8; see also Rowlands 1998, 14). I will now detail how power shifted to the benefit of expatriate and professional women in the local women's organization of Fateh, the Women's Social Work Committees.

Demobilization of Grassroots Organizations

Construction of the PA's governance helped to bring the professional women's elite to the fore in Fateh's women's grassroots organizations, at the expense of the rural and refugee women activists. The Oslo Agreement and the establishment of the PA triggered a process that led to the demobilization of all grassroots organizations in the Occupied Territories, including those involved in the women's movement. The donor agenda in support of "peace building" and the growing power of the diasporic elites over the locals were also factors in marginalizing grassroots organizations and their local cadres. The NGO-ization of the latter would add insult to injury.

Before its establishment as a governing authority, the Palestinian leadership worked to "control the street" and, in particular, to control Fateh. Under the PA, the attempt to control Fateh continued, with methods that ranged from recruiting students linked to the security apparatus to sabotaging internal student elections in educational institutions. Attempts by Oslo supporters to manipulate internal elections, whether for Fateh or the popular unions linked to the PLO for women, writers, or students, did not produce the desired degree of control, and the resentment, conflict, and division within Fateh continued to escalate, which led to the loss of its support among many social groups.

The internal decay within Fateh had a major effect on its women's organizations. The attempts of different groups, from the returnees to the supporters of the Oslo process, to build new power bases within Fateh led to further fragmentation. The main division was between those who supported the Oslo Agreement and those who opposed it. The leadership of the Women's Social Work Committees (WSWC), the grassroots Fateh women's organization, took a position critical of Oslo in alignment with the influential Fateh figure Marwan Barghouti, who was advocating the path of "struggle" and "resistance" against Israeli oppression. The pro-Oslo political leadership of Fateh attempted to dilute this opposition by expanding the number of women in the WSWC. The addition of more women seemed on the face of it to be an attempt to increase their representation in a significant decision-making body, but in reality it was an attempt to rein in and weaken the organization. Rawda, an active WSWC and Fateh member from a refugee camp, criticized the new members: "The women they added have no political awareness, no organizational experience, and they know almost nothing about the political organization of women. Many other members were more deserving to be in their place, but they were chosen to create patronage and not for any personal merit. They wanted to control Fateh locally by using women" (interview).

The enlarged body "elected" a new leadership group of thirteen members that did not include Rabiha Deyyab, head of the WSWC.

The widespread criticism of this move reached the president, who mandated the restructuring of women's participation in Fateh, leading to the creation of a new entity named *tanzim al-mar'a* (Women's Organization). This new group was strongly contested by activists in the WSWC who perceived it as a means of excluding the militant activists who came mainly from villages and refugee camps in favor of "professional" women who "never sacrificed their time and lives as we did. . . . They wanted to put all women in a small hall to fight each other. The WSWC is the women's organization of Fateh, so why create another body and this time isolated from its base? They just wanted to marginalize us" (Rawda, interview). The attempt to create a parallel women's organization came to an end with the eruption of the second intifada in 2000, but by then, the biggest grassroots women's organization was already demoralized, divided, and losing its vision.

The process of creating the PA posed a dilemma for many leaders of grassroots women's organizations. If they joined the PA structure they might lose the power base they had managed to build; if they didn't join the PA they would be leaving the dividends of the process to the undeserving. It did not take long for almost all the women leaders who supported Oslo to join the PA bureaucracy. Uncertain about the durability of the PA and its institutions, however, they did not want to take the risk of leaving their institutional bases to other figures. As they sought simultaneously to exercise the powers of their new governmental posts while still heading their nongovernmental organizations, the latter suffered. The lack of internal elections made it easy for them to keep both posts, although the pressure on many to prove themselves as professional femocrats meant that they had little time for their grassroots organizations. For example, Deyyab, the head of the WSWC, was put under tremendous pressure to choose between that post or her position as general director in the Ministry of Youth and Sports; she had to fight to preserve both "as the men do." Thus, the PA co-opted these women and the lack of democracy paralyzed their organizations.

Once the PA was functioning, the WSWC oriented itself toward making claims on the "state" like the rest of the women's NGOs, a track that alienated the organization from its previous vision and programs. The WSWC had a wider outreach than the women's organizations affiliated with the leftist parties. Like the Islamists, the WSWC targeted villages and refugee camps and managed to organize educated young women. Urban professional and academic women were more inclined to join leftist women's organizations, seeing the WSWC as conservative and lacking a feminist agenda. One activist explained its popularity among rural and refugee women: "We use a simple language the people can understand, we give each one what he or she would like to hear—if they are religious we use religious language, if they are leftist we use a leftist language. The most important thing was how to mobilize people to join the struggle, but with women we paid special attention to providing services for them and their children. Women were lacking everything. They have no services in the villages, no employment, and the level of poverty is striking" (Rawda, interview).

For Fateh women, the gender agenda was understood as fulfilling women's basic needs through the provision of services, especially for poor women. However, the successful cadres and those most respected were not the ones who organized or mobilized women, but rather the ones involved in the political organization's underground and militant activities. In Fateh there is a clear distinction between the military wing and other mass-based organizations, including the women's organization. Being a member of the women's organization is an insufficient criterion for inclusion in the party's higher ranks. Those who joined the women's organization were labeled Fateh members "to show our popularity" (Tina, interview), but very few women were actually members in the Fateh political organization. In order to be a member, women had to prove themselves as "*bint* Fateh"—a daughter of Fateh (Tina, interview). A real "daughter of Fateh" was constructed as masculine, tough, with short hair, simple trousers, and a long shirt with long sleeves; as Islamism became popular, a headscarf was added to the image. She had to be discreet, talk little, and remain staunch under interrogation. Some women who managed to become heads of militant cells were given male *noms de guerre*. As Salwa recalls: "I was known by the name of Abu Mohammed [Mohammed's father].[13] I talked, walked, and behaved exactly like a man. If I showed my femininity, they [men] would take me for a weak, easy-to-crack person. I was tough, very tough. I had to show them that I am not less than them, as a tough strong man. I only realized that I am a woman and that I have to be proud of it after the establishment of the PA, when I attended a conference on what our 'gender agenda' should be under the PA" (interview).

When the PA was established and many leftist women's organizations and NGOs started to demand that it champion women's rights, the WSWC felt at a loss. Rawda explains the dilemma felt by many women activists in Fateh:

> We in Fateh are not like women in the leftist organizations who raised women's issues from the very beginning of their work. We were more oriented to the national cause. We never dealt with or spoke about what the social status of women should be once we have a state; that was postponed 'til after the liberation. When the PA was established we realized our *matab* [impasse]—now there was no national struggle, now it was a state-building era and we had no vision about what we had to do. We thought of enlarging the WSWC's Executive Committee, we thought of adding more highly educated professional women to help us to draw up a mission statement and manage our organization. We have great women militants who sacrificed a lot during the struggle, but they are not highly educated, they are not *motakhassissat* [professional]. We had very little money; we needed to raise funds for our organization. The PA didn't give us any financial help and we were obliged to register as an NGO to fund-raise for our own activities. We hoped that might open new avenues and provide new contacts. (interview)

13. It is a common practice in Palestinian culture to give the name of the first male son to his parents; thus, Abu Mohammed means the father of Mohammed. Salwa was appointed head of a police station in Gaza but was removed when a prisoner in the station escaped.

At the time of this writing, the WSWC has still not solved its dilemma. The women in the organization are highly political—they know that if they hire outside professionals it might diminish their own power and move the organization in a direction over which they have no control. Yet at the same time they need the expertise of professionals in order to effectively manage the process of NGO-ization.

Between State and Civil Society: The Role of Women's NGOs

The role played by Palestinian NGOs before the Oslo Agreement differs significantly from their role in the post-Oslo phase. Before the formation of the PA, Palestinian society was organized in and around political parties and mass grassroots organizations. NGOs were linked to these parties under the umbrella of the PLO, which encouraged and financially supported the parties and their satellite organizations. While the PLO and its political parties were banned by Israel, some of their satellite bodies were allowed to operate, since they were seen as service-providing organizations. Between the end of the 1987 intifada and Oslo, the NGO sector was the main channel of foreign aid supporting the delivery of services at the grassroots level, including clinics, schools, kindergartens, and income-generating projects. The result was that these NGO actors grew in importance, acquiring even more power than their parent parties.

The role of NGOs in the West Bank and Gaza shifted under the influence of the state-building process initiated by the Madrid Conference in 1991. The period from 1988 to 1994 witnessed a proliferation of overtly feminist women's organizations (Women's Affairs Centers in Nablus in 1988 and then in Gaza in 1989; the Women's Study Center in 1989; the Women's Affairs Technical Committee in 1991; the Women's Center for Legal Aid and Counseling in 1991; the Women's Study Program at Birzeit University in 1994; see appendix A) (Jad 2000, 44). The growing number of institutions propagated a new discourse on women and women's status, but within the context of a steady decline in women's mobilization. An unpublished study of five women's mass organizations by the NGO Panorama revealed that their membership declined by 37 percent after 1993 and the new enrollment rate in 1996 did not exceed 3 percent, most of it in the WSWC, the Fateh women's organization (probably for patronage reasons) (Jad 2000, 44).

Understanding the effects of the state-building dynamics on different forms of organization in civil society provides key insights into the actual process of demobilization of the Palestinian women's movement. The dual dynamics of state building and NGO-ization redoubled the fragmentation and demobilization of all social movements. The limited life cycle of "projects" induced fragmentation rather than generating what Tarrow (1994) has called "sustainable networking," whereby ties established between organizations and individual participants are maintained over time. NGO-ization also has a cultural dimension, spreading values that favor dependency, discourage self-reliance, and introduce new modes of consumption.[14] It precipitated changes in the composition of the women's movement elites (Goetz 1997) that resulted in a major shift in power relations. I use Radtke's and Stam's (1994) definition of power as the "capacity to have an impact or produce an effect" so that "power is both the source of oppression in its abuse and the source of emancipation in its use" (8; see also Rowlands 1998, 14; Agarwal 1994).[15] My study shows a shift

14. It is common to read advertisements in Palestinian newspapers for collective community actions organized by youth groups, such as cleaning streets, planting trees, and painting walls, tagged by a little icon indicating the name of the donors funding these projects. It is also noticeable that many NGO events are held in fancy hotels with expensive catering, the distribution of glossy print materials, and the employment of "presentable" youth, whose image has gradually supplanted that of the activist as a peasant.

15. Along with Radtke and Stam (1994), Rowlands (1998) differentiates between two types of power: "power over"—controlling power, which may be responded to with either compliance or resistance—and "power to"—generative or productive power (manifested as resistance and/or manipulation), which creates new possibilities and actions without domination. This power can be what enables the individual to maintain a position or sustain an activity in the face of overwhelming opposition, or to take a serious risk (14).

from "power to" women in the grassroots to "power over" them by the new elite.

My concern here is to avoid the dichotomies of traditional/modern and authentic/Westernized (Ahmad 1992; Abu-Lughod 1998). I also avoid judging the NGOs in terms of the class they represent, what Pringle and Watson (1992) call "representation" politics. I intend, instead, to provide an in-depth analysis of how women articulate their agendas in this particular form of organization. If the diversity of women's organizations reflects the diverse positions of women in society, it is important to examine how different forms of women's organization reflect different interests (Yuval-Davis 1997; Molyneux 1998, 2001), how these interests are articulated, how the participating activists engage with other female constituencies and activisms, and how all these processes are shaped and reshaped in a context of unfulfilled national struggle and unachieved state formation. My assumption, reflected in my theoretical approach, is that different organizational forms manifest and articulate different gender interests.

If we compare the size of the older societies and unions with that of the constituencies of contemporary NGOs, a decline in the participating population is apparent. The prevailing NGO structure involves a board of between seven and twenty members and a highly qualified professional and administrative staff whose size is usually small, depending on the number and character of the organization's projects. The practical power of decision-making frequently is not in the hands of the board but rather with the director. The power of the latter stems from his or her ability to fund-raise, be convincing, appear presentable, demonstrate competence, and deliver the well-written reports that donors require. Communication and English-language skills are vital, in addition to proficiency with modern communication equipment (computer, mobile phones).

As for the internal "governance" of NGOs, a survey of more than sixty Palestinian NGOs found that most of their employees do not participate in decision-making due to "their passivity or their lack of competence" (Shalabi 2001, 152). Nor do the "target" groups participate in decision- or policy-making. When administrators were asked why this was so, they answered that they themselves were part of the society, they knew it, and they could make determinations about its needs. In many women's NGOs, staff members do not even know how their target groups' budgets are distributed. According to Shalabi, the internal governance of the surveyed NGOs was "a mirror reflection of the Palestinian political system based on individual decision-making, patronage and clientelism," and the lack of rules governing organizations' internal relations. In some cases, a union dispute erupted and was settled in a "way very far away from the rule of law" (154).

The highly professional qualities required of administrative staff for donor communications may not directly affect the links between an NGO and local constituencies, but most of the time they do. Referring specifically to the Palestinian experience, the traits of successful cadres in the grassroots organizations—the women's committees that were branches of political formations that sustained the first intifada—differed considerably from those required in NGO staff. The success of the cadres lay in *organizing* and *mobilizing* the masses, and was based on their skills in building relationships with people. They succeeded in this because they had a cause to defend, a mission to implement, and a strong belief in the political formations they belonged to. For a cadre, it was important to be known and trusted by people, to have easy access to them, to care about them, and to help them when needed. The task called for daily, time-consuming, tiring effort in networking and organizing. The cadres knew their constituencies personally, as communication often depended on face-to-face, individual human contact. NGOs, by contrast, depend primarily on modern communication methods such as media, workshops, and conferences, and globalized rather than local tools. These methods may not be bad in themselves but they are mainly used to "advocate" or "educate" a "target group," usually defined for the period needed to implement the "project." Here the constituency is not a natural social group; rather it is abstract, receptive rather than interactive, and the "targeting" is limited by the project time frame. This temporality of the project and the constituency makes it difficult to measure the impact of the intervention, and also jeopardizes the continuity of focus on whatever issue is involved.

It is important to recognize these differences in order to clarify the prevailing confusion between social movements and NGOs, because if it is to have weight or, in political terms, power, a social movement must have a large popular base. According to Tarrow (1994), what empowers social movements is that "at their base are the social networks and cultural symbols through which social relations are organized. The denser the former and the more familiar the latter, the more likely movements are to spread and be sustained" (2). He adds, "contentious collective action is the basis of social movements; not because movements are always violent or extreme, but because it is the main, and often the only recourse that most people possess against better-equipped opponents. Collective action is not an abstract category that can stand outside of history and apart from politics for every kind of collective endeavor—from market relations, to interest associations, to protest movements, to peasant rebellions and revolutions" (3). The same can be said of women's movements. To put "'women's movement[s]' into context, we have to ask first, what a 'women's movement' is and how can we distinguish it from 'women in movement'" (Rowbotham 1992, in Jackson and Pearson 1998, 226).

There are different views as to what constitutes a women's movement. It could be a mobilizing engine to demand female suffrage, with a leadership, a membership, and diffuse forms of political activity that qualify it as a movement, as distinct from forms of solidarity based on networks, clubs, or groups. And according to Molyneux, it implies a social or political phenomenon of some significance, due both to its *numerical strength* and to its capacity to effect change, whether in legal, cultural, social, or political terms. A women's movement does not have to have a single organizational expression and may be characterized by diversity of interests, forms of expression, and spatial location. It is, however, composed of a substantial female majority, where it is not exclusively made up of women (Molyneux, cited in Jackson and Pearson 1998, 226).

Thus, it seems preferable to reserve the term "movement" for something broader than a small-scale association. As I argued earlier, the typical structure of NGOs debars them from serving as mobilizing or organizing agents, so that however much they proliferate they cannot sustain and expand a constituency, nor tackle issues related to social, political, or economic rights on a macro- or national level. Were they to undertake these aims, they would have to stop being NGOs.[16] When, in 1998, women's NGOS undertook such a national initiative in a model parliament, the constraints on NGOs in mobilizing and organizing became clear.

Legal Reform and Social Change in Project Form: The Model Parliament Experiment

In early 1998, a project titled "Palestinian Model Parliament: Women and Legislation" was launched by the Ramallah-based Women's Center for Legal Aid and Counseling (WCLAC) to achieve a set of goals including legislation guaranteeing human rights and equality for Palestinian women, and broader participation in building a civil society based on the foregoing principles, justice, and the rule of law. More immediate objectives were also set, including the encouragement of public discussions on legislation and democratic principles, and the improved dissemination of legal information. Emphasis was placed on raising public awareness through the media and lobbying officials in decision-making positions.

The project brochure explained its rationale:

> The presence of an elected Palestinian Legislative Council refreshes the hope of Palestinian women to claim Palestinian rights, to build the independent state and a democratic civil society. The current era of construction and the necessity to prepare for the future make it the duty of women to immediately and actively participate in establishing the foundation of legislation based on respect for human rights and the principles of justice and equality, which represent the will and interest of the people. (WCLAC 1998)

---

16. In the middle of a debate in Egypt on *khul* (a woman's right to be divorced if she gives up her financial rights), a prominent feminist activist was asked if her center was taking part in the debate. She replied, "We don't deal with such 'projects.'"

Soon afterward, the Center decided to launch a national campaign for this cause targeting all social groups in Palestinian society, and all men as well as women. Before implementing the project, the Center approached many women's organizations to participate: "We asked for a meeting and presented the idea in order to decide who can do what. We expected that each organization would take the part that is related to their projects" (WCLAC director, in a meeting with WATC in 1998). A preparatory committee group was formed, made up of a media committee (*i'lam*) and a negotiation and lobby committee (*mofawada wa daght*) run by WCLAC staff members. A handbook on negotiation and lobbying techniques was produced and training workshops on the use of those techniques were organized. After a round of preparatory events, a total of five model parliament sessions was scheduled in five different cities. The concluding session, in Ramallah, would focus on arriving at final language for proposed legislation (WCLAC 1998).[17]

An important component of the campaign was the production and distribution of an array of glossy print materials and huge billboards announcing the project's main slogan: "Don't walk in front of me, I cannot follow you. Don't walk behind me, I can't wait for you. Walk beside me and be my ally" (*la tamshi amami aad la atba'ak; la tamshi khalfi qad la antazerak; emshi bi janebi wa kon halifi*). "Total equality" was the campaign's *mot d'ordre* and the guiding principle of its training programs. On a theoretical level, "total equality" is seen by some as requiring "gender-neutral legislation," while others argue that women need sex-specific laws and protections (Phillips 1993, 45). Eisenstein (1989), for example, argues that total equality has, so far, silently privileged the male body: when men and women are treated the same, it means that women are treated as if they were men; when men and women are treated differently, the man remains the norm,

17. Three sessions for the 1998 Model Parliament were held in the West Bank: in the North (Nablus) on February 21–22; in the South (Hebron) on March 2–3; and in Ramallah on March 11–12. Two sessions were held in Gaza City and a central-area session was again held in Ramallah on April 25.

as compared with which the woman is peculiar or lacking. Feminism has been endlessly locked in an equality/difference dichotomy (Scott 1988; Phillips 1993, 45). Eisenstein suggests that, instead of the difference between male and female, we need to recognize the many differences among women and among men, as well as between the two. In this respect, I could not find any material indicating that there was awareness in Palestine of the debate in international feminist circles around the "total equality" agenda, and I got the same impression from my interviews with the staff and other people involved in the model parliament legislative project. The whole "equality versus difference" discourse (see, e.g., Pateman 1988, 1989; Phillips 1993; Eisenstein 1989) does not feature prominently in the Palestinian context, where understanding women's situation is based mainly on activist experience and the relations grassroots organizations develop with their constituencies.

The model parliament sessions were publicized as the culmination of the national campaign for an "open democratic forum" in which everyone could participate. Accordingly, many invitations were issued to individuals and institutions, including the religious establishment and activists in the Islamic movement, women's organizations, representative figures of various social groups, government bodies, political parties, and Members of Parliament. The preparatory committee "wanted to include people from different social and political backgrounds . . . and the people who accepted our invitation were considered members in the Parliament" ('Othman 1998, 62).

The WCLAC organizers saw the campaign as "just a project," and seemed unaware that what they were dealing with was intimately related to the concepts of Palestinian nationalism, national identity, and citizenship, and they were not attuned to the contending discourses around those concepts. Some of the organizers saw it as an "exercise" to train legislators in how to tackle women's rights in a legal framework and to train the public in participating in the discussion around the drafting of new laws (Hammami and Johnson 1999). Others saw it as a consciousness-raising practice to conceptualize laws closer to the ordinary expectations of the public. Still others saw it as a "test" to evaluate who was with "us" and who against. What was clear was that there was no consistent view as to what should be the outcome of the project or "anticipation as to its results" (Siniora 2000, 2). However, there was a major shift after the Islamists attacked the project as an externally driven bid by "Westernized, donor-driven, Marxist feminists to change the law of *shari'a* for Muslims" (Al-Huda Association 1998). The project's proponents felt compelled to restate its primary goal, abandoning the achievement of "total equality" for the more "neutral" aim of securing "freedom of expression." Many academics and supporters of women's rights who sought to defend the model parliament engaged in this discursive shift.

The project triggered a range of reactions. Some, mainly middle-class, asserted that it was not the time for such issues and that the Occupation must come to an end first. Some mainstream activists saw the project as driven by foreign—specifically Western—funding to divert people's attention from the daily realities of life in Palestine. The PA, represented by the governor of Ramallah, who was invited to address the model parliament's concluding session, readily provided police protection for the conference and presented itself as a guarantor of the very "freedom of expression" it nominally sought.

As for the Islamists, their reactions were varied as well. The Islamic establishment, represented by clergy in the Ministry of Religious Endowments (*wizaret al-awqaf*) and the office of the Supreme Judge (*qadi al-qudat*), were most keen to stand against the call to disband the *shari'a* courts and apply *shari'a* family law in civil courts. They presented a memorandum to the Palestinian Parliament condemning the proposed changes and urging the MPs not to accept them ('Othman 1998, 81). Most importantly, the clergy questioned the "legitimacy" of women and the public at large—and even Parliament itself—in addressing or debating issues seen as subject to their jurisprudence. In other words, the *'ulama'* (religious clergy) claimed the prerogative to rule in matters involving *shari'a*. Their position was founded on the duality of the Palestinian legal system, in which civil courts exist side by side with religious ones, and they argued that Parliament only had authority over the former.

Hamas was more belligerent, engaging in a campaign through mosque services and various publications to silence and defame those who wanted to step over one of the "red lines" of *shari'a*. The attack focused on delegitimizing women activists involved in the project as "inauthentic," as members of a marginal non-Muslim minority (Christian[18] or secular/atheist), and as puppets of their Western benefactors (Al-Huda Association 1998, 4, 6). The attack distinguished carefully between the "new centers"—i.e., NGOs—and other women's societies, which were said to deserve respect and appreciation (3). Organizations such as the Women's Affairs Technical Committee (WATC) and, in particular, the WCLAC were attacked by name in leaflets and in Friday sermons. The project thus propelled the WCLAC and the women's movement in general into a highly contested public arena where Islamist discourse—empowered by the failure of the PA to bring about national independence or social change—gained clear hegemony. Islamists were further empowered by the PA's flagrant efforts to marginalize them, which only served to weaken the nascent Palestinian legal structure (Sayigh and Shikaki 1999; Kayed 1999). As a more immediate consequence, some women activists involved in the project found it difficult to resume their daily service in poorer areas. Others, especially lawyers, were no longer welcome to work in *shari'a* courts. Many had to explain or distance themselves from what had happened. According to Manar Mohammed, a Fateh activist in Gaza, "women did not want to let us in, they said you are the *sorreyat* [the model parliament was known as *al-barlman al-souwari* in Arabic], you work to divorce women from their husbands" (interview).

Nevertheless, the project did achieve important gains, such as articulating a general agreement among Palestinians that existing "personal status laws need serious consideration" (Siniora 2000, 6). It popularized the notion that ordinary people should be involved in

---

18. It happened that the lawyer who reviewed the draft laws and submitted her recommendations, which included a civil family law, as well as the head of WCLAC and the project director were all Christians.

changing laws and legislation, and not legislators and experts alone. It enabled women to test their strengths and their weaknesses and provided invaluable lessons in better networking, mobilization, and organization. It also showed up the many contradictions in Palestinian nationalism and its relation to religion (Hammami and Johnson 1999; Welchman 2003).

The hostile reaction to the model parliament project caused deep anxiety among members of the different women's organizations. Some who were part of the WATC coalition felt that they had been dragged into an overt confrontation with the Islamist movement they had neither planned for nor wanted at that particular time. On the other hand, they did not want to take a stand against the WCLAC's vision, since many of them shared some or all of its goals, if not its strategy. The GUPW, for example, found itself in a situation where it had to "confirm" that it did not support the abolition of *shari'a* but was interested in its reform. More importantly, the project left bitter feelings and a lack of trust among the different women's organizations. It also led to a sharper polarization between women's NGOs and mass-based organizations. The project did not help create a women's front, but rather led to further fragmentation. It is not hard to see this as a case in which the fear that the universal citizen "threatens to shut down the awakening recognition of group identity and difference" was realized (Phillips 1993, 87).

Two years later, Randa Siniora (2000), executive director of WCLAC's model parliament project, presented a paper in English to an international conference on Islamic family law in the Middle East and North Africa in which she offered important conclusions and lessons learned from the project. It was clear, she said, that the "initiative [was] by all means beyond the scope of one group or one organization. . . . [S]uch initiatives need to be planned in total partnership with our allies . . . and broad-based coalitions are needed, including links with the grassroots segments of society" (7, 9, 10). Most crucially, she argued, "it is only when political parties realise that it is in their own interest to adopt a social agenda that real change will be effected concerning the social and legal status of Palestinian women. The NGO community in Palestine cannot and should not take sole responsibility for advancing social change and legal reform. The role of the NGO community is to facilitate and assist in the process; it should play the role of a catalyst" (13).

Conclusions

Successive colonizers subordinated Palestinians as a whole and rural people in particular to the urban elite. In turn, Palestinian nationalists, in their ideas and their practice, treated women as auxiliary to men and delimited their role mainly to the domestic sphere. Of particular relevance, urban elite women treated rural women as their subordinates, the object of their charity and "uplifting." This pattern was a central reason for the failure of the urban elite women's movement of the 1930s and 1940s to engage with women in rural areas, thus denying itself a truly popular base. Women, divided along class and regional lines, acted not as a unified body, but focused on their own parochial interests. Furthermore, the unstable political situations long endured by the Palestinians and their leadership tended to militate against any serious push by women for social change.

The emergence of the secular, nationalist PLO in 1964, and especially after the Arab defeat of 1967, was pivotal in consolidating Palestinian national identity based on core tenets of struggle, sacrifice, and return. The new mode of Palestinian nationalism constituted women in contradictory images of the "traditional, sacrificing mother" whose main role was to (re)produce her nation by providing male fighters, and of the "revolutionary militant" who should join hand in hand with her brothers in the struggle to liberate the nation. This contradictory construction was contested by women activists who started to challenge the prevailing gender order by pressuring their organizations for more equitable legislation and policies.

The "revolutionary" era in the diaspora and the Occupied Territories was an important phase in the development of the Palestinian women's movement, during which women's activism was successful in bridging the gap between urban elite women, those in rural areas, and refugees. This linkage spurred the wider organization and mobilization of women at the grassroots level and the formation of new cadres who, for the first time, did not come from privileged backgrounds.

The Oslo Agreement and the emergence of the PA triggered a process in which civil society organizations shifted from sustaining their communities to claiming their constituents' rights. This shift brought the elite urban professionals back to the fore at the expense of the rural and refugee leadership. The merger between the structures of the PLO and the PA ultimately led to the marginalization and fragmentation of grassroots organizations and elites alike, ceding both discursive and functional space to the already expanding influence of the Islamists.

3

Between Faith
and Feminism

Islamist Women of Hamas

WHILE THERE IS A CONSIDERABLE VOLUME of writing on contemporary Islamist movements (Hroub 1996, 2000; al-Hamad and
al-Bargouthi 1997; Abul-Omrein 2000; al-Taheri 1995; Abu Amr
1994; Litvak 1996; Schiff and Ya'ari 1989; Hilal 1998; Munson
2003), there has been only sketchy reference to their gender ideology
and very little attention has been paid to female militants themselves.
In this chapter, I study and give voice to the Islamist women of Hamas
(the Islamic Resistance Movement), who are not considered by many
feminists to be important contributors to Palestinian women's activism. I argue that this is an important omission, particularly in view of
their growing activism in civil society.

The aim of this chapter is to contextualize and explore the changing discourse, structure, and gender ideology of the Islamist movement in the West Bank and Gaza from the late 1970s to the present
and to examine Islamist women's activism within Hamas. The Islamists' changing need for women to play roles in the public sphere has
resulted in a transformation from near total apathy and demobilization to more inclusion and much greater activism. I argue that secular
feminist movements influence the direction of the debate on gender
and women's rights in Islamist movements and many of the positions
and views of the latter are formed in reaction to secular feminism. I

71

have found it difficult to describe and make sense of Islamist "feminism" without scrutinizing the rejoinders it offers to modern, secularist principles. Thus, the idea of a fixed "inner logic" of Islam explains the position of Islamist movements less accurately than does an examination of how Islamist women engage with their secularist counterparts whose positions actively inform Islamist discourse. I focus on Islamist women in the West Bank and Gaza, the discourses they employ to promote their vision, their daily practices, and their positioning within the Islamist movement.

I use the phrase "Islamist movement" to refer to a sociopolitical movement founded on an Islam defined as much in terms of political ideology as in terms of religion (Mitchell 1969 quoted in Roy 1999, 39); "Islamists," then, denotes the members and supporters of such a movement. In Palestine, the Islamist women's movement comprises women active within Hamas as well as in other Islamist bodies. However, Islamist women have been mobilized into a movement only in Gaza, and there is little coordination between Islamist organizations in Gaza and the West Bank.

This chapter begins by contextualizing the Palestinian Islamists within the international debate on Islam and Islamists. One of the most important elements is the fusion between Islam as a religion, and nationalism (whether pan-Arab or country-specific) as a secular and modern construct. In this context, the debate over whether the Palestinian national movement is secular (i.e., modern) or a conflation of Islam and secularism (i.e., traditional) is analyzed and critiqued.

The growing influence of Islamist movements in the Middle East is usually examined in the context of states' withdrawal from providing vital social and economic services to their citizens. This frame does not fit in the case of Palestine, where a sovereign nation-state never existed. However, the socioeconomic and political transformations produced by the Israeli Occupation were important in promoting the Palestinian Islamists directly and indirectly. Hamas, founded in 1987, thus shifted from an exclusionary religious movement into a powerful rival and alternative to the secular Palestinian national movement represented by the PLO or the PA. The ability of Hamas to shift its position to a nationalist stance and expand its movement into a nationwide one was crucial to its reaching wider constituencies and gaining more popular support and legitimacy. Hamas has deliberately used the conflation between Islam and nationalism to "nationalize" Islam and confine it to the territorial context of Palestine, and to "Islamize" Palestinian nationalism.

In reacting to and emulating the secular and leftist political groups, the Islamists learned how to adjust their appeal to attract a wider constituency. With the collusion of the Israeli Occupation and the Jordanian regime, the Islamists in Palestine managed to build an impressive infrastructure of cultural, social, economic, and political institutions that proved crucial in sustaining the Islamist movement.

The pivot from accommodating the Occupation to full-fledged resistance through spectacular military actions was a turning point in the history of the Islamists in Palestine; it brought them uncontested popularity. Once established as a broad, popular national movement, Hamas altered its structure to act as a legal, political party. The Islamic National Salvation Party, established by Hamas in 1995 (and dissolved after Hamas came to power in the legislative elections of 2006), was an important vehicle for the Islamists' pursuit of a more sustained and organized constituency in the eventuality of power-sharing through democratic processes such as elections. This shifting perspective was a crucial factor in compelling the Islamists to pay more systematic attention to recruiting and organizing women. In competition with the secularists, and in reaction to their stance on recruiting and integrating women into their organizations, the Islamists began to target women, in particular highly educated women, and to integrate them into their party structure at all levels.

The link between gender ideology and religious fundamentalist movements such as Hamas is one of great consequence to their quest to build the moral society based on the moral family. In an attempt to explain the growing power of the Islamists and the lack of a visible role for Islamist women in the national resistance, I examine what I term the "gendered structure" of the movement and the evolving nature of Hamas gender ideology. The rigid, formal division of labor confining women to the domestic sphere as the reproducers of a "moral" nation gave way to more open-ended interpretations of texts, enabling women to open up a wider space in the public arena. This was not haphazard; it was the outcome of the work and activism of Islamist women within the movement against the background of the achievements women had realized in society at large and which the Islamists could not reverse. It was also the product of and reaction to the pressure exercised by secular feminists in their critique of the Islamists' attempt to freeze the gender order through the immutable rules of *shari'a* law.

In this chapter, I present an analysis of the construction of Islamist women's discourse and its interplay with universalist feminist discourses, local discourses, and modes of activism within Palestinian society and women's movements. I outline the development of the terms of engagement between the Islamist movement and the political organizations under the umbrella of the PLO, and Fateh in particular. I also trace the development of the relationship between Islamists and the Palestinian Authority after the Oslo Agreement in 1993. A historical account of the evolution of Hamas's political ideology in its rivalry for power and ideological hegemony with other national and secular groups will prove necessary, as will a detailed account of the fluctuations between religious and political national principles in Hamas's discourse.

Islam and Its So-Called "Resurgence"

Many studies have shown that what has been widely called the "resurgence" or "revival" of Islam—the "return" to an Islamic lifestyle and a growing religiosity—can be seen in virtually all Muslim societies, affecting culture, social relations, economic affairs, and political life (e.g., Esposito 1983; Burke and Lapidus 1988; Zubaida 2000; Karam 1998; Ayubi 1991; Beinin and Stork 1997; Hunter 1988; Haddad and Esposito 1998). Some Islamists themselves are among those who promote this concept of "resurgence," often in the course of rejecting the label "Islamic fundamentalism" as a foreign notion. The Islamist Palestinian historian Khaled Abul-Omrein (2000), for example, uses the term *al-madd al-islami* (Islamic resurgence) in discussing the different phases "of the history of Islamic activism between strength and weakness and spread and decline" (18). I refrain from using the terms "Islamic resurgence" or "revival," as they can be taken to imply a static, ever-present Islam waiting to be reactivated (see, e.g., Davis 1987, 37; Roy 1999; al-Azmeh 1996). The phenomenon of growing linkages between religiosity and politics cannot be understood with reference to the traditional systems of thought and action, but represents an effort to generate and legitimate new forms of political and social action in radically changing societies. It is, thus, a novel and modern phenomenon (Burke and Lapidus 1988; Zubaida 2000; Dekmejian 1988; Hunter 1988; Kandiyoti 1991b; Roy 1999; Karam 1998; Ayubi 1991; Beinin and Stork 1997).

The corollary debate on the role of Islamist movements has been rendered very complicated by two different developments. On one hand, "neo-Orientalist"[1] approaches (Bill and Springborg 1990; Lewis 1964, 1988; Kedourie 1992; Crone 1980; Gellner 1983, 1992; Pipes 1983, 1992; Vatikiotis 1983, 1987) cast the modern Middle East and regimes in the region as blighted by the "medieval failure to develop stable politics that continues to be one of the difficulties Muslims face in modernizing" (Pipes 1983, 187–88, in Sadowski 1997, 18). Crone, for example, has argued that, as a religion, Islam is essentially "monotheism with a tribal face" (quoted in Sadowski 1997, 17–18). Thus, Muslim societies are depicted as incompatible with Western notions of democracy, secularism, or even the nation-state. In the same fashion, the resurgence of political movements claiming Islam as an ideology is explained in terms of an "immutable" Islam

---

1. The thesis that Middle Eastern societies are resistant to democratization has been a standard tenet of Orientalist thought for decades, but in the 1980s a new generation of Orientalists adopted a new vocabulary that allowed them to embed their work in a wider, international debate about the relationship between civil society and democratization. This updated approach sought to prove not only that Muslim countries have the most terrorists and the fewest democracies in the world, but that they always will (Sadowski 1997, 14).

distinct from its economic, political, and social context. This exceptionalism may also be explained in cultural terms (Salamé 2001, 3) or in terms of culture shaped by sociohistorical factors (Sharabi 1988).

On the other hand, the "good governance" agenda, which has become dominant since the 1980s, emphasizes formal democratization and the promotion of civil society (Norton 1993, 1995; Kramer 1992; Salamé 2001; Waterbury 2001; Hudson 1996; Ibrahim 1993, 1995; al-Sayyid 1993; Zubaida 1992). Controversy erupted between scholars who entertain the possibility that modern forms of civil society can develop in the Muslim world, and those who invoke Islam to justify the presence of a strong despotic state ruling at the expense of civil society in which autonomous social organizations are unable to curb the powers of the state (Turner 1984; Ayubi 1995). It was further argued that groups within Islamic societies were weakly organized and lacked strong corporate identities. Social associations in the Middle East have tended to be informal, personal, and relatively inefficient in winning support and extracting resources from the populace, and have proven too feeble to challenge the power of the state and constitute a civil society (Springborg 1975, cited in Sadowski 1997, 35; Ayubi 1995). In this setting, modern organizations such as unions, peasant associations, and professional syndicates only provide window dressing that obscures the continuing struggle of atomized clients to secure the sponsorship of elite patrons.

The prevailing view shifted as a consensus emerged among Western and Middle Eastern scholars that Middle Eastern states are weak and, as a result of economic crises, getting weaker (Bill and Springborg 1990; Lewis 1964, 1988; Gellner 1983, 1992; Kedourie 1992; Vatikiotis 1983, 1987; Ayubi 1995; Salamé 2001; Roy 1999). These writers concur that the frailty of the state partly reflects and partly encourages greater assertiveness by social groups; while states are paralyzed, movements like the Islamists appear to have seized the initiative. Some think the growing energy of social groups can be harnessed to help forge democracies in the region (Norton 1993; Kramer 1992; Salamé 2001; Waterbury 2001; Hudson 1996). It has, however, been argued that certain such structures (such as NGOs) have been privileged while others (the Islamists in particular) remain ostracized from these formations of power (Ibrahim 1993, 1995; al-Sayyid 1993; Ayubi 1995; Massad 2015). There is also a more fundamental debate as to whether Islamist organizations can ever be part of civil society in the Middle East (Norton 1995; Kramer 1992; Ayubi 1995; Hudson 1996). Neo-Orientalists assert that a proliferation of social movements will discourage any trend toward power-sharing or greater tolerance in the region, and may in fact breed civil war and anarchy.

Arguing against such views, Sami Zubaida (1993), for example, has criticized the ahistorical generalizations so characteristic of Orientalists by showing how many authors erroneously invoke the notion of a continuous historical essence of Islam (see also Abu-Lughod 2013; Massad 2015).[2] Zubaida (2003) points out that these authors ignore specific socioeconomic and political developments and conjunctures, and questions the existence of *a* "Muslim" society, arguing that "modern Islamism is a political ideology quite distinct from anything in Muslim history, which, in recent years, has become a dominant idiom for the expression of various and sometimes contradictory interests, aspirations and frustrations" (31).

Whether or not they used the language of "resurgence/revival," many scholars attributed the phenomenon of growing religiosity and the politicization of Islam to a common set of socioeconomic, political, and cultural factors such as the failure of the postcolonial nation-states in the Middle East to achieve sustainable levels of development, the spread of political repression and socioeconomic injustices, the rise in the influence of the petro-dollar after the oil boom in 1973, military defeats, the failure of secular nationalisms, political corruption, and state withdrawal from service provision (Eickelman and Piscatori 1996; Lapidus 1988; Kandiyoti 1991b; Zubaida 2000, 2003; Dekmejian 1988; Roy 1999; Salamé 2001; Hunter 1998; Beinin and

2. Zubaida (1993) specifically addresses writings by Badie (1986), Gellner (1992), and Vatikiotis (1983) on the emergence and development of nation-states in the Middle East.

Stork 1997; Sadowski 1997; Kramer 1997; Turner 2003; Stowasser 1987; Haddad and Esposito 1998; Abu-Lughod 2013; Massad 2015). In Palestine, however, not only has there never been a state, there is a further complication in that Israel, as an occupying power, has been deeply invested in the elimination of the secular, nationalist PLO. As capitalist democracies supported Islamists who fought communism during the Cold War, so the Israelis had an interest in nourishing the influence of the Islamists in order to weaken the PLO and ultimately break up the national movement (Usher 1997; Beinin and Stork 1997; Schiff and Ya'ari 1989). Alongside these influences, Hamas has also managed, to a great extent, to mutate from being a religious, political movement to projecting itself as a broad-based national movement in which Islam becomes the core of Palestinian national identity.

Gender, Islam, and Islamists: Contested Definitions of Feminism

Islam and Islamists have attracted the attention of many feminist scholars. Discussions of gender relations in Muslim societies often reflect a preoccupation with culture and ideology (Hale 1997, 234; Abu-Lughod 2013; Massad 2015). Many feminist scholars have criticized those discussions of the relationship between gender and religion in which Islam is seen as immutable, singular, and ahistorical (Keddie 1979; Tucker 1993; Hammami and Rieker 1988; Kandiyoti 1988, 1991b; Ahmed 1992; Moghadam 1993; Abu-Lughod 2013; Massad 2015). They highlight the strategies of resistance, adaptation, and accommodation that women everywhere employ in situations of oppression or subordination (Hale 1994, 234). Other theorists, however, argue that there can only be a single reading of gender in Islam, and that it is unable to accommodate women's demands (Moghissi 1993, 1994, 1995). Within the vast study of women and gender in Islam or in Muslim societies, some have argued that women's rights proliferated and were buttressed by Islamism. Mir-Hosseini (1999, 3) suggests that the different approaches to studying gender in Islam be classified in three ways. The first approach is based on varied interpretations and reinterpretations of the sacred texts, which are invoked as sources of authority and legitimacy for particular ideologies or stand-points on women's rights, gender roles, and relations. The second is that of local and national political ideologies with their local historical particularities, which produce their own discourses on women and gender roles. The third is that of the lived experiences of individuals and local communities, which reveal the structures of opportunity and constraint affecting women. Perspectives vary from seeing Islam as the main cause of women's subjugation to invoking it as the panacea for women's problems based on the argument that Muslim societies have denied women their rightful status by misconstruing the Proph-et's message of equity within the legal system (Beck and Keddie 1978; Bodman and Tohidi 1998; Fernea 1985; Göçek and Balaghi 1994; Haddad and Esposito 1998; Stowasser 1987; Kandiyoti 1991b, 1996; Karam 1998; Mir-Hosseini 1999; Afkhami 1994, 1995). I intend, in this chapter, not to deal with the first type of approach but to con-fine myself to the second and third sets of debates. I analyze Hamas's gender ideology and its impact on gender relations, as well as the lived experience of Islamist women in the Hamas political structure.

I reserve the term "Islamist women" for those who belong to an Islamist movement and who are actively engaged in the public sphere in promoting what Keddie has called an "Islamic state that would enforce at least some Islamic laws and customs" (quoted in Karam 1998, 16). In the Palestinian context, the different forms of Islamic dress signal the heterogeneity of the Islamist groups and their politi-cal projects. Hamas advocates the gradual Islamic reeducation of the masses through *da'wa* (proselytizing), until the masses themselves call for an Islamic government. Like the seminal pan-Islamist Party of Liberation (*hizb al-tahrir*)—founded by Taqi al-Din al-Nabhani in Jerusalem in 1953 and now active in dozens of countries—Hamas also encourages the forceful seizure of state power as the main instru-ment of re-Islamization of the state and society (al-Bargouthi 2000, 43–46). Whether or not they subscribe to those specific beliefs, all Islamist women agree on some form of Islamization (that is, greater Islamic consciousness and practice) of both people and government. This process involves steps ranging from giving classes in mosques, universities, and homes to demanding the application of *shari'a* through various institutions (Karam 1998, 235). In practice, the pursuit of Islamization has inevitably developed against and in relation to secular nationalism.

Islamist women, whether active in Islamist movements or independent, have triggered a debate among feminist scholars over what might constitute feminism in the context of religious or fundamentalist movements that openly reject the principle of total equality for women. Saba Mahmood (1996) singles out "two core issues around which feminism's discomfort with religion is articulated: the first is the claim that religion is a largely male enterprise, and has historically granted women a subordinate position; the second is the more recent phenomenon of the resurgence of politico-religious movements (in the US, the Middle East and South Asia) whose goals are considered to be inimical to women's interests" (2). Taking the term "feminism" to mean any movement that consciously rejects gender-discriminatory thinking and practice and takes action to eliminate gender injustice, the notion of "Islamist feminism" has validity. Karam (1998), for example, advocates it for those women who are Islamist because they situate their political and social agendas firmly within a framework of political Islam, and who are feminist because they are aware of the particular oppression of women, which they actively seek to rectify with recourse to Islamic principles. They emphasize equity in terms of access to resources and rights (Levy 1996) and complementarity, as opposed to calling for total equality (Karam 1998, 10, 235). Karam defends the use of the term "feminist" for Islamist women as making a useful distinction within Islamist movements between those who do and those who do not support equity for women. She adds that the definition indicates possible points of intersection with other women activists (10). Karam also makes a distinction between Islamist feminists—who shy away from the "feminist" label—and Muslim feminists—who use Islamic sources such as the Quran and the *Sunna* (the Prophet's actions and sayings) to argue that the discourse of equality between men and women is valid within Islam (11; see also Abu-Lughod 2013, 175).

In a similarly inclusive manner, Mir-Hosseini (1999, 6) understands "feminism" in its widest possible sense—as a general concern with women's issues, as an awareness that women suffer discrimination at work, in the home, and in society, and as a series of actions aimed at improving women's lives. She also values the term politically as a means of identifying Islamist women. She retains it because she sees that it is important to locate women's demands in a political context that is not isolated from women's movements and experiences elsewhere in the world. Recognizing feminism as an integral part of contemporary politics, she argues that only through participation in global feminist politics can Muslim women influence its agenda and benefit from it (7). Accordingly, Mir-Hosseini urges a reexamination of the approach that uncritically identifies Western feminism with the modernization paradigm. She states that for Muslim women to participate in global feminism, the debate must "make room for the emergence of feminist theories based on the actual politics of gender in Muslim societies in which religion is a paramount element" (9).

Badran, however, pointing to the uneasiness many activists feel in espousing the term "feminism," suggests an alternative: "gender activism" (1994, 202). She distinguishes between feminism as a political practice and feminism as a term of identity. She notes that there are some women who articulate and practice forms of feminism but who adamantly refuse to take on a feminist identity. For these women, Badran proposes "gender activist," reserving "feminist" for those who embrace it.

In light of these different perspectives, an analytical approach that distinguishes between patriarchal gender relations within the family and religiously sanctioned patriarchal codes would be useful. It is important to avoid a simplistic conflation of Islam and cultural nationalism in the course of advocating an "authentic" culture (Kandiyoti 1991b; al-Azmeh 1988; Hale 1997). It is also crucial to avoid, as Hale (1994) suggests, overemphasizing the theoretical at the expense of paying close attention to actual, lived experiences under Islamist rule and how it affects the daily lives of people in general and of women in particular. White (2002), in her study of Islamists in Turkey, drew similar conclusions: while the Islamist movement there provided women with strategic opportunities within the constraints of class, it also presented a paradox of contradictory expectations that supported both activism and patriarchy.

Islamists between "Authenticity" and Universalism

Here a quick word on *asala* (authenticity)[3] is in order. Islamists and Islamist movements often invoke cultural authenticity against "Westernization" to undermine those who challenge the predominantly male-dominated religious hierarchies. As will be seen when analyzing Islamist women in Hamas, even some Islamist women are frequently accused of cultural inauthenticity when they attempt to reconcile Islam with human rights. *Asala* is invoked here, according to al-Azmeh, "at the expense of an appreciation of conjectural and historical realities" (1993, 72).

The debate over cultural authenticity versus universal rights for women has provoked controversy among feminist scholars (Moghadam 1994a; Kandiyoti 1991b; Molyneux 2001; Hale 1994; Benhabib 1999; Phillips 1993, 2002; Nussbaum 2002; Abu-Lughod 2013; Massad 2015). It entails the interrogation of the viability of cross-cultural values as a means for assessing women's rights and empowerment. Some agree that such a framework is required to weigh whether any of these cultural values are worth preserving (Nussbaum 2002,

---

3. Lexically, *asala* indicates salutary moral qualities such as loyalty, nobility, and a sense of commitment to a specific social group or a set of values. It also indicates a sense of sui generis originality in association with those qualities. Considered as an attribute of historical collectivities, Arab, Muslim, or any other, *asala*, according to al-Azmeh (1996), becomes a central notion in a Romantic conception of history whose defining feature is a vitalist concept of nationalism and of politics. Al-Azmeh argues that *asala* discourse is "consequently an essentialist discourse, much like the reverse it finds in Orientalism, in discourses on the primitive, and in other discourses on cultural otherness. In common with these discourses, the discourse on authenticity postulates a historic subject which is self-identical, essentially in continuity over time, and positing itself in essential distinction from other historical subjects" (82–83).

52). Those who are critical of cross-cultural models invoke the need for diversity and the avoidance of "paternalism" by those who apply the practices and values of one group to others, who refuse to recognize the legitimacy of difference, and who seek to impose the practices of the dominant group (Phillips 2002, 119). The invocation of a cross-cultural set of rights blurs cultural diversities that seem to insist that norms of justice are always relative to the society in which they are formed, reflect values and practices particular to that society, and are based in no universal truth outside local standpoints. Cultural authenticity is repeatedly invoked by Islamists to rebuff the universal rights discourse and a more critical stand on the two approaches is important. No monolithic understanding of culture is able to override the internal consensus in some societies that their customs of male dominance are practices "the society" wants to sustain (Phillips 2002, 137). In the same vein, universal rights should be based on a thorough understanding of the historical, social, economic, and political framework of a society as well as the full participation of women in debating and agreeing on which rights should be defended and for whom as a precondition to setting an agenda for all women.

The Shifting Nature of Palestinian Nationalism

Arab nationalism has from its origins invoked Islam as a basis for legitimacy. Neither Islam nor nationalism is a fixed idiom, and I argue that the brand of Islamism contesting for power in the Palestinian national context is, to a great extent, a product of the failure of the secular national movement to deliver on its promises of national independence and state building. I argue that one of the elements that eased the transition to a "fusion" between Islam and Palestinian nationalism was the defeat of the Palestinian national movement and the ability of Hamas to identify itself with the struggle to gain Palestinian national rights.

The linkages between religion and secularism in the construction of Palestinian nationalism have been the subject of a virtual debate between two influential scholars. On the one hand, Budeiri (1994) argues that the fact that Fateh "resorts to religious symbols and ideology to mobilise and enlist support casts doubt on the often repeated assertion that Fateh, and by implication the Palestinian national movement, is a secular force" (12). Islam, Budeiri assures us, was and continues to be one of the paramount elements of Palestinian national identity, especially inside the Occupied Territories. He argues that "the Islamic movement in Palestine was instrumental from the very beginning of the British Mandate in assimilating a nationalist discourse. It is indeed difficult to establish a demarcation line separating Islamists from their 'nationalist enemies'" (7). Islam, as a symbolic reference point, functions in his description as a cultural reservoir drawn upon in the national call for resistance, which tends to undermine secularism. Given such a view, no wonder the leader of the national movement during the British Mandate, Haj Amin, was put in the same basket with Izz al-Din al-Qassam,[4] seen as both "religious" and "Islamic."

In contrast to Budeiri, Hilal (2002) does not recognize Islam as a central factor in the construction of Palestinian national identity, whether under the Mandate or in its modern formation in the 1960s. Defining secularism as a clear separation of political institutions from religious ones—"in a national political field it implies that organizations, identities and ideologies have distinct paradigms, dynamics, and determinants that differ from those pertaining to the religious field" (1)—he asserts that the confrontation with Zionist and British rule generated an essentially secular Palestinian identity in the form of a *national* individuality transcending that of religion, sect, and locality. According to Hilal, at no stage did Palestinian nationalism resort to religious discourse or mythology to maintain its hegemony. "This does not contradict," he says, "the fact that most Palestinians have been and are still religious in the popular meaning of religiosity" (1).

4. A religious and nationalist leader in Haifa, Izz al-Din al-Qassam was among the first to declare the British the main suppressors of Palestinians' national aspirations. His killing by British police in 1935 was a key precursor to the Palestinian revolt of 1936–39.

While I agree with Hilal that the PLO did not return to Islam merely as a meta-political point of reference (Salamé 2001, 8), it did accept that marriage, divorce, and inheritance should be based on the popular understanding of Islam. Gender relations within the Palestinian community under the political control of the PLO were governed by *shari'a* and not secular law. Gender relations were the blind spot of commentators on Islam and secularism who failed to see that in matters of gender and the family there was more continuity than discontinuity between the two ideologies. This confirms Kandiyoti's opinion that the ambiguities of modernity are most apparent when it comes to the issue of the role of women in the body politic (1998, 283). In the meantime, Hilal, who distinguishes sharply between religion and nationalism in the Palestinian context, does not provide an answer as to why a "mainly" secular movement needed religious idioms to legitimize itself.

One of the diagnostic criteria for unmasking the nature of a national project is to examine its construction of gender and gender relations, yet many writers and scholars who have written on Hamas and Palestinian nationalism are silent on this question (e.g., Hroub 1996, 2000; al-Hamad and al-Bargouthi 1997; Abul-Omrein 2000; al-Taheri 1995; Abu Amr 1994; Litvak 1996; Schiff and Ya'ari 1989; Hilal 1998; Munson 2003). Those who insist Palestinian national identity was based mainly on secular idioms have to homogenize this identity; they do not want to see how nationalism and its multiple identities are permeated by class, gender, and religion (Anthias and Yuval-Davis 1989; Kandiyoti 1991b). Kandiyoti, for example, demonstrates that "although many (nationalisms) were influenced by the ideas of the enlightenment and were of secular persuasion, they unwittingly endorsed the notion that any changes in the position of women could only be condoned in the national interest" (1991b, 410). Nationalist ideologies need an "ideal woman," but her defining traits sometimes conflict. Fateh perceived gender relations and the ideal woman as carrying, as Kandiyoti puts it, "their own ambiguities and tensions" (1998, 282). The ideal woman was portrayed as a peasant: fertile, modest, and "authentic." At the same time, however, the "modern woman" was portrayed as the disciplined, de-eroticized body, the "sister of men." In other words, the Palestinian national movement portrayed women as the "privileged repository of uncontaminated national values" (Kandiyoti 1991b, 410). Such models of women have persisted through the establishment of the PA and on to the present day.

Fateh always resisted challenging the patriarchal control of women within the PLO. The many attempts by activists in the General Union of Palestinian Women to promote and protect women's rights in divorce, marriage, and inheritance failed. They attributed this failure to the refusal of the head of the PLO to endorse any such move or, according to Samira Salah, "to question the flagrant abuse and exploitation of some of the Fateh fighters whether in the uncontrolled practices of polygamy, the failure to recognize their children from undeclared marriages, or the many cases of domestic violence" (interview; Naila Ahmed concurred, in very similar words).

This might serve to explain the ease with which support for a secular PLO was transformed into sympathy for, and in many cases even allegiance to, the Islamist movement. The increasing politicization of gender and religious identities might call into question the "progressiveness" of secular Palestinian nationalism and the unity of the Palestinian national identity. The increasing popularity of Islamism has its roots not only in cultural or ideological premises but also in important changes that occurred in the West Bank and Gaza after the Israeli Occupation in 1967.

The Israeli Occupation and the Formation of a New Elite

The "new" Palestinian Islamists are different from those active during the British Mandate or the era of Jordanian rule. The old generation of Muslim Brothers came from the wealthy urban strata, the new one mainly from the peasant refugees in the Gaza Strip. The founders (e.g., Ahmed Yassine, Ibrahim Yazouri, 'Abdul Fatah Dokhan, Mohammad Hassan Sahm'a) were schoolteachers and minor members of the clergy. Members of the new generation (e.g., Mahmoud Zahar, 'Abdel 'Aziz al-Rantissi, Salah Shihada, 'Issa al-Nashar, Isma'il Abu Shanab,

Mossa Abu Marzouk) were trained as doctors, engineers, headmasters, and university teachers at Arab universities (Abul-Omrein 2000, 257; al-Bargouthi 2000, 57–59). Their supporters consisted mainly of students, especially from poor and conservative families, as well as clergy and professionals (al-Bargouthi 2000; Abul-Omrein 2000).

There is little reliable data about their constituencies. Just before the eruption of the second intifada in September 2000, the Development Studies Program at Birzeit University recorded support (among individuals aged sixteen years and above) as running at 33.3 percent for Fateh, with 17.6 percent backing radical Islamist groups (13.9 percent for Hamas and 3.7 percent for Islamic Jihad). By February 2002, support for Fateh had dropped to 23.6 percent, while support for Islamist groups had risen to 24.8 percent (20.9 percent for Hamas and 3.9 percent for Islamic Jihad). Those embracing secular left-wing groups remained around 5 percent.[5] The quality of the political leadership in Hamas played and continues to play an important role in its popularity. Sheikh Ahmed Yassine, Hamas's co-founder and spiritual leader, was a well-respected figure, seen as charismatic, humble, close to the poor, ascetic, clean-handed, and with an open heart to all those in need.[6]

The fluctuation of popularity for Hamas relates to the progress of the peace process through the PA, which acted as a catalyst for economic and social mobility. With the rise in hope after the Oslo Agreement in September 1993, many contended that Hamas's days as a hegemonic force were numbered. Not only had the peace agreement restored the PLO's standing, but, more importantly, international funds were pledged to underwrite the deal; that would replenish the PLO's empty coffers and so lubricate the networks of support and patronage through which authority could be consolidated (Usher

5. Development Studies Program, Birzeit University, Poll No. 1 (August 31–September 2, 2000) and Poll No. 6 (February 2–9, 2002).

6. Yassine's personal qualities were important in legitimizing his leadership, especially in contrast to Arafat whose reliance on patronage and acceptance of corruption was well known.

1997, 343). With the failure of the peace process and the spread of corruption within the PA, Hamas's popularity soared. Its standing was also related to a trend of growing religiosity among Palestinians.

A distinction needs to be made between religiosity and political Islam, since the former does not necessarily imply political mobilization. The degree of religiosity in a society can only be understood as part of a complex array of beliefs and does not necessarily imply any inevitable social or political vision linked to Islamist politics. Thus the growing influence and power of Hamas does not have an inevitable trajectory—it depends to a great extent on circumstantial factors. As discussed in chapter 2, the deterioration of the economic situation after Oslo contributed to the popularity of the Islamists with their service-provision institutions. The concurrent political decline of the PLO in turn had a significant effect on the internal dynamics of Palestinian Islamism. It is this economic, national, and political background that provides the context for an examination of the fluctuating power and influence of the Islamist movement in the West Bank and, in particular, in Gaza where it originated.

The questions about the links between religion and politics addressed above lead to other questions relevant to this study: If the religious element no longer appears as a meta-political point of reference, why is the reference to religion politically useful? Why is the national secular discourse in retreat while the religious discourse is gaining ground? Some scholars assert that contemporary Islamists are seen as the only means through which dissidence of any sort can be expressed in most Muslim countries. Modernist, nationalist, secularist, and communist ideologies have been contaminated by association with past colonial powers or more recent neo-colonialist endeavors (the United States in Israel and the Soviet Union in Afghanistan) (Lawrence 1987, 32). In the sections that follow, I focus on the role of the Israeli Occupation in shaping the reconstruction of Palestinian nationalism in its new Islamist hue.

To understand the political power of Hamas, one must look beyond its religious texts to take account of the various contexts in which the Islamist movement is embedded and the kinds of creative dialogues it has had to engage in within Palestinian society. Indeed, the Palestinian Islamists under Jordanian rule in the West Bank were different from those under Egyptian rule in Gaza or under the Israeli Occupation after 1967. The role of the successive states, the distorted processes of modernization and development, and the presence of rival political groups shaped to a great extent Hamas's vision, ideology, political orientation, and positions on gender.

The Changing Relationship between Islamism and Nationalism in the West Bank and Gaza after 1967

The Palestinian Muslim Brothers decided not to participate in the national struggle in the wake of the 1967 War and the Occupation of the West Bank and Gaza due to what Abul Omrein (2000) calls "their utter quantitative and qualitative weakness, [and] the weakness of their parent organisation in Egypt which deprived them of important support. Their numbers were small and they found difficulty in attracting new members when people were still attracted to Nasser" (175). It was decided, then, to recruit new members through home visits and religious lessons in the mosques. Thanks to the spread of *tarbeya wa da'wa* (education and proselytizing) among youths, in particular those between the ages of fifteen and twenty (177; see also Schiff and Ya'ari 1989, 221–22; Hroub 2000), a new movement started to emerge. In this phase, the Brothers' aim was to transform the new members from infidels into believers and to forge links between younger and older members. I could find no record of any interest in recruiting women or directing any specific activities toward them during this period.

Reconstruction of the moral individual was seen as essential, a core element of which was the responsibility of the male guardian for his womenfolk, summed up in the saying, *"kolokom ra'i wa kolokom mass'olon 'an ra'iyatehe"* (you are all guardians, and you are all responsible for your own subjects) (Maysoon, interview). In this sense, Hamas was in line with Keddie's (1999) assertion that "most religio-political movements support a return to a more patriarchal and gender-unequal view of religion and society" (12). It is worth noting here that in contrast to the defeats and crises usually used as explanatory idioms for the rising tide of Islamists in the Middle East, in the Palestinian case, the defeat of 1967 gave a boost to the national and secular PLO.

The following decade witnessed a massive expansion in the popularity of the PLO, especially after the municipal elections organized by the Israeli authority in 1976, which brought a younger generation of leaders to the national leadership. According to the Israeli military governor in Gaza, "[W]e extend some financial aid to Islamic groups via mosques and religious schools in order to help create a force that would stand against the leftist forces which support the PLO" (quoted in Usher 1997, 340). According to Schiff and Ya'ari, it was thought that "the fundamentalists posed less of a threat to stability than the nationalists did, and any damage they might cause, would be more than offset by the good they would do in finally neutralizing the PLO" (1989, 224).[7] There is agreement that the Islamists, at least in the first and second phases of Islamist activism, did not pose a threat to the Israeli authority, and that only when they did begin to constitute a threat were they outlawed in 1989. In addition, the Islamists were allowed to control the religious institutions because that put them beyond the control of the PLO (al-Bargouthi 2000, 28).

During this period, the Islamist movement was focused on institution building and aggressive expansion, in particular among students in Palestinian universities (Ababneh 2014). Three important religious institutions already existed in this period. The Islamic Compound (*al-mojama' al-islami*) was built in 1973 in Gaza and legalized by the Israeli Authority in 1979; the Islamic Society was formed in 1976; and the Islamic University was established in 1978–79. These institutions played a crucial role in spreading the movement to a great many people, especially Gazans, through the provision of vital social services. The Islamic Compound, which provided an important protective cover

7. This account is strongly contested by the Islamists, who note that the Israeli authority allowed many other nationalist secular and leftist organizations to emerge and be active (Abul-Omrein 2000, 226–30).

for all sorts of activities by the Brothers (Abu 'Amr 1989, 33–34), extended social and material services and "cultural amenities" to all sectors of Gazan society. These included the establishment of Islamic libraries all over Gaza, an annual Islamic book fair, the local reprinting of important Islamic books, the establishment of many kindergartens to raise children with "Islamic values," the founding of a Quranic school (*madrassa tahfiz al-Qur'an*) in 1976, specialized supplementary classes for students in mosques, and Quranic recital competitions (*mossabaqat hifz al-Qur'an*). Proselytizing and recruitment took place through group visits to the Aqsa Mosque in Jerusalem, religious sermons, communal Ramadan meals, and the spread of the new phenomenon of *'eitikaf* among young men (withdrawal from social activities to spend nights praying in mosques) (Abul-Omrein 2000, 179; Usher 1997; al-Salehi 1993). Young men grew beards, wedding ceremonies took a more modest turn, and soccer teams formed up to join the Islamic League, whose players wore long pants and were never heard to curse (Schiff and Ya'ari 1989, 226). The young men were taught about self-sacrifice, pride in the simple life, obedience, and discipline.

All these activities took place in a climate of economic decline, as the Israeli labor market was being purged of thousands of Palestinian casual workers, which increased their appreciation of the social services provided by the Muslim Brothers through a fund to support poor students studying in Gaza and abroad, people whose homes had been demolished by the Occupation army, and families whose breadwinners had been imprisoned by the Israeli authority. The Brothers established a blood bank and many health clinics, and occasionally distributed free medicine. The *mojama'* modeled many of its activities on those that used to be sponsored by secular and leftist groups, such as volunteer work campaigns, summer sea camps, and sports training and competitions, as detailed in a *mojama'* brochure distributed in Gaza at the time. Most of these activities were designed for men.

The Islamic Compound also ran religious courses (*doross*) for women in Gaza and organized exhibitions of *libass islami* (Islamic dress) (Abul-Omrein 2000, 181). The Center for the Rehabilitation of the Muslim Girl (*markaz ta'heel al-fatat al-moslema*) opened in

1982, providing workshops in sewing and embroidery, according to the same brochure mentioned above. In this phase, local mosques also initiated some activities directed toward women, such as gender-segregated religious instruction and book exhibitions. Women took to covering their heads and wearing robes (*jelbab*) over their clothes (Abul-Omrein 2000, 179; see also Usher 1997; al-Salehi 1993). The Islamists' target was the cohort of young, educated women in their thousands looking for suitable jobs.

The establishment of the Islamic University in Gaza was another important step in the spread of the Brothers' influence. Many Gazan students used to study in Egyptian universities. After the first Camp David Agreement was signed in 1977, Egyptian universities stopped accepting students from Palestine, which led some Islamists to seek funds from the Gulf countries, Saudi Arabia, and Jordan to build a local university in Gaza. The Islamic University's first faculties—*shari'a* and *ossol al-din* (sources of religion)—began teaching in the 1978–79 academic year. With 7,000 students, it was the largest university in the Occupied Territories.[8] It played a major role in the recruitment of students for the movement and in organizing, for the first time, student Islamic blocs (*kotal islameyya*) in all Palestinian universities. It also served as a venue where Islamist activists were exposed to the discourses of nationalist, secularist student blocs. Competition with their rivals helped the Brothers learn how to "nationalize" the Islamist discourse (as will be explained later) to suit a wider audience of students, and also how to compete in open democratic elections (Ababneh 2014). It was through borrowing the activist methods of secular and nationalist groups that the Islamists reinvented themselves.

8. In the 1998–99 academic year, 9,272 students were enrolled in the Islamic University of Gaza (then the only institution of higher learning in the Gaza Strip); by way of comparison, 4,276 students were enrolled in Birzeit University. In the 2003–4 academic year, 13,390 students were enrolled in the Islamic University, again more than doubling the 6,317 students at Birzeit. In the same year, approximately 43 percent of the students at IUG were women (www.iugaza.edu), compared to 51 percent at BZU (www.birzeit.edu).

According to Ahmed Atawneh, who headed the Islamist student bloc at Birzeit in the late 1990s, competing with other groups drew their attention to "the importance of the women's vote, and how crucial [it was] to recruit female students to support the Islamic blocs," especially in universities such as Birzeit, where "conservative families won't send their girls" (Abul-Omrein 2000, 187; see also Ababneh 2014).

By 1980, the first Islamic student *kotla* was well established at the Islamic University, and in 1981, all the Islamist blocs in the West Bank universities convened for the first conference of the Union of Muslim Students in Palestine (*ittihad al-talaba al-moslimeen fi falastine*) (Abul-Omrein 2000, 187). The success of the Islamist bloc at such a prominent secular and liberal university as Birzeit was an important milestone. One of the founders of the Birzeit Islamic student bloc recalled how, in the first student elections in which the Islamic blocs participated, they ran under secular names: the Students' Work Bloc (*kotlet al-ʿamal al-tolabi*) at Birzeit University, and the Independent Bloc (*al-kotla al-mostaqilla*) at Al-Najah National University. In those first elections, the Islamists won 43 percent of the vote at Birzeit; the next time, they ran openly as the Islamic Bloc and took 36 percent (al-Madhoun 1987, 36). Secular and nationalist students denounced the Islamist blocs for having what Abul-Omrein dubs "a backward vision of Islam, a backward stance vis-à-vis women, and something alien to the national movement" (2000, 186). Ahmed Atawneh summarizes this period when the Islamists first became alert to the advantages of recruiting female students:

> From the early eighties until the intifada, the Islamists were not participants in the national struggle against the Occupation. Their task was social work aimed at incorporating the maximum number of people into *ahkam al-islam* [the rules of Islam], whether men or women, by organizing popular festivals in the universities, lessons in the mosques, book fairs, and distribution of Islamic books and publications, including cassettes. We were urging many girls to veil. We wanted to create a general atmosphere to encourage more women to

veil. Veiling was a marker to show that this society was in the process of transformation; and veiled students were crucial to that process. In order to demonstrate this transformation, we used to organize a march every year before the student elections, with two lines, one for males and one for veiled females, just to show their growing number, as *da'aya lal-fikra* [publicity for the idea—i.e., the idea of the Islamization of society]. (interview)

In the six universities in the West Bank and Gaza at the start of the 1980s (Birzeit in Ramallah, Al-Najah in Nablus, Hebron University, Bethlehem University, Jerusalem–al-quds University, and the Islamic University in Gaza) as well as in the many intermediate schools and technical colleges, the Islamists either controlled the student councils (Hebron, Jerusalem, Gaza) or posed a serious challenge to nationalist and leftist student groups (winning 25–40 percent of the vote in the others, with the exception of Vatican-operated Bethlehem University). In each university, the Islamist students insisted on having a dedicated space to use as a mosque, which also functioned as a meeting place for the Islamic bloc and a venue for their collective activities (communal meals during Ramadan, handwritten magazines inside the mosque, and collective prayers), and a rallying point for ordinary student projects such as volunteer work. The Islamist student blocs were less likely to join confrontational demonstrations against the Occupation forces than other student blocs, focusing more on confronting secular liberalism. Bassam Jarrar, an outspoken Islamist leader in the West Bank, said that he targeted Birzeit University because it was a "moral challenge" due to its "modernization" (*'assrana*) and mixed classes, the active representation of political parties, and the unveiled majority of its female students. It also posed a religious (*'aqa'edi*) challenge, since its curriculum was seen to be "against Islam" (Jarrar quoted in Abul-Omrein 2000, 187).

Control of religious institutions gave the movement access to an important source of revenue. The preeminent *waqf* (trust or endowment) in the Occupied Territories, which was then and remains affiliated with Jordan, was keen, as was Israel, to sequester its assets from the control of the PLO (al-Bargouthi 2000). Those assets were "a rich source of economic power" in Gaza, according to Schiff and Ya'ari (1989). "About 10% of all real estate in the Strip—hundreds of shops, apartments, garages, public buildings, and about 2,000 acres of agricultural land—belonged to its trusts, and the *waqf* . . . employed scores of people, from preachers and other clerics to gravediggers" (224). Schiff and Ya'ari also report that during the two decades from 1967 to 1987, the number of mosques in Gaza more than doubled, from seventy-seven to 160 (225).

Although the Muslim Brotherhood did not attempt to build a front organization along the lines of the Islamic Compound (*mojama'*) in the West Bank, many of its members held key positions there, in the small Islamic College in Hebron (funded by Jordan) and in a score of charitable societies. They also controlled the allocation of welfare to 10,000 needy families in Nablus, granting loans and scholarships, hiring lawyers for detainees, paying compensation for property damaged by the Israeli army, and running orphanages, homes for the elderly, and even an independent high school (Schiff and Ya'ari 1989, 226). Thus, thanks to the support of Jordan, the approval of Israel, and funds from the Gulf, the Islamists managed to build an impressive infrastructure in Gaza and, to some extent, the West Bank.

Some of the female students recruited in this second phase went on to play important leadership roles among Islamist women; prominent examples include Maysoon al-Ramahi, head of the Islamic Al-Khansaa Society in the West Bank, and Amira Haroun, a leading figure in the politburo of the Islamic National Salvation Party in Gaza. These female students were recruited at the initiative of the male students, who were eager to win their votes in student elections, but spurned "immoral" mixed parties and picnics. Instead, they promoted cultural activities such as exhibitions of Islamic dress (in lieu of traditional embroidery), Islamic book fairs (as opposed to "progressive" and Marxist book fairs), mosque lessons for women, and collective prayers. Like the nationalists and leftists, they also employed more direct methods such as helping new students find lodgings and get acquainted with their new environment. They targeted the "more modest, more conservative girls," as opposed to "the more fashionable [ones]" who "like to mingle with boys" (Ahmed, interview). Like Fateh, the Islamists attracted students from lower-class, rural, and refugee backgrounds.

The focus of mosque lessons for women was Islamic values as they relate to women's issues, captured in slogans such as "*al-nissa' shaqa'eq al-rijal*" (women are sisters to men) and "*al-islam karram al-mar'a*" (Islam honors women) (Maysoon, interview). Women were also taught *ressalat al-umoma* (the message of motherhood) and how crucial their role was in building the good Islamic family. It was common in the mid-1980s for male Islamist students in engineering or chemistry to rally against the entry of women into those disciplines, which they saw as counterproductive to women's role as the mothers and reproducers of the nation. Islamist women were often challenged by liberal and secular students, who would provoke them by questioning their reasons for engaging in education if they saw child-rearing as their main role. Islamists would reply that women saw education as a guarantee for the future that did not contradict the supremacy of motherhood. In Maysoon's words:

> As a Muslim woman, I don't worry much about unemployment or hardship, that part is covered by *qawamat al-rajol* [a man's responsibility as head of the family]. All I care about is that a man does his best to meet his obligations; if he doesn't manage to provide a decent life, then it's up to me to help and support him. This doesn't contradict the fact that I studied engineering, because I want my daughter to get her degree too, since it's a safeguard against changing times when women might have to provide for themselves. Besides, I didn't get my degree solely for economic reasons—it also helps me build my character by asserting my presence.

The Islamists could not ignore the valuable lesson Palestinians learned after the 1948 *nakba*, that education is the only defense against unpredictable change, especially for rural girls. While Hamas sought to enforce patriarchal norms through gender segregation, it also advocated education for women, which in some cases gave them an opening to public life. Gender segregation itself yielded new employment opportunities for educated women outside the traditional professions (e.g., teaching and nursing), such as jobs as photographers and waiters at weddings, where most veiled women, especially the unmarried ones, take off their veils.

The Decline of the PLO and the Islamization of Palestinian Nationalism

The years following the expulsion of the PLO from Beirut in 1982 saw a gradual erosion of its prestige and control, despite the increased level of activity and involvement of its constituent groups in the Occupied Territories. While continuing to pay lip service to the strategy of *kefah mossallah* (armed struggle), the PLO in actual practice focused on political action and building institutions, taking advantage of Israel's tolerance of protest and civil rights–oriented activities, which the authorities believed would contribute to a state of normalization (Budeiri 1994, 14). While the PLO was increasingly absorbed in international diplomatic activity, the Islamists wasted no time in elaborating a new ideology in which nationalism would be brought to the fore.

The Muslim Brothers had originally rejected nationalism as a secular, exclusivist, and selfish value. Hassan al-Banna (1946–49), their founder and leading ideologue, saw nationalism as a foreign implantation designed to break down Islamic unity in order to speed up the Western takeover of Islamic lands. Yet, given the spread of nationalism in Egypt, al-Banna tried to reconcile it with Islam by investing a pan-Arab patriotism with at least some Islamic meaning. He saw Islam as a religion that gives man a true love for his homeland and the strength to fight for it (Gershoni and Jankowski 1995, 80–83). The Islamic *umma* (community) needed the existence of the Arab nation, which would provide the spiritual power to achieve its own liberation and redemption, which in turn would lead to Arab unity and ultimately the restoration of the united *umma* in one supra-territorial and supra-racial homeland (76–77, 94–96).

During the 1980s, a vehement challenge to the Brothers' passivity in the Palestinian struggle against the Occupation arose from within its own ranks ('Awwad 1989, 49). The younger generation of the Muslim Brothers had new role models as the electronic media brought news of Islamist triumphs in various countries to the refugee camps of Gaza and the villages of the West Bank. These populations were fully cognizant of the triumph of the Islamic Revolution in Iran in 1979, the exploits of the Islamic Resistance in Southern Lebanon, the victories of the *mujahedeen* in Afghanistan, the militancy of various Islamist groups in Egypt engaged in violent conflict with the Sadat regime and its successor, and Hafez al-Asad's brutal suppression of the Muslim Brothers in Syria. All this stood in sharp contrast to the quietism and withdrawal from public space preached by the Brothers' traditional leadership (Budeiri 1994, 14; Abul-Omrein 2000; al-Bargouthi 2000). This disparity resulted in a politically inspired split that led to the birth of the Islamic Jihad movement. Its establishment signaled the beginning of a new campaign of violent attacks on Israeli civilians, settlers, and army personnel. Thus, no sooner had the PLO laid down the banner of armed struggle than it was taken up by the Islamist forces.

The young leaders of Islamic Jihad, 'Abdel 'Aziz Odeh and Khalil al-Shakak, bitterly charged that, in the face of the heroic struggle of the Palestinians, the Muslim Brothers' movement lacked critical thinking and cultural openness and was "morally bankrupt" (Abu 'Amr 1989, 114). According to Hroub (2000), one of them said that, "contrary to the Brothers, our priority is not indoctrinating the masses but direct action"—that is, resisting the Israeli Occupation in Palestine (126).

Islamic Jihad joined words with deeds and conducted several spectacular military operations against Israel in 1986 and 1987. According to Budeiri (1994), they gave the Islamic movement as a whole the credibility it had hitherto lacked. Now there was a framework where those who desired violent confrontation with the enemy were welcome. The banners under which these actions were undertaken were Islamic, though the actions were not unlike those carried out by nationalist groups in the not-so-distant past. Islamist thinkers later close to Hamas went further by asserting that there were intimate ties between Fateh and Islamic Jihad, a relationship seen by Abul-Omrein (2000) as a "highly explosive equation that combines radical nationalism with religious radicalism" (222). Thus, the martyred figure of old Sheikh Izz al-Din al-Qassam was reanimated and reconfigured by Islamic Jihad to symbolize the combination or recombination of Islam and nationalism, and his name was given to a local mosque in Gaza over which Islamic Jihad had clashed with the Muslim Brothers (224). It is interesting to note that the Brothers reacted against Islamic Jihad as an alien "other," much as the PA would do, later on, in response to Hamas. According to Abul-Omrein, the Muslim Brothers denigrated Islamic Jihad as "a Shiite Iranian bridge to Palestine," "an obstruction in the path of the Islamic movement," and "allies of the secularists" against the Brotherhood (225). However, many observers, including members of Hamas, now agree that the daring military operations Islamic Jihad carried out in 1986 and 1987 had stolen the Brothers' thunder.[9]

The intensification of the national struggle as manifested in the first intifada propelled the Palestinian Muslim Brothers to reincarnate themselves as the Islamic Resistance Movement (*Haraket al-Moqawama al-Islamiyya*), known by its acronym, Hamas. As a political force formed outside the field of the PLO, Hamas realized that in order to compete with the national movement led by Fateh, it would have to wholeheartedly join in and direct the intifada, borrowing Fateh's forms of organization, its modes of struggle (e.g., armed resistance), and the subjects of its discourse, while rejecting its secularism and its operative position that peace negotiations were the only way to achieve self-determination (Hilal 1998, 55; Budeiri 1994).

The first intifada began on December 9, 1987, in the Jabaliya refugee camp in the Gaza Strip, when an Israeli truck crashed into two

9. On October 15, 1986, members of Islamic Jihad attacked a crowd of Israeli soldiers and their families who were celebrating their graduation from basic training in front of the Wailing Wall in Jerusalem; one person was killed and seventy injured. In May 1987, a group of six Islamic Jihad prisoners escaped from the most heavily guarded Israeli prison in Gaza. They opened fire on the Israeli soldiers at the facility, killing four. Some characterize this incident as the beginning of the first intifada (Abul-Omrein 2000, 249).

vans carrying Palestinian workers, killing four of them. That event served as the catalyst that sparked rebellions throughout the Occupied Territories. Following the violent deaths of the four workers, the first leaflet aimed at redirecting popular anger by calling for a general strike was distributed by Islamic Jihad on December 11. Three days later, a leaflet produced by the Brothers and signed "*Haraket al-Moqawama al-Islamiyya*" announced the birth of Hamas.

The Islamic Resistance Movement embarked on a radical process of Islamizing the familiar national symbols, which included modifying the Palestinian national flag by emblazoning it with the *shahada* (the Islamic profession of faith) and naming it the "Islamic flag." An image of the familiar outline of Palestine was used in posters, graffiti, and emblems as a symbol of the integration of the patriotic and Islamic messages. The original emblems of both the Egyptian and the Palestinian Muslim Brotherhood show the Quran amid two crossed swords, with the word *wa-a'eddu* (make ready) written beneath them (figs. 1 and 2). In the Hamas logo (fig. 3), the Aqsa Mosque replaced the Quran and two Palestinian flags were added, encircling the crossed swords, with the silhouette of Palestine at the apex and its name written underneath. The two flags, as noted, bear the profession of faith: "There is no God but God" and "Mohammed is the messenger of God."

The liberation of Palestine was thus to constitute a step on the road to Arab unity, and the struggle itself would unite the Arabs. Hamas declared that the liberation of Palestine and the growth of Islamism in the Arab world would render the hope of Islamic unity as realistic and attainable. The intifada itself would play an important role in this process by returning the Palestinians to their full Islamic identity and by rallying Muslims all over the world behind the Palestinian struggle (Hamas Charter, Articles 15 and 33).

This linkage between Islam and Palestinian nationalism has been spelled out more explicitly in many scholarly studies over the past two decades. Both Munson (2003, 44) and Litvak (1996, 5) assert, for example, that the Hamas Charter clearly signals a development in which Palestinian nationalism becomes an integral part of Islam. In

1. Egyptian Muslim Brothers emblem.

2. Palestinian Muslim Brothers emblem.

3. Hamas emblem.

other words, the universal call to prepare for a struggle for the sake of Islam is now directed to the more specific Islamic struggle for Palestine. According to Litvak (1996), Hamas shifted from the traditional vision of the Muslim Brothers who saw Palestine, in al-Farugi's words, as the "heart of the Arab world and the knot of the Muslim peoples" (al-Farugi 1983, quoted in Litvak 1996, 11), and advocated instead the unambiguous consecration of Palestine, extending the sanctity of Al-Aqsa Mosque in Jerusalem, "the pearl of Palestine," to Palestine as a whole, which is traditionally known as the "land of *al-Isra' wal-Mi'raj*" (the place of the Prophet's ascension to heaven). Hamas maintains that this is what distinguishes Palestine from all other Islamic lands and makes it the inheritance of all Muslims (Litvak 1996, 11; al-Hamad and al-Bargouthi 1997, 30–32).

As Hamas Islamized Palestine, it also nationalized Islam, yet it confined its activity to the land of Palestine and did not seek to act as a transnational, universal religious movement. But does this Islamization of the Palestinian national identity exclude non-Muslim Palestinians? To mobilize maximum resources and present itself as the movement of all Palestinians, Hamas has paid careful attention to the Christians in Palestine. A leaflet distributed by Hamas in July 1991 addressed the issue in the following terms: "Palestinian Christians are an integral part of the Palestinian people and the Arab nation and part of its civilizational identity. They have the same civil rights and duties as the rest of the Palestinian people. Respect their feasts and religious festivities and participate in them when possible. Urge them not to leave the country under the criminal policies of the Israeli Occupation. Encourage them to be part of political life and political institutions. Establish a bridge with their religious leaders and consult with them on the general affairs of the country" (Hroub 1993, cited in al-Hamad and al-Bargouthi 1997, 176; see also Hroub 2000; Litvak 1996). Hamas sees Palestinian Christians as an integral part of the Palestinian people, as culturally Muslim and sharing so much in the way of customs, values, and aspirations—a position very similar to that of an older generation of Arab nationalists of Christian faith such as Michel Aflaq and George Antonius. However, while there is no confessional interfaith conflict in Palestine, what Hamas proposes falls short of acknowledging Palestinian Christians as full citizens with equal rights; otherwise, there would be no need for the message quoted above. Needless to say, there is no Christian representation in Hamas's social and political institutions, as there was in the PLO. It is unclear what the legal status of Christians will be if an Islamic state in Palestine is established, or how Christians would be represented within a *majlis al-shura* (consultative council) instead of a parliament.

Complementary to the process of nationalizing Islam and Islamizing Palestine, Hamas also invented many cultural "traditions." Similar to Fateh's revolutionary songs with their martial beats and patriotic lyrics, Hamas produced a multitude of cassettes of national-themed religious songs, distinctively drum led and performed by men only. Through religious education and socialization, Hamas gradually implemented Islamic dress, very similar to that of Iranian and Shiite women in Lebanon (a long coat and scarf of darker colors). The traditional folkloric dress (*thub*) came to be seen as less Islamic, in particular because of its colorful embroidery; besides, according to Samira, a leading figure in the Islamic Al-Huda Society, "it gives some women a chance to wear it tightly close to their bodies and its belt defines their shape" (interview). Hamas agents also invented the "Islamic marriage" in which the guests are gender-segregated and hired performers provide entertainment that strictly adheres to religious codes (Abul-Omrein 2000, 181).

Thus, Hamas's transformation into a militant national resistance movement brought the old national ethos—fusing struggle, sacrifice, and suffering invested with sacredness and inviolability—back to the very core of Palestinian national identity. Within this formulation, any act that detracts from the struggle is considered sacrilege, if not treason. As described in chapter 2, this reconstruction of Palestinian national identity conflicts with the PA's parallel attempts, shaped around narrow definitions of loyalty and gains. Once again, women's purity has become a mainstay of the ethos of suffering, sacrifice, and struggle; immodest dress and conduct dishonor the memory of the martyrs and unwittingly aid the enemy's designs to corrupt the nation, while women's preoccupation with trivia and fashion is an insult to those who fight for liberation (Hammami 1990; Moghadam 1994a; Taraki 2003). Islamists also rail against the work of women's NGOs, with their extravagant promotional campaigns, conferences, high salaries, and lavish donor funds (i.e., profits) instead of sacrifice and suffering while the Occupation rages on unabated.

In the struggle for grassroots support at colleges and universities, Islamists rubbed shoulders with Marxists and often borrowed their concepts and methods. I argue that this is where they gained their political education, not from religious texts. As I have already indicated, Islamists succeeded in establishing themselves in the students' movement, triggering a bitter rivalry with the nationalists that involved some violent episodes. While it is beyond the scope of this study to evaluate the democratic practice of the Islamists in all Palestinian institutions, the analysis below suggests that it is difficult to pass judgment without also considering the attempts of other groups to control other institutions.

The conflict around the control of the Islamic University of Gaza is revealing as an example of the intense rivalry between the Palestinian Muslim Brothers and the secular nationalist groups. The IUG was built with donations collected by the Islamists, in consequence of which they perceived it as "theirs." As background to the struggle for control of the university, in 1979, both Fateh and the Brothers wanted to take over the Palestinian Red Crescent Society, which was seen as controlled by the Communists. Islamic University student activists belonging to Fateh and the Brothers formed a short-lived coalition that won four out of twenty-one seats in the student council that year, while a rival coalition of the left (Communists, DFLP, and PFLP) took seventeen seats. The result was contested amid accusations of fraud, while Fateh and the Islamists prepared for further elections, which never took place (Abul-Omrein 2000, 206–7). According to Abul-Omrein, students set fire to the Red Crescent Society, cinemas, and other entertainment venues in Gaza (208). Subsequent attempts by the non-Islamist groups, including Fateh, to gain dominance within the Islamic University, involving students, staff, and administration, were all unsuccessful. On June 4, 1983, groups close to Fateh and the leftist parties attacked the university, which led to the injury of more than two hundred students (Abu 'Amr 1989, 72). In 1984, another attempt was made to hold democratic elections for student council seats, but this too failed and culminated in the assassination of the university's vice president, allegedly by members of Fateh. The next year, one of Fateh's leaders in Gaza was physically attacked by a group of Islamists (al-Zahar, in Abul-Omrein 2000, 217). In 1986, female IUG students affiliated with the Marxist PFLP tried to organize some events to promote their party. According to Ismail Haneya, who later became a prominent Hamas leader, when the students invited speakers from outside the school, they were accused of "breaking the rules and attacking the university administration" and expelled (quoted at 209). This was followed by an attack on an Islamist female student, which led to a series of back-and-forth reprisals. Ultimately, there was an assassination attempt on Hamas co-founder 'Abdel 'Aziz al-Rantissi for his role in expelling the leftists. It is worth noting that female Islamist students, like other nationalist and leftist female students, were an integral part of all the preceding struggles over the control of Islamist institutions in Gaza. It is important to keep this background of conflict in mind when discussing the spread of the veiling campaign during the first intifada, in which Islamists were accused of bullying leftist women.

With the outbreak of the first intifada in December 1987, women of national and secular inclination were increasingly obliged to wear headscarves. Youths in the streets, looking for a "national" role to play, took initiative to coerce schoolgirls and young women to cover their hair, including verbal harassment and stone-throwing. While obligatory veiling was not explicitly called for in the Brothers' religious and political directives at the beginning of the intifada, their proselytizing efforts in previous years had made it easy for many young men and boys to take the control of "their women" into their own hands. This "national" duty was facilitated by the Islamists' obsession with protecting their militant members against infiltration through mingling with women, whether by the Israelis or other political groups.

Many women cite December 1988 as a watershed of the hijab campaign (Hammami 1997, 199). By then, it was a matter of principle for some women not to wear the headscarf. But then, on September 19, 1990, a *mythaq sharaf* (covenant of honor) was signed between Hamas and Fateh to establish new rules for relations between the two organizations based on "the right of each party to carry out its activities without intimidation . . . the release of Islamic University staff salaries . . . the return to constructive dialogue to end disputes, [and] respect for the nation's beliefs (*'aqidat al-umma*), its mosques, and the properties of its citizens" (Hamas [ca. 1990], 142–44). The signing of this covenant signaled a new phase in Palestinian democratic practice and a rare instance of pluralism that solidified the internal unity of the Palestinian polity against the Occupation. However, it failed to stop all confrontations, especially in light of the deep discord between Hamas and the PA over the peace process and its political consequences.

In this context of rivalry, mutual mistrust, and physical attacks between the different factions, perhaps one can understand why the youth of Gaza felt provoked to force young women to wear hijab. The dispute was predominantly about whose vision and political power should prevail, that of the Islamists or of Fateh and the nationalist secularists. As the next chapter describes, several developments over the following years shifted the balance toward the Islamists.

4

The "New Islamic Woman"

Gender Discourse and Islamist Politics

THE LESSON Hamas learned from its experience in the first intifada and from its reading of the rise and fall of the PLO's power was to maintain consistency between its ideological line and its political activity. In practical terms, this meant emphasizing Islamist discourse alongside paramilitary resistance. When Hamas initially took action through the intifada, it employed peaceful means, adopting military tactics from 1992 onward (Hroub 2000; al-Hamad and al-Bargouthi 1997). The combination of political and military action boosted Hamas's popularity considerably, which was hard for the PA to ignore after its founding in 1994. Unlike the PLO, there was no place for women in Hamas's military wing. This fact—significant though it was—made it easier for secular Palestinian groups and international observers alike to dismiss and ignore the contributions of Islamist women's activism, which might have been thought undeniable. As a consequence of this denial, the character and practice of Islamist women's activism became matters of easy and largely erroneous assumption, rather than study and analysis.

The relationship between Hamas and the PA was conditioned by the relationship between the PA and Israel. Hamas rejected the peace process that started at the Madrid conference in 1991 and culminated in the 1993 Oslo Agreement, which called for the establishment of partial Palestinian self-rule through the PA in the Occupied Territories. The PA sought to co-opt the opposition, in particular

Hamas, by offering a share in the leadership. Hamas turned the offer down.

In February 1994, a Jewish settler in Hebron entered the Ibrahimi Mosque during dawn prayers and opened fire, killing thirty worshippers and injuring a hundred more. In April that year, the first attack by Hamas on Israeli civilians inside the Green Line defining the 1949 borders of the State of Israel started a wave of suicide attacks. Hamas now became a target of both the PA and Israel, eroding the PA's legitimacy, especially with the paralysis of the peace process and the growing Israeli policy of collective sanctions and reprisals.

The PA followed a dual approach in its direct relations with Hamas: opening lines of communication and negotiations and cracking down when diplomacy failed. In the meantime, the PA waged a media campaign against Hamas, questioning its loyalty by accusing it of cultivating relations with and owing allegiance to Iran (Schulz 1999; Hroub 2000, 107). Thus, Hamas was depicted as the alien "other." The PA scored points against Hamas by capitalizing on the pivotal quandary the movement faced. Hamas could either pursue guerrilla activities, risking a clash with the PA that might lead to civil war, or freeze such activities, which would undermine its credibility as the spearhead of an alternative path of resistance.

Hamas, in turn, followed a multipronged strategy with the PA, ranging from verbal attacks against it, to attempts to gain its sympathy (or, more specifically, the sympathy of its police force), to liaising with it to resolve problems on the ground and avoid civil conflict. Hamas drew a red line for itself—avoid a civil war at any cost—which enabled the PA to crack down on Hamas when the latter launched military actions against Israel (Hroub 2000, 107–8; al-Hamad and al-Bargouthi 1997). On November 18, 1994, "Black Friday," the PA police opened fire on Hamas demonstrators in Gaza, killing fourteen (al-Hamad and al-Bargouthi 1997, 249; Hroub 2000, 103–9). The assassination of several Hamas military leaders followed, along with a large-scale PA campaign of arrests of group members. In 1996, for example, nine hundred members, including a number of leadership figures, were jailed and, in many cases, tortured. The PA also raided

Hamas mosques, agencies, charitable societies, and civil society institutions, including the Islamic University of Gaza. It placed restrictions on Friday sermons, the use of the mosques (which the PA had placed under the control of its *awqaf*), and the activities of alms collection (*zakat*) committees. Hamas could do little more than issue press releases condemning what was happening (al-Hamad and al-Bargouthi 1997; Hroub 2000, 108).

The attacks on Hamas amounted to violations of basic civil liberties, and in some instances exceeded those committed by Israeli forces under the Occupation, which greatly undermined the PA's credibility in the eyes of many Palestinians, including those in Fateh itself. On March 7, 1996, two hundred security and police officers attacked the Islamic University and other schools. Ultimately, the Netanyahu administration's assumption of power in May 1996 and its refusal to carry out Israeli obligations under the Oslo Agreement prompted the PA to mitigate its policies concerning Hamas, but its belligerence had already played into the movement's hands.

To better function as a political movement, Hamas had already separated its military wing and its political operations. On December 11, 1995, Hamas announced the establishment of *Hizb al-Khalas al-Watani al-Islami* (the Islamic National Salvation Party)—often referred to as Khalas (salvation)—which functioned as a legal opposition party. Despite plans to establish its headquarters in Jerusalem, the Salvation Party operated in Gaza only. Frequent PA crackdowns on the party and its journal, *Al-Rissala* (The Message), made expansion into the West Bank and Jerusalem impossible.[1] The Israeli policy of comprehensively dividing the Palestinian territories hinders the movement of leaders and cadres between the West Bank and Gaza, while the targeted assassination of Islamist leaders, including those of the Salvation Party, further obstructs its growth and structural development.

1. As of this writing, all legal institutions belonging to Hamas have been closed by the PA, despite many protest demonstrations. According to Amira Haroun, the twice-elected head of the Salvation Party's Women's Action Department, this has forced the party to focus on "consolidating our presence in Gaza."

However, these persecutions, whether by Israel or the PA, have caused Hamas's popularity to soar.[2]

The party's founding mission statement indicated that it was a Palestinian political party operating in accordance with Islamic doctrine and adopting the *majlis al-shura* (consultative council) in its internal structure (Roy 1999, 44). Islam was presented as an integral system of life and a solution to all problems. The statement stressed the need for participation in political-cultural activity and social-economic construction, and the protection of religious values and civil rights, including those of women, laborers, and cultural societies. For the first time in the Brothers' history, the language of "rights" was used for different social groups, in particular for women and other disadvantaged groups who had rarely been targeted by the Brothers' activism. The use of "rights" language will be dealt with later. First, I examine the position of women within the Salvation Party and the ways in which their roles differed from those played by nationalist and secularist women within the structure of the national movement.

Mainstreaming Gender à la Islamism

Islamist women grapple with the need to combine two paradoxical expectations: as model mothers and obedient wives, and as model political activists. It is the same dilemma that nationalist and secularist women are still struggling to solve. Hamas's contradictory gender ideology, like that of the nationalists, stresses the traditional role of women in reproducing the nation. While the movement is keen to promote an updated image of Islamic womanhood, it is clear that this image potentially contradicts the longstanding conception of the Palestinian woman as the fertile "womb."

The Salvation Party opened its doors to the "new Islamic woman," who is well educated, professional, politically active, and outspoken—in

2. In a poll organized by PCRD (Palestinian Center for Research and Dialogue) immediately after the 2004 assassination of Sheikh Ahmed Yassine, 31 percent of respondents said that they would vote for Hamas in the next election, versus 27.1 percent for Fateh; 70.1 percent said that Hamas's popular base would increase.

sum, modern—while also a good, committed Muslim (*moltazema*). Even the veil is seen as a signifier of modernity since it is different from "traditional dress." As members of the party's Women's Action Department put it, the "new Islamic dress"—a long robe of plain color and a white or black headscarf—is: "different from the *thub* [traditional peasant woman's dress] which is used by our mothers and grandmothers"; "it means different things; it is a unifying symbol to our followers and members; if I see a woman wearing it, I know immediately that she is *ukhot*[3] [a sister]"; "it indicates that we are educated and not like our mothers, who are mostly illiterate"; "it gives us *heiba* [respect] as the dress of our *'ulama'* [clergy]; it is economical, simple, and modest" (Amira, Youssra, Maysoon, Kholod, interviews). From this perspective, Islamist dress is regarded as superior to the *thub* because it is a uniform of conviction, unlike the blind adherence to tradition that is presumed to explain choice of dress among the masses. Implicit in the Islamist veiling style is participation in a national social movement that lends the wearer a heightened sense of status, both moral (vis-à-vis secularists) and social (vis-à-vis women who merely cover, but do not veil). However, despite its political cachet, behind the social force of veiling "one can discern the familiar principle of *himaye*, guidance and protection by (and from) men" (White 2002, 223).

Unlike some other Islamic parties, as in Turkey for example, in which Islamist women, once married, lose their "voice" when they retreat to the security and seclusion of the patriarchal family (White 2002), the party and its women's department made an important venue available for a category of women who were well educated (with a bachelor's or postgraduate degree) yet had limited access to a restricted, male-dominated labor market. In this sense, it is important to trace the identity the party provided for women so that they could manage their dual roles as activist in the public sphere and as mother and wage earner.

3. It is worth noting that Fateh also used to call a woman member *ukhot* (sister), while in the leftist parties she is called *rafiqa* (comrade).

While education is an important facilitator of class mobility, the fact that the majority of Islamist women are refugees, educated in Gazan or other Arab universities, and hold a conservative outlook limits their chances of employment. For example, the NGO sector, which functions as an important employer of educated women, requires proficiency in foreign languages and managerial and administrative skills. The Salvation Party took upon itself the role of a "developmental party" to "mainstream" gender in its structure at all levels.

The Women's Action Department (*da'erat al-'amal al-nissa'i*) was established as one of thirteen departments in the party managing all aspects of activities and administration, from public relations to cultural and political affairs. Unlike the women's organizations in the national movement, it was clandestine and therefore had to take a different form. The Women's Action Department was able to fully integrate women into the party's political organs, whether in the leadership or the popular base.

The popular base of the Salvation Party was represented in the general conference (*al moatamar al 'am*), whose members were elected from among the party members in each of Gaza's five geographical regions. The general conference in turn elected the central *majlis al-shura* (advisory council), which set the party's basic policies (executed by a politburo, also elected). However, there was no clear projection of the future role such a body would play in an eventual Islamic state. Roy, for example, problematizes the role of such councils and declines to equate them with elected parliaments in non-Islamic democracies. In an Islamic context, he writes, "what matters is the function of the 'counselling'" (1999, 44–45). In other words, it is important to determine whether such councils act as legislative and decision-making bodies, or merely provide consultative guidance, since, in a religious context, God alone legislates. In Hamas's case, while some of the institutional names were Islamized, the structure of the party was very similar to that of the secular nationalist organizations, in which there is a general assembly that elects a central committee to formulate and follow the policies to be implemented by an executive body.

In 2003, for example, the *majlis al-shura* was composed of fifty-two members, of whom eight (15.3 percent) were women—five of them refugees and three from Gaza City; five married with children and three single. The elected women were all well-educated, holding degrees in physics, chemistry, medical science, education, and English from universities in Jordan, Egypt, Syria, and Gaza. None had been active in a political party before. Only one of the twenty-one total of women in the *majlis al-shura* and politburo had male relatives in the party, which suggests that they mostly established their credentials on merit as educated activists.

In each region, there is a five-member *hay'a idareyya* (administrative committee). There are two heads in each *hay'a*—one for men and the other for women—who organize contacts and events. The female members of these committees are not there to enforce gender segregation but rather are fully incorporated members of party bodies. As Amira Haroun, the head of the Women's Action Department, put it, "It's not about segregation. We discussed this issue in the party several times—it's because the women previously didn't know the male candidates and vice versa. So, on this level, women members vote for women and male members vote for men. Once they all reach the general conference, they all [males and females together] choose the male and female members of the *majlis al-shura* and then the politburo" (interview).

In the politburo (*al-maktab al-seyassi*), thirteen out of the eighty-five members were women (two unmarried). The share of female representation in the politburo and the *majlis al-shura*—15.3 percent in each case—was much higher than the respective figures in all PA and PLO political bodies, whether filled by election or appointment.

In the Palestinian National Council, for example, which is formed by nomination according to a party quota in which Fateh holds the majority determined by a formula in which Fateh controls no less than a majority of the seats (50 percent plus one), women represented 7.5 percent (fifty-six out of 744) in 2000. And in the elected Palestinian Legislative Council of 1996, they represented 6 percent (five out of eighty-eight) (Jad 2000, 54; SIDA 1999, 20). There were no women representatives in the Executive Committee, the highest level of the PLO, until August 27, 2009, when Hanan Ashrawi was elected.[4]

In the Salvation Party, the primary task of the Women's Action Department was to include women in public life by getting them involved in party activities. According to Amira Haroun, "We have a yearly plan to *damj* [integrate] women, politically and culturally, into the society" (interview). The department was keen to increase women's membership in the party, which, according to Amira and Youssra, was around 27 percent of the general conference in 2003.

To facilitate this integration process, the party and its satellite societies ran a massive network of kindergartens for a minimal charge to parents, and poorer women and the wives of political prisoners were exempt from paying any fee at all. Running kindergartens was a task long undertaken by nationalist and secularist women's organizations, which they abandoned after 1993 and the post-Oslo shift in donor agendas. The vacuum left by these organizations was not filled by the PA when it was established in 1993 but by Islamist organizations. By running a network of kindergartens, the Islamists solved a major problem for working mothers and women activists.

It is important to note that the two women who managed to make it to the party's top level were both unmarried. According to Youssra and Amira, members of both the politburo and the Women's Action Department, the politburo's work was very diverse, intense, and time-consuming. Many feminists identified the scheduling of political meetings as a hindrance to women's participation, since they were usually set for the convenience of men (Waylen 1996). When asked

4. The same could be said of women's representation in the leadership of Palestinian political parties, which was relatively low despite the impressive activism of many women's organizations. In the late 1990s, women were severely underrepresented in the Central Committees of the Popular Front for the Liberation of Palestine (10 percent); the Democratic Front for the Liberation of Palestine (19.5 percent); FIDA (a DFLP faction that broke away in 1990) (19 percent), and Fateh (only 5 percent) (SIDA 1999, 21).

about the timing of their meetings and whether they were suitable for women, Youssra and Amira pointed to the veil as a facilitator, even during late hours. As Youssra explained: "We have certain days when we discuss our general plans within the party at these meetings; we collectively choose the best time for all of us, men and women. But even if we have to be late sometimes, it's not a problem for us; since we are *moltazemat*, no one approaches us to do any harm. Our people know that we work for their benefit and we are well respected for that" (interview). In this case, the veil facilitates mobility for the politically committed woman, providing the necessary validation to break taboos that would ordinarily bar an unmarried woman from going out late at night. If the maintenance of her virtue depends on her behavior, her behavioral signals mark the unapproachability and inviolability of the Islamist woman.

The Women's Action Department used various methods to recruit women. Its members worked face to face with their targets, building cells in the refugee camps as entry points. Their task was facilitated by the existence of large numbers of political prisoners, a special focus of their activities which included the prisoners' families. The department organized an annual campaign of demonstrations against the Israelis and the PA on behalf of these prisoners (now forgotten by almost all nationalist and secular women's organizations). According to Youssra, they demonstrated against the PA because of its "lack of democracy," and also to protest the PA's "constant harassment of the party offices and its journal," as well as "the arrest of its leaders"[5] (interview).

In the party's yearly plan, activities directed toward women combined both a national and a gender-specific agenda. The department targeted women with a higher education for recruitment through

5. In 2001, the PA banned all Salvation Party activities, including the publication of its journal, *Al-Rissala*, and raided its local offices to confiscate all of its documents, computers, and other equipment. According to Amira, the party was functioning at a very low level from its headquarters in Gaza City.

cultural and educational activities, while vocational education and material support targeted the poorer and less well educated women. The department organized many *dawrat* (workshops) in *tathqif seyassi* (political socialization), very similar to the kind of programs conventionally offered by secular leftist (Marxist) women's organizations. There was a program called *al-multaqa al-nassawi* (women's encounter), aimed at *al-tawassol wal-taf'eel* (linkage and mobilization), that targeted women lawyers, writers, journalists, doctors, and accountants. In addition, there was a permanent annual course in *i'dad kader* (cadre formation, also retaining its original Marxist flavor) which sometimes lasted all year.[6] These types of programs were innovative in comparison to those run by nationalist and secularist women's organizations, which failed to target this category of women in such a systematic and sustained manner.

While Islamist ideology and activism opened doors for women, they tended to be revolving doors for less-educated women who were often unable to sustain an activist or professional life or even to support themselves or their families. Many were the wives of political prisoners (a large majority of Palestinian political prisoners come from the Islamic movement). When asked what the department did for such women, one leader answered: "We do our best to try to attract these women to our activities. We organize workshops to train them in different professional skills so they can support themselves. But in many cases they simply drop out. Their imprisoned husbands pressure them not to follow the courses, not to leave their homes, especially if they are serving a long sentence. We couldn't do anything to help. This is a sensitive family matter" (Youssra, interview). When Youssra and other women were asked if they use their power within the party to pressure their husbands to change their mind about their wives' participation, the answer was negative. This reaction could be attributed to

6. The curriculum of the course in cadre formation covered "modern" and "scientific" subjects such as self-assertiveness, self-building, effective communication, political awareness, socialization, program designing, and collective picnics.

the contradictory values promoted by the Salvation Party: involvement versus motherhood, obedience, and family unity.

As for specific women's issues, the department organized an annual one-day "women's conference" in which men and women presented papers on gender issues. They covered hot topics raised by secular, nationalist women's groups or dealt with specific problems that women face in their various fields of activity, such as work, political life, and culture. Some of the workshops were directed at the male members of the Women's Action Department, focusing on topics such as socialization or involving, for example, a thorough discussion of *shari'a* family law. According to Amira Haroun, "Some topics elicit fierce resistance from men, as in the discussion of *shari'a*, while other topics, like mixing [male and female], are contested, and some male members are provoked by the gender segregation in our activities" (interview). As one male member put it, "as a party that supports the development of women, we should abolish segregation in the party" (Zaid, interview).

I will address the attitude of the party and the Islamist women concerning *shari'a* later, but it is important to note here that the motivations behind the call to reform *shari'a* are in essence a desire to change the internal power relations between males and females within the family structure. Male members are receptive to change and support "mixing," which enhances the image of the party and its women as "modern," while they continue to resist deeper, less visible changes within the family. Support for mixing is not shared by all Islamists, many of whom encourage the segregation of students in the university, which suggests that even the veil is not enough to transcend gender barriers.

The annual women's conferences were a vehicle for the presentation of the Islamists' ideology on gender, and it is noteworthy that figures in the highest level of Hamas leadership were keen to attend and "to show their support" for Islamist women. Sheikh Amhed Yassine gave a speech at the first conference in 1998. At the second women's conference in 1999, Mahmoud al-Zahar, a prominent Hamas leader, presented a paper, setting a precedent that has yet to be repeated—as far as I know—in the history of the Palestinian women's movement to date.[7]

Sheikh Yassine again attended the fifth conference in 2003, as did Dr. 'Abdel 'Aziz al-Rantissi, when the establishment of the Islamic Women's Movement in Palestine was announced before an audience of more than 1,500 men and women. This announcement marked Hamas's intention to link all the Islamist women's institutions and coordinate and channel their efforts to represent the Islamic vision for women. This included eight women's organizations: the Muslim Women's Association; the Women's Action Department of the Salvation Party; the Women's Action Department in *al-mojama' al-Islami* (the Islamic Compound); the Islamic bloc (female students), Female Student's Council in the Islamic University; The Palestinian Mothers' Society; Family Care Society; The Women's Unit in the Arab Institute for Study and Research; and the Mothers of Martyrs Society.

While the presence of the top leadership at the Islamist women's conference could be interpreted as a potential opening, an encouragement of women's public role and women's activism, it could also be interpreted as a potential closure, a hardening of positions and a retreat into interpretations of Islam that might affect women negatively. The fifth conference in 2003, for example, was also used to launch a massive attack on the draft reform of the penal code which favored a more egalitarian approach to the penalties imposed for adultery and violence against women within the family. The standing law imposed harsher punishment for adultery on women than on men and was relatively tolerant of domestic violence. The point of the attack was that the proposed reform was not based on *shari'a*, which reflected an escalation of the Islamists' demands; i.e., that not only family law but the penal

7. Political leaders would ordinarily attend the opening ceremony of these women's conferences and then leave before the participants got down to work. The presentation of a theoretical paper demonstrates a much more significant involvement. The contents of Mahmoud al-Zahar's paper will be discussed in a later section.

code should be based on *shari'a*.[8] And with the support of the Islamist women, the leadership used its power to stall an open and critical discussion of the law at the conference. Thus, the party reaffirmed its formal position that *shari'a* is derived from sacred sources and is thus fixed and immutable (Zubaida 2003, 1). This putative "freezing" of *shari'a*, however, is subverted by Islamist women in their ordinary activism and their daily interaction with other women's groups.

Ultimately, in securing women's representation within the Islamic National Salvation Party, the Women's Action Department was a catalyst for the inclusion of even more women activists in the party and further broadening its constituencies. And in order to achieve that goal, it was necessary to take the women's needs into consideration. The kindergarten network was an important facilitator and so were the various programs aimed at cadre formation and skills development for different categories of women. WAD proved extremely successful in mobilizing a large number of women to defend the party against PA harassment, in defending the party line on the preservation of *shari'a*, and in discrediting other secularist and feminist women's groups that were also calling for legal reforms. In so doing, they borrowed a great deal from the secular women's organizations, modeling their internal structures and running similar types of projects and programs.

The new adherents whom the party brought into the movement included university graduates and professional women, which helped Hamas transition from a male-dominated underground paramilitary organization to a popular political movement. The top leadership's backing of the decision to create an Islamic women's movement was a significant milestone in the history of the overall Palestinian women's movement, as women became a strategic concern for the national movement for the first time and under the banner of Islam. However, since *shari'a* was held to be fixed and immutable when the movement

8. Under this attack, the Palestinian Parliament halted discussion of the draft law (Palestinian Information Center, July 16, 2003.

was announced, women's demands for more egalitarian treatment under the law were effectively stalled.

The Gender Ideology of Hamas

While Hamas's gender ideology is expressed in terms of fixed and immutable religious principles, it is, nonetheless, possible to demonstrate that it is contradictory and in constant flux. This is a result of ordinary socioeconomic factors and, as I have proposed, a reaction to the challenge presented by the discourse of feminist nationalist and secular women, as well as Islamist women's activism within the movement. As argued in chapter 2, the universalist discourse used by women in NGOs is alien not because it is "Western" but because it was not founded on a deep understanding of the situation of the women whose interests these organizations claimed to be representing. Moreover, in the aftermath of the Oslo Agreement, this universalist discourse was reproduced and diffused in the absence of a power structure to support it, whether through the women's movement or through the national secular political movement.

The lack of attention to gender ideology and its impact on gender relations in the study of Islamist movements in the Middle East by male scholars has been widely criticized. Baron (1996) states that "most male observers of fundamentalism, or Islamism, see 'the activist' as male and the central message as political or economic" (120). In many books written on Islamism, be they Arab, European, or Israeli, it is astonishing to note how the Islamists' gender ideology was mostly ignored (Hroub 1996, 2000; al-Hamad and al-Bargouthi 1997; Abul-Omrein 2000; al-Taheri 1995; Abu-Amr 1994; Litvak 1996; Schiff and Ya'ari 1989; Hilal 1998; Munson 2003). It has largely been the task of women writers to examine the impact of Hamas's gender ideology (Hammami 1991, 1997; Taraki 1989; Jad 2000; Pavlowsky 1998; Milton-Edwards 1996; Abu-Lughod 2013). Even in women's writings, Islamist women were ignored as actors, and the focus was mainly on the manifest impact of the gender ideology of the Islamist movement, particularly in relation to the veil. One publication that professed to detail the different components of Palestinian women's activism completely ignored Islamist women and their organizations (SIDA 1999, 48–50). This is a common tendency in the study of religious and fundamentalist movements worldwide. Hawley (1994) asserts that "it surprised us that the matter of gender ideology had received so little attention in the nascent literature on comparative fundamentalism" (25). Guarding against this neglect, Keddie (1999) warns that "such studies are still considered something apart by most male scholars, and not as something that deeply affects politics and society so much that they cannot be dealt with adequately without taking cognisance of gender questions" (17).

The conflict over gender and the "ideal" woman is not a neutral, exclusively religious aspect of Hamas's ideology. As Papanek (1994) explains, the ideal woman goes hand in hand with the ideal society, although the specific status of women depends very much upon the specific vision of the ideal society (see also Kandiyoti 1991a, 1991b; Moghadam 1994). If the ideal society is an independent Islamic state, the ideal woman is a good Muslim, modest, pious, and *moltazema*. A woman's role is to complement her man, rather than to function fully as an equal to him. In light of this consideration, it is important to trace how gender is perceived and reconstructed by Hamas and how these processes differ from comparable processes in the secular national movement. It is also important to recognize, however, that some of the tendencies we see in Hamas are by no means unique to Islamist movements.

In what is considered a classic volume on fundamentalism and gender, John Hawley and Wayne Proudfoot (1994) attempt to explain why fundamentalist religious movements are so obsessed with women and gender. They argue that "the construction of gender is an important part of the meaning of fundamentalism and their perspective on gender casts a uniquely revealing light on the nature of fundamentalism as a whole" (27). The authors offer three explanations for fundamentalists' obsession with gender: otherness, nostalgia, and religious machismo. In reference to the first, Hawley and Proudfoot explain that "in groups led by men whose identity is constructed in important ways by their confrontation with an external 'other,' great weight falls on the need to control the other 'others' in their midst" (27). According to Karen McCarthy Brown (1994), women are seen by fundamentalist movements throughout most of the world as "playing the role of designated 'other' in sociocultural contexts defined by men, and thus they tend to carry the projections of all that is undesirable or threatening in human existence: sexuality, emotion, pollution, sin, and mortality" (188).

Fundamentalist gender ideologies are also explained in the context of encounters with the "other," such as the imperialist Christian West. The critique that Christian missionaries made of the treatment of women in Hindu and Islamic societies has paved the way for a virulent fundamentalist rejection of the supposed degradation that has come with the liberation of women's roles in the societies that unleashed those missionaries onto the world. According to this line of thinking, divorce, prostitution, open homosexuality, flagrant exhibitionism, and pornography clearly expose the moral destitution of Western modernism. Many Muslims have held that the purpose of such "Crusader imperialism," latterly in collusion with Zionism, was to visit these effects upon Islam. The chain reaction proceeds according to what Yvonne Haddad (1985) calls an "Islamist domino theory." First, "female public exposure" is condoned, and this leads—via such horrors as dating and homosexual marriage—to "deep dissatisfaction, a criminal climate, a disquieting sense of insecurity," and, ultimately, to "uncontrolled inflation, more frequent cases of rape, and the threat of depression and bankruptcy" (287, 302–3). The defense against this is to make a woman a "queen crowned in her kingdom and her home," where she will be responsible for the transmission of Islamic values to her children, and not allowed to stray from that role (287).

An almost invariable component of fundamentalism is devotion to the cause of restoring an idealized past, a mythical age that never was, or in any case was never quite what it is now claimed to have been (Roy 1999; Zubaida 1997, 2000, 2003). Visions of such a past typically lay strong emphasis on the role women played in the perfection of that bygone time. The reason is that in every society the disparity between the sexes is a source of social and cognitive tension.

In any account of the golden age, that tension must be wiped out if the past is to seem ideal. Since men primarily control the construction of this idealized past, their solution is to portray the women who inhabit it as self-sacrificing and generous—they yield before men to produce greater harmony. Not only do they acknowledge the limits of their place in the social fabric, they glorify it. Hence, a special place is reserved in fundamentalist movements for women who articulate the virtues of this attitude in the present day, depicting it as a healthy alternative to the futile and ultimately demeaning struggles that come with trying to be a "modern woman" (Hawley and Proudfoot 1994, 30; White 2002). Thus, the evocation of the traditional family and the moral values on which the nation was putatively built, and a set of values that pivot on chaste, maternal womanhood become crucial. The same is true for men: the motifs of otherness and nostalgia, both prominent features of fundamentalist consciousness, "reinforce each other and meet in a conservative ideology of gender that reconstructs an idealized past and attempts to reshape the present along the same lines" (Hawley and Proudfoot 1994, 32).

Hawley and Proudfoot argue that, for the rhetoric of religious machismo to succeed, its proponents often find it helpful to invoke the presence of women who need defending. Often these are real women: mothers and wives who need to be shielded from too much contact with the corrupt outside world. Such helpless women may also be symbolic—territory, culture, and history that have been desecrated by the attacks of modernity are frequently depicted by fundamentalists as female. As Hawley and Proudfoot state, "these two kinds of women, the symbolic and the real, reinforce one another. Symbols of endangered womanhood can be more easily sustained if they are nourished in an environment where real women must depend on men to defend them, and the converse is also true" (33). Hence, the characteristic militancy of fundamentalist groups is not, after all, just a metalanguage for a stance of opposition to modernity. It is an active force that helps make "traditional" gender roles second nature in fundamentalist religion (34). "Traditional" here is used in the sense not that the fundamentalists retain usages that were common in earlier

times (although this is sometimes also true), but that they participate in an actively constructed past. As suggested by Eric Hobsbawm
(1983) in his introduction to *The Invention of Tradition*, such usages
are intended to reflect unchanging archetypes, rather than emerging
in an organic way from processes that would properly be called "custom" (2–3).

In the context of the Middle East, more specifically, Leila Ahmed
(1992) presents the Islamist preoccupation with women as a struggle
over culture, and Islamist discourse on women as a discourse of resistance; what is being resisted is the colonial and postcolonial assault on
Muslim religion and culture in which the crusade against "backward"
practices such as veiling constituted an important element, especially
in the late nineteenth century. In other words, if the imperialists saw
the custom of veiling and the position of women in Muslim societies
as proof of the inferiority of Islam and a justification for their attempt
to subjugate Muslims, Islamists now invert the terms of this discourse
and stress the importance of veiling and the return to indigenous
practices as a form of resistance.

Pursuing the same logic, Lisa Taraki (2003) goes further and
views the Islamist preoccupation with women's dress and conduct
not only as a form of resistance but also as a way of taking the ultimate historical revenge; i.e., demonstrating by counter-example the
moral bankruptcy of the West and the superiority of Muslims. To the
Islamists, the price of imperialist supremacy was the moral decay of
Western society. And what could symbolize moral decay more starkly
than the degraded American or European woman who has no respect
for marriage or the family, who bares her skin for all to see, and who
gives her body without resistance? In focusing on issues crucial to the
Arab Muslim's value system (the centrality of family, virtue, and modesty in women), the Islamists strike a responsive chord in conservative
Arab society, which by and large subscribes to the Islamists' diagnosis
of the causes of Western society's ills. They also restore a measure of
pride and self-respect to Arabs, and assure Muslims of their moral
superiority despite their economic and political subjugation.

In the same vein, Deniz Kandiyoti (1991b) notes the agreement among scholars that the historical antagonism between Islam and Christendom created an area of cultural resistance around women and the family, which together came to represent the inviolable repository of Muslim identity. She observes that Islamic authenticity can be evoked to articulate a wide array of disaffections, from revolt against imperialist subjugation to class antagonism. This opens up the possibility of expressing such antagonism in moral and cultural terms, with images of women's purity exercising a powerful mobilizing influence, as in the case of the populist discourse of the Khomeini regime in Iran, which singled out Westernized elite women as the most dangerous bearers of moral decay.

Bringing socioeconomic factors into the debate, Valentine Moghadam (1993) argues that the increase in female education and employment has slowly weakened the system of patriarchal gender relations, creating status inconsistency and anxiety on the part of the men of the petite bourgeoisie. Taraki (2003), looking at modernization in Jordan, argues that what characterized the latter half of the twentieth century was the breakdown of the barriers that had kept women out of sight and therefore out of (the male) mind. While women had always been physically visible in the fields and in the marketplace, they had occupied their place within a sexual division of labor that upheld the patriarchal order. The entry of women into the wage labor force, the educational system, and the public domain in general challenged the traditional order, especially as unrelated men and women were thrust together in work and social situations far from the watchful eyes of the family.

Taraki (2003) explains that increasing economic need has forced men to acquiesce in women seeking employment outside the home, and state-sponsored mandatory education for girls has meant that resistance to female education is no longer a viable option. Limited choices in these areas, therefore, are compensated for by ensuring that when women go out into the gender-integrated world, they do so with the minimum of social risk. She concludes that the Islamic movement in Jordan, in making women's dress and conduct a cornerstone of its social agenda, expresses what individual men fear and need: fear of losing control over their women and the need to be assured that other men cannot lay a claim to them (214). Thus, the failed promises of post-independence developmentalism could be interpreted not as merely a concatenation of technical failures, according to Kandiyoti (1996), but as moral failures requiring a complete overhaul of the worldviews underpinning them. She states that it is "against this background that some oppositional movements have been advocating a 'just' Islamic order, invoking notions of authentic Muslim womanhood as part of a broader critique of Westernization and consumerism" (24).

Turning to Palestine, many scholars invoke socioeconomic and political factors to explain the spread of politicization and mobilization of women by the national secular movements in the 1970s and 1980s, which led to the massive participation of women in the first intifada (Taraki 1989; Jad 1990; Hasso 1997; Hammami 1997; Kuttab 1993). The establishment of a number of Palestinian universities beginning in the mid-1970s attracted many young women from rural and poorer backgrounds to higher education. Enrollment in secondary schools and universities has been steadily growing since 1975.[9] Nationalist student activism in these universities was crucial in attracting young women to the secular national movement. The persistent demand by Palestinians in rural areas for girls' education, touched on in chapter 3, contradicts depictions of rural men as implacably conservative, fearful of modernity, and intent on controlling their women.

In addition, the threat posed by colonization was always apparent and empowered the nationalists and the secularists from the mid-1930s to the end of the 1980s. This is not to ignore the deterioration

9. Female enrollment in secondary education, for example, was successively 58, 61, 75, 71, and 90 percent in 1975, 1980, 1985, 1990, and 1995 (Ghali 1997, 37, table A1).

of the economic situation beginning in the early 1980s in the West Bank and Gaza, which led many educated young women to seek work in the unprotected informal sector of private workshops, which provoked the call to control women. However, the question remains as to why the Islamists' momentum surged in the late 1980s and not before.

The growing influence of the Islamists can be explained only with reference to a series of interrelated factors: the decline of the Palestinian national movement accompanied by the withdrawal of the grassroots organizations from service provision; the NGO-ization of women's organizations which ruptured their organic links with the grassroots; and the nationalization of Islam and the Islamization of the Palestinian national identity by the Muslim Brothers.

Central to this latter process was the Islamization of gender. Rema Hammami has made the case that the 1987 intifada was the first time "that an issue, specifically veiling, once relegated to the arena of religious behaviour had been mobilised as a nationalist issue" (1997, 194). She asserts, rightly, that the campaign for hijab demonstrated the ability of Hamas to conflate its social ideology with Palestinian nationalism, wielding the threat and the use of violence against women to impose the veil. Women gained little support from the national leadership of the intifada, which failed to stop the campaign in time.

From this, it may seem that Hamas's gender ideology was a fixed concept stemming from a conservative and misogynistic religious platform. Again, women, in this view, were perceived as victims of the imposition of something they did not want. While that might be true for some women in the leftist organizations, it is still important to understand why it was difficult to reverse the course of events when, after the establishment of the PA, the national leadership of the intifada issued many leaflets, with the concurrence of Hamas, delegitimizing the attacks on women.[10] In other words, why do we witness an

---

10. Many leaflets were issued to condemn any threat or act of violence against unveiled women, be it throwing stones or eggs or any other potentially intimidating behavior (see Hammami 1997, 200–201).

increase in the number of veiled women and girls if veiling is a symbolic form—if not a signifier—of adherence to the textual tradition of Islam advocated by Hamas? In her study on the Palestinian Federation of Women's Action Committees (PFWAC), Hasso (1997, 259) indicated, for example, that 80 percent of her sample presented themselves as religious. She also showed that many had worn hijab in response to social pressure since the first intifada, but that some also indicated that they wore hijab as a matter of personal conviction. While Hasso's research focused on a secular leftist women's group, I shall focus on a group of women who, as far as I know, have not yet been researched, and who do not perceive themselves as "victims of the veil," but rather as full-fledged agents in representing its principles.

I argue that in order to understand the gender agenda of Hamas, one must explore the factors that link gender and nationalism. Hamas's gender ideology cannot be separated from the colonial use of gender or the rivalry with other nationalist groups or, to a lesser extent, the scriptural texts. Other factors as well, such as the conservative elements of Palestinian nationalism in its secular form, as explained above, could be invoked to elucidate Hamas's gender ideology (Jad 1990; Massad 1995; Hammami 1997; Budeiri 1995).

I would argue that the orthodoxy[11] displayed by Hamas in the first intifada cannot be explained as a misrecognition of indigenous culture as it arose in the context of a reaction to the increasing intimidation of women aggravated by the Israeli Occupation. Hamas, in contrast to Fateh, spelled out its gender agenda at an early stage. This practice is a common feature of religious movements that place a great deal of emphasis on the family unit. The Israeli writer Amnon Cohen (1982), in his well-known essay "The Moslem Brothers," said the movement

11. Bourdieu (1977) distinguishes between doxa and orthodoxy. In doxa, there is a quasi-perfect correspondence between the objective order and the subjective principles of organization (as in ancient societies), and the natural and social worlds appear self-evident. The doxa is thus distinguished from the orthodox and the heterodox, which imply the awareness and recognition of the possibility of different or antagonistic beliefs (see Eagleton and Bourdieu 1992, 111–21).

had "fixed repressive ideas about women and how they were expected to conduct themselves. Women were not permitted to use makeup or to over-adorn themselves, they were to veil their faces, and were not to appear in public 'half naked.' This, the Brothers maintained, was clearly laid down by Islam" (182). This strict gender agenda and moral system softened as Hamas grew and became more popular. It also evolved in relation to the sort of pressure exercised by Islamist women on their leaders and the level of "empowerment" these women achieved through their activism within the movement.

The Moral Nation Needs Moral Women

Chandra Mohanty (1991) warns against the analytical leap of perceiving the widespread practice of veiling as indicative of women's sexual oppression and control. Rather, she urges us to understand it by questioning its meaning and function in various cultural and ideological contexts. However, Rema Hammami (1990) has shown that the spread of veiling in the course of the first intifada had national significance—in the face of the death and destruction brought down on the people by the Israeli Occupation, women had to show respect for the martyrs. She also blames the leftist groups for not stopping the veiling campaign. According to Hammami's argument, all women are put in a single category—those who are oppressed by the veil—whether they adopt it or reject it. This "homogenization of women, irrespective of their class, race, religious and daily material practices, might create a false sense of the commonality of oppressions, interests, and struggles between and among women" (Mohanty 1991, 68). In fact, it resulted in the denial of voice and agency for Islamist women. I problematize the presumption of homogeneity by analyzing how the Islamists' old orthodoxy differs from the new.

In the first place, contrary to claims made by authors such as Cohen (1982) above, the intimidation of women is in itself an artifact of the Occupation rather than the result of a fixed conservative culture that "oppresses women." Hamas's focus on military activism should be highlighted to better understand its position vis-à-vis women's piety and veiling at any particular moment. Secondly, the veil has different meanings for different women according to their self-perception, class, and ideology. Finally, a more nuanced approach to understanding the meaning of veiling is important in the elaboration of an oppositional political strategy.

During the first intifada, a new formulation of the issue of women's piety and modesty was deemed essential in order to "protect" the nation. In fact, this formulation had been spelled out clearly a few years before the intifada, in the secret booklets Hamas used to distribute to its male members to warn them about the interrogation and torture practices widely used in Israeli prisons. Hamas believed that the detailed confessions extracted from PLO prisoners, as weak secularists lacking faith, had been disastrous for the armed struggle against Israel. It was feared that the Islamic endeavor would suffer a similar fate unless its disciples were taught to steel themselves against the worst physical and psychological pressure the Israelis could apply. Resistance, unyielding internal strength, and a sense of self-empowerment were vital to withstand torture and interrogation.[12] By 1987,[13] the Brothers had founded two organizations in preparation for paramilitary resistance: the Palestinian *mujahedeen* and *al-jihad wal-da'wa*—known together by the abbreviation *Majd* (glory). The latter was a highly secret group concerned with "intelligence and pre-emption" (*istikhbarat wa rad'*). Its mission was to protect the

12. This policy changed after the Israeli crackdown on Hamas in 1989 and 1990, under which many Hamas members were subjected to severe torture. As a consequence, "the talk about [maintaining] the utmost internal strength and empowerment was demystified by the reality on the ground; very few people proved able to withstand the violent physical and psychological torture, while the majority collapsed. The new policy was that if a member went out on a military operation he should execute his mission and withdraw safely, or resist to the end if he was encircled, with surrender not an option" (Abul-Omrein 2000, 353). This might be understood as the most pertinent background for the suicide bombers, rather than the supposed "death culture" so frequently cited in Israeli and Western media.

13. There are contradictory accounts of the founding date of these organizations—some give 1982, others 1984 or 1985 (see Abul-Omrein 2000, 196–97).

movement from any penetration by the Israelis or by other Palestinian organizations; collect information on the Israelis; gather information on any agents of "moral corruption" in the society, from suspected collaborators to drug dealers, thieves, and prostitutes; increase awareness of security matters through booklets and leaflets; and interrogate collaborators to determine whether to punish or to "liquidate them" (Abul-Omrein 2000, 197).

Prior to the intifada, Majd took on the "liquidation" duty. In a booklet addressed to its militant members, the movement declared that those who proudly defied their interrogators would be rewarded as though they had died for the glory of Allah. But those who broke under interrogation would never know forgiveness, for they had done worse than damage the organization. In clear rivalry with other nationalist organizations, the movement sought to be more solid, moral, and faithful, signifying that it was empowered by God and Islam. In this context, if it were known that confessions were made under Israeli torture, that would deter new candidates from joining the military wing and undermine Hamas's attempts to distinguish itself from other, "less faithful" groups. It could not be claimed that Islam was superior to secularism unless Hamas members were known to "spit out their blood and teeth under the whip" (Schiff and Ya'ari 1989, 232). An iron will, the handbook preached, was all one needed to withstand deprivation, whippings, electric shocks, and threats: "We must remember that the enemy's strength is naught compared with Allah's grace" (*The Jihad Fighter Facing Interrogation and Torture*, cited in Schiff and Ya'ari 1989, 232).

An early Hamas handbill stated that Shin Bet (Israel's internal security service) was trying to entrap potential collaborators by using hashish and other drugs as bait, and that it caught young women in its net by having "stray dogs" (Palestinian collaborators) seduce them. Young girls were encouraged to take along an older, trustworthy chaperone when going to hair salons, boutiques (small clothing businesses run by young, educated women, often in their homes), and shoe stores (231). Thus, the leaflet highlighted what became known as the *isqat* policy.[14] Young men were warned off alcohol, pornographic magazines, and loose women who tried to flirt with them in the street. Thus, strict moral conduct, piety, and modesty were instrumentalized as important tools for national resistance and weapons of the underground. As described by Schiff and Ya'ari (1989), "Just as the PLO had to grapple with the problem of its permeation by Israeli agents, so Sheikh Yassine's aides looked for ways to prevent penetrations by double agents and to keep new recruits from falling under the Israelis' sway. A prisoner was best off telling his interrogators from the start that he was privy to secret information but would die under torture rather than reveal it" (232). Religion itself was a source of great strength in the contest with Shin Bet, who saw the Hamas people as "exceedingly tough nuts to crack" (230).

This national security policy has had serious implications for the social order—women's mobility has been greatly reduced and more social pressure has been placed on women who might make any "suspicious" moves. The way women talk, walk, and act all came under close social scrutiny. A survey on living conditions in Palestinian society indicated that 56 percent of women surveyed in Gaza and 47 percent in the West Bank said they were unable to move about freely within their communities (Heiberg and Øvensen 1993, 306–7). Another consequence of this policy was the crackdown on collaborators, drug dealers, and prostitutes. Fateh, in its rivalry with the Islamists, sought to take the lead in this policy of "purification" of the society, thus participating actively, in Gaza, in forcing women to veil. According to Naima el-Sheikh, head of the Fateh women's organization in Gaza, who adopted Islamic dress herself: "I cannot tell who is Fateh and who is Hamas who harass women to 'urge' them to veil, but I can tell you that our own male members in Fateh were pressuring us in the

14. The Arabic word *isqat* has various literal meanings, most pertinently to "tumble" or "fall," as into a trap. In the Palestinian context, it refers specifically to the methods used by the Israelis to manipulate or seduce victims and force them to work against their people's national interests.

organization to veil, they used to tell us Hamas people are not more 'moral' than us" (interview).

Fateh also took the lead in killing "loose women." Between 1988 and 1993, 107 women were killed in the Occupied Territories, eighty-one of them in Gaza; these women had been deemed "morally suspect" rather than confirmed as collaborators (Be'er and Abdel-Jawad 1994, 89–90). The Islamists' military organization was not the main perpetrator of these crimes; rather, Fateh groups came first, followed by groups related to Fateh, and then groups affiliated with the PFLP. These "morally suspect" women were seen as betraying not only their families' honor but their nation's honor, and their elimination was cast as a national duty. Thus, the imperative to uphold the moral order in the face of the colonial power was more or less the same for religious national movements such as Hamas and the nationalist secularist groups.

However, the security policy alone is not sufficient to explain the insistence on hijab as a moral code for women. It is also possible to see it as a score-keeper in the Islamist rivalry with secularist, non-veiled groups. Hijab is a unifying cultural marker for the movement and a signifier of its growing strength among Hamas followers, or, as Keddie (1998) suggests, it may primarily be a way of asserting communal identity, rather than a strong religious marker. Hijab became an important symbol used to forge a new, "modern" identity and open new possibilities for women within and outside the movement. The different meanings of hijab should not be reduced to that of simple marker of Hamas's gender ideology. Rather, the group's ideology changes as the power of Islamist women alters within the movement.

In 1988, Hamas published its *mythaq* (charter), in which it spelled out its formal position on gender in Articles 17 and 18. Article 17 states that "Muslim women have a role in the liberation struggle that is no less important than the role of men: woman is the maker of men, and her role in guiding and educating the generations is a major role." In the same article, women are presented as passive targets for the "'Masons,' 'Rotary Clubs,' intelligence networks—all centers of destruction and saboteurs. . . . And the Islamists should play their role in confronting the schemes of those saboteurs, i.e. protecting [women]."

Article 18 stresses that "the woman in the house of the *mujahed* and the striving family, be she a mother or a sister, has the most important role in caring for the home and raising the children with the ethical character and understanding that comes from Islam." The woman is advised to be economical, avoid careless expenditures, and "keep in mind that money is blood that must flow only in the veins to sustain the life of children and parents equally." Women are thus admonished to "give" to their family and nation instead of "taking," a notion Hamas emphasizes to differentiate Islamist women from secular activists. In this vision, women are portrayed as dependent on men, confined to their homes, and segregated from public space. However, this does not reflect how Islamist women were active participants in the student blocs of Hamas and other Islamist associations. The tension between Hamas's gender vision and what Islamist women actually do will be presented in the following sections. Through their own involvement in the movement, these women managed to change the prevailing gender vision to make a space for themselves.

Demobilization within Mobilization: Hamas's Gendered Structure

In this section I analyze the contradiction between the marginalization of women in Hamas's organizational structure and their mobilization in civil society. Islamist women were a crucial force in increasing Hamas constituencies within the student movement, although their activism was not recognized within the movement structure in the West Bank. Regardless of that oversight, independent activities in student politics went unchecked.

Hamas's structure for the inclusion of women in the West Bank differs from the structure in Gaza. I argue that this gendered format might have been an important factor in demobilizing women in these areas, especially when Hamas became a hegemonic political power in the Palestinian polity during and in the aftermath of the first intifada. The Salvation Party of Gaza had no equivalent body in

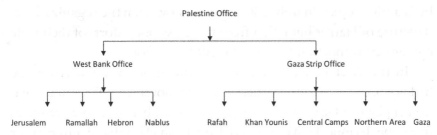

4. Organizational structure of the Muslim Brothers movement in Palestine.
Source: Abul-Omrein 2000, 194–97.

the West Bank, nor did the West Bank have any mobilizing and organizing entities for other social groups such as students and workers.
While party members were seen in the different activities of the intifada (organizing strikes, funeral processions, confrontations with the
Israeli army), female Hamas members were not visible participants.
(Veiled women participants were not necessarily Islamists.) The reason
for their absence could be explained by the fact that Islamist organizations were targeting males.

Before the first intifada, the Brothers' organization in the Gaza
Strip was divided into five regions as shown in Figure 4. Each region
formed a local *majlis al-shura*, and each regional *shura* elected its
administrative committee (*hay'a idareyya*) as well as representatives
to the general *shura* council (one for each fifty members of the local
shura). It was only later, in the mid-1980s, that a general *shura* council
was formed for the West Bank. Together, the councils in Gaza and the
West Bank form what is called the Palestine Office Regional Office
(*maktab falastine al-maktab al-qotri*).

During the first intifada in 1987, changes were made to this
structure, some in response to the Israeli crackdown on Hamas and
others in relation to the development and expansion of Hamas's activities (Abul-Omrein 2000, 194–97). I did not find any indications in
Hamas documents or from interviews that women were participants or
targeted for recruitment, whether as candidates or as electors. Islamist
women had to wait until the establishment of the Salvation Party at
the end of 1995 to be incorporated into Hamas. The activism shown

by Islamist women in universities did not flow from the organizational structure of Hamas but rather from the grassroots efforts of their male colleagues, competing for votes in school elections.

In the West Bank, once a female student left the university, she had no place to go in the structure of the movement. The same situation applied to Gaza, where the growing number of female graduates from the Islamic University and later from Al-Azhar University or other schools had no place to go other than to work in the social institutions belonging to the Muslim Brothers. In late 2003, Hamas leaders announced their intention to form an Islamic women's movement and female students joined forces with mainstream political organizations like the Salvation Party (only in Gaza).

Organizing students and linking them to political parties is crucial in Palestine, where youth in general and students in particular play an important role in boosting the national movement and the struggle against the Occupation. Any attempt to understand why the Islamists did not seek to organize female students in their central organizations, whether under the name of the Muslim Brothers, Hamas, or the Salvation Party, must acknowledge that these institutions carried the imprint of the conservative gender ideology of the movement familiar from its inception. This is especially true with respect to young unmarried females.

In examining the structure of the Islamic student blocs in the universities, I found that there is a female students' committee (*lajna-talebat*) in each one of them. These female students' committees are tasked with mobilizing female students to support the Islamic blocs and recruit people into the movement. There are no mixed bodies to coordinate the different activities of the male and female students, but rather two parallel, equal bodies (Ababneh 2014), although there is some coordination at the top level of each bloc between the few active female members and the male leaders. According to an activist in the Islamic student's movement: "We can ask for a mixed big meeting in the universities for both sexes when we have a common goal to achieve, such as a major protest against the university administration or a flagrant violation of our right as an Islamic bloc to organize our activities, but we don't have a mixed structure for students" (Ahmed, interview). The lack of any mixed body of activists affects female graduates more sharply than it does their male peers, particularly in the West Bank, where the Islamic institutions are fewer and less concentrated than in Gaza.

What women have available in the West Bank are a few charitable societies. Examples include the Al-Huda Islamic Society and the Al-Khansaa Society, both in Al-Bireh/Ramallah; Hanieen in Nablus; the Muslim Woman's Society in Jerusalem; and a similar society in Hebron. Structurally, these organizations resemble the old-style women's charitable society described in chapter 1. Most have a director (*modeera*) and an administrative committee (*hay'a idareyya*) of five to eleven members, elected from a general assembly (*hay'a 'amma*) of between one and three hundred members. Like the old charitable societies, their focus is not on organizing women but on providing a limited number of work opportunities in home economics, embroidery, and catering. In the latter, they have been largely successful, establishing a "network of relations with the PA ministries, banks, and many private enterprises" (Samira, interview). According to Samira, the revenues from their activities cover their expenses, in addition to which they manage to attract substantial donations from Islamist businessmen who see their activities as in line with the Islamic duty to support the poor, orphans, prisoners' and martyrs' families, and the needy in general. These societies receive no foreign funding, which gives them legitimacy in attacking and delegitimizing other women's organizations, in particular those working with women's NGOs.

They also organize their own cultural activities as an alternative to those of the nationalist and feminist women's groups. For instance, Women's Day, commemorated internationally every March 8, was replaced by the Festival of the Muslim Woman (*mahrajan al-mar'a al-moslema*). The date was selected for the "pragmatic" reason that it comes before the end of the academic year. According to Samira, "This is to recruit female students to help organize the festival, otherwise it would be difficult to find them or bring them together later on" (interview). The Festival of the Muslim Woman and similar events tend to attract a huge number of women and their children. Samira gave an estimate of 2,000 to 2,500 women, plus their children. These rallies are the female version of the usual proselytizing of the Muslim Brothers, in which women are urged to follow the rules of their religion and encouraged to be good, committed Muslims. Again, as in the old type of women's charitable societies, the women who attend these rallies are not asked to undertake any political activity in a party organization.

The Muslim Brothers in the West Bank do not bother to organize women after they graduate from school or university, since they view women's role as mainly belonging in the domestic sphere. As Ahmed put it: "Women graduates have no place to go and this is because of the prevailing conservative vision in our oriental society. But also, in the thinking of many Islamists, women's role is still limited to her home and family, so the focus and expectation after graduation is that women will go back to their homes. This is the rule among Islamists in the West Bank. Any exception will depend fully on the woman's husband's wish after marriage, whether to allow her to be active or not, and many choose not to" (interview).

The absence of mobilizing structures for Islamist women in the West Bank could be mitigated by the apparent coordination among Islamists around the territory in Hamas's all-male underground militant organization. Islamist women are not part of the underground structure (all Islamist women interviewed claimed that they had no connection to Hamas). There is no legal, official unifying structure in the West Bank as there is in Gaza; however, it was difficult to determine whether the lack of any unifying body for Islamist women is due to the leaderships' lack of interest in organizing Islamist women in the West Bank (in contrast to Gaza) or to the women's own priorities. When Islamist women in the West Bank were asked if they coordinate their activities or programs, the answer was negative. However, as one asserted, "when possible, we attend each others' rallies and conferences" (Maysoon, interview).

Women's charitable societies are aligned in a general union of which Islamist societies form a part, but there is no overall coordinating body. The delay in setting up a structure similar to that of the

Salvation Party could be attributed to the PA's constant harassment of the party's activities. The same treatment is inflicted on Islamist figures in the West Bank—in parallel with the targeted assassination of their leaders by the Israeli Occupation forces. The Israeli policy of physically separating Palestinian cities and villages is creating additional obstacles to any Islamist attempts to establish such unifying structures. The absence of a mobilizing body for Islamist women in the West Bank has meant that they participate in political activism to a significantly lesser extent than their counterparts in Gaza.

An Ever-Evolving Gender Vision: "The Text Does Not Prohibit"

The observation that "the text does not prohibit" was a recurrent theme throughout my interviews with Amira, Maysoon, Samira, and many other women militants. What they meant was that many restrictions on women's roles are not actually based on Islamic religious texts, which are open to various interpretations, which makes it possible to carve out a wider legitimate space in the public arena. The daily reality of life for women eager for work, education, and political participation shaped a growing critique inside the movement. Islamist women, while fully complicit in disseminating the movement's gender ideology, are, however, also the first to push the envelope and expand their public space.

The evolution they spurred was accompanied by a change in Hamas strategy after the peace process began, when it shifted from a primarily underground paramilitary organization to form a political party. With the establishment of the Islamic National Salvation Party in 1995, Hamas started to pay more systematic attention to recruiting women in order to widen its popular base. With its new emphasis on the legal political struggle, like that of other national organizations, it was difficult for Hamas to ignore the conditions in which women live and bar them from political life. Yet the movement unhesitatingly attacked the claims for women's rights made by secular nationalist women's organizations. Thus there were both internal factors pressuring Hamas to deal with women's issues and external pressures, coming from feminists' demands and the equal rights discourse, which offered a serious challenge to the Islamist discourse.

What, then, are women's rights from an Islamist perspective? Here the answer will come not from the male leadership of the party but rather from its women. I draw on materials associated with a 1997 workshop and three conferences—held in 1998, 1999, and 2000—that clearly illustrate the shift that took place in Islamist women's experience within the party, their daily practices, and their definition of women's rights.

The first conference concentrated on delegitimizing other women's groups in order to present the women of Hamas as the true, authentic voice for women's interests. In the second conference, we find an admission that the Islamists had no vision or agenda for women's issues, but at the same time were making an attempt to reinterpret religious texts to allow a new reading that would incorporate what women have achieved in society due to the processes of modernization. It is crucial to note that in the process of formulating a new reading of religious texts, a parallel process of "de-Islamizing" the discourse on women's rights took place. As will be explained, the Islamists adopted new terms such as "sustainable development" that had predominantly been used by foreign donors and feminist activists. By the time we get to the third conference, the concept of sustainable development was itself brought under scrutiny and the applicability of the concept to Palestinian society questioned. Also, for the first time, a "modern" and this time avowedly "feminist" critique of the liberal rights approach was used. These conferences were landmarks in the passage of Hamas gender ideology from the utter rejection of feminism to borrowing and selectively incorporating positions advocated by feminists. This resulted in the recuperation of those positions by the Islamists (i.e., they were Islamized) while at the same time, their Islamic discourse was de-Islamized and considered within a contemporaneous framework.

From Rejection to Engagement

The Women's Action Department of the Salvation Party proved to be energetic in pushing the boundaries of the Islamist women's space within the party structure and in society at large. On April 24, 1997, its initial publication appeared—a booklet that was the outcome of a one-day workshop (*youm derassi*) titled "Palestinian Woman: Where Next?" For the first time in the Brothers' history in Palestine, the booklet filled the gaps of their gender agenda and inverted some of its previous positions. Its introduction states that the workshop's raison d'être was that women's role "became a preoccupying issue for those many who are keen to see women occupying a distinguished position in the society side by side with men" (WAD 1997, 1). The booklet asserts that the "waves that have surfaced in our society lately all claim to uplift women, as they see fit, but women, who stand on their rights in Islam, do not accept these claims. We as Muslim sisters, aware of our great religion, have to stand up strongly and courageously to clarify and spread our ideas in our advancing society. We are the preachers for the true uplifting *nahda* [renaissance] for women through the true, deep, and correct understanding of our religion. This will be the true victory for women" (WAD 1997, 1).

Many papers were presented during the workshop by Hamas cultural leaders, both women and men, in a systematic attempt to delegitimize non-Islamic women's groups. They did this by depicting women's NGOs as a Western ploy to weaken the nation and betray it by "smothering" Israel's existence over the heart of the *umma*. They rejected the call to foreground the gender agenda as inappropriate when the national agenda was at stake. In one presentation, Nehad Khalil (1997), a prominent cultural and political analyst from *Al-Rissala*, the Salvation Party's journal, voiced his skepticism about the motives and "foreign funding" of the various NGOs engaging in rights-based advocacy in Palestinian society. He linked their proliferation to the West's desire to create a political environment more accepting of Israel, and the need of some Palestinian party cadres for employment and personal "enrichment, through funding, and fame" (3, 4). Condemning the diversion of attention toward issues that "don't fit with the existing social and economic structures," he rejected the recourse to international conventions, arguing that it was "understandable when we talk about human rights violations by the

Israelis" to gain international support, "but when we dialogue internally as Palestinians about liberties and women, we have to start from our culture, heritage, and daily reality" (4, 5).

In my interviews, many Islamist women expressed the same skepticism about universal rights for women. Maysoon, for example, stated: "Isn't it weird to hear the same discourse from many women's organizations all over the Arab world and the Islamic world? How come all women's needs and aspirations are all the same across a spectrum of different societies with different contexts and needs? Where is the specificity of each society, where are the variations between them and among women themselves? This is a standard blueprint strategy pushed not by women but by foreign donors" (interview). However, the 1997 workshop did not outright reject the prevailing discourse on women's rights, and there was a range of views among those who did seek to claim new rights. Some participants (mainly from Gaza) called for the prohibition of polygamy and the right to divorce within *shari'a* law, while others called for restrictions on polygamy without an outright prohibition.

After rejecting feminists' calls, Nehad Khalil (1997) scorned the position of the PA:

> The Authority has no special agenda for women. It adopts neither a liberal vision, nor a conservative one, let alone a religious one. The PA is keen to talk about women's rights and equality superficially, as window dressing. This is mainly to give the impression to the world that our society is modern and respects women and their rights. This lack of an agenda is reflected in the contradictory behaviors of the PA. While we have a woman minister and a woman ambassador in the PA, the Ministry of the Interior issued a rule to ask women to get the consent of their guardians to issue their passports. (7)

Finally, after asserting that "Islam dignified women and gave them their rights," Khalil acknowledged that Islamists had paid little attention to women's interests once the struggle against the Occupation erupted. In this, the Islamists were like the nationalists before them. All the same, Islamists could not ignore the matter; in Khalil's words:

"the issue is on the table now, there is a debate about family law and its reform, on early marriage and its prohibition" (7).

I see Khalil's paper as an admission by an Islamist that delegitimizing "others" is no longer a viable practice. Most importantly, it raises the need to know what women's actual situations are. This call was reflected in the recommendations in his paper: to establish a study center focused on women's issues, and for intellectuals and researchers to direct more attention to the laws, ideas, visions, and studies of the secularist women's groups (8).

A paper presented by Khitam Abu Musa (1997) inverts the gender vision of the Hamas Charter of 1988, interpreting Islam as the source of all of women's rights: education, the free choice of a husband, inheritance (widely denied by custom), mobility (to participate in the call for the rule of God and *jihad*), proselytizing, and social or professional work (17–21). Turning to a particularly controversial issue—"mixing with men"—she concludes, "[T]hus, now we can see that Muslim woman was moved to prove herself in all aspects and fields of life. Islam allows women to meet men, and to engage in dialogue if she is committed to the *adab shar'eyya* [the conventions of *shari'a*]" (21). According to Amira Haroun, who addressed the question of *adab shar'eyya* in an interview, this is to be understood in terms of adopting Islamic dress and maintaining respectable manners in line with religious customs.

In interpreting Islamic tradition and *shari'a* in support of her position, Khitam Abu Musa (1997) draws on the authority of the religious text to underscore that "women's urge to develop *intilaq* [to flourish] and participate in social life with all that entails, including meeting men, is an approach *decided* [emphasis added] by the Islamic *shari'a* and the Prophet's *Sunna* [deeds]" (21). She also uses the concept of "public good," declaring that "Islam *mandates* [emphasis added] women to go out and participate in social life because the opening up of public work for women is for the good [*al-khayr*] of the spread of a serious, beneficial life for more Muslims. This begins with the request for and provision of education; the aiding of a husband in earning a living; the participation in beneficial social work or political activism that supports goodness and fights the trivial" (22). This vision is not shared by all women in the Salvation Party; it seems more pertinent to the needs of educated women who want to abolish the gender segregation code in order to take advantage of more opportunities in the labor market. Less educated women have a different perspective: "In the party, they are irritated when we insist on being separate. The party says that as a developmental party there is no harm in mixing, but this is against our traditions" (Zaina, interview).

In an attempt to "purify" the new Islamists' position, it has been important to detach Islam from the oppression of women and claim that such negative behavior is due to the "Palestinian mentality" and "backwardness." According to Salah Bardaweel (1997), former editor-in-chief of *Al-Rissala*, one trend represents "ignorance and limited vision characterized by sharp contradictions and imbalances while the other recognizes women's value and assigns them ethical and moral status." He claims that the latter is "less known due to the underdeveloped phases which Palestinian society went through," but studies of Islamic revivals during different periods show that Islamic leaders "gave women more attention by providing for her education, culture [*tathqifiha*], and the development of her capacities in her house, society and nation" (28).

The Women's Action Department booklet documenting the workshop's proceedings included a section on international conventions pertaining to women and the resolutions of the World Conference on Women held in Beijing in 1995, as well as recommendations for the party. Recommendations on the "dissemination and the advocacy" of women's issues included the formation of Palestinian feminist *nassawi* (cadres) through debates and Islamic workshops; the study of contemporary universal conventions from a comparative perspective; the embodiment of women's rights in practice; and the creation of an educational program to sensitize men to women's roles (WAD 1997, 44).

Beginning a year after that first workshop, the Women's Action Department organized a series of five conferences to study women's situation on a "scientific" basis. Research papers were presented by a range of scholars and educators at these conferences.[15] Meticulous attention was given to the concerns of Palestinian feminists related to legislation, work, education, political participation, communication, and women in the media, in which an Islamist vision was formulated *in response* to other platforms. An overarching vision crystallized around the rejection of the idea that religion is the cause of women's subjugation, and the dismissal of civic legislation (*qanon wad'i*) for women. Islam was seen as the path to "fairness and justice" (Amira Haroun, interview). In this context, daring and novel religious interpretations were presented by the party's top leaders.

Mahmoud al-Zahar (1999, 4), a prominent figure in Hamas, argued in a paper he presented that women in Islam have equal rights to men in all aspects of work, but their labor must differ in two respects: when it might lead to a contradiction in *shari'a* and when certain work might not be suitable for women's capabilities and characteristics (*qodorateha wa khossosseyateha*), although he left those unspecified. Al-Zahar formulates a brilliant combination of the public and the private around the controversial issue of men's dominance (*qewama*) in the family—a concept that flagrantly contradicts the notion of equality raised by the feminists, since it puts women under men's authority. He interprets men's supremacy based on economic and managerial rather than political terms, stating that "*qewama* does not mean absolute authority, but means that a man takes the responsibility to provide for the material and emotional needs of the family, to provide protection and care, and to administer [*yassos*] the family according to principles of justice." Al-Zahar links *qewama* with another principle as applicable, he argues, to the private sphere as it is to the public: *al-shura* (consultation or deliberation). As he puts it: "Muslims should not understand that *al-shura* and *al-qewama* are a state of tyranny or despotism [*halat istebdad*], but are something in which all members

15. In addition to the conferences in 1998, 1999, and 2000 that I focus on, there were two more in 2001 (on women's role in the second intifada) and 2003 (on the redrafting of the penal code), to whose papers I did not have access.

of the family participate in their own way [*shorakaa'*] as part of the family's management. Like the state, the family can only be built on *shura*" (4).

Al-Zahar sees authoritarianism in the family as a sort of extremism (*tatarrof*); the loss of *qewama* as chaos (*ifrat*); and both as potential causes of the collapse of the family, the society, and the state. Thus, democratization à la Islamism is, again, not only a concern in the public sphere, but also very relevant to the private sphere of the relationship between husband and wife, as well as between parents and children. This "new" interpretation was echoed by one of my interviewees. In Maysoon's words: "In my family, we are used to discussing and deliberating our daily plan. I encourage my children to choose what they want to eat, to wear, to do, and to study and, of course, we allow my girl to choose who she wants to marry. But the man she wants has to come in the open to ask for her hand and not meet her secretly. Once everything is in the open, we facilitate all the steps. Our religion is *yosser* [easygoing], not *'ossr* [hard to follow]" (interview). Maysoon refers not only to her family's daily democratic practice, but also to what has become a common trend among Islamists in facilitating the marriage arrangements for young couples. The new approach endeavors to minimize marriage expenses by eliminating unnecessary and extravagant expenditures (such as wedding parties in hotels, grand banquets, flowers) and involves a reduction in the dowry (*mahr*) a bride's family should expect to receive.

Many other papers were presented in these conferences that also tried to formulate a more progressive gender vision on the basis of *al-shari'a*. However, while the starting point is the text of the Quran, the call for new interpretations is always linked to the needs of society and the "spirit of the age" (*roh al-'assr*). Religious discourse was gradually minimized in favor of a more "modern" and temporal discourse. The usual empty, repetitive, faith-based spurning of other women's groups was criticized as a "traditional" Islamic stance. Another paper by Nehad Khalil (1999) articulated a well-grounded knowledge of the development discourse in Palestine, in particular of the sustainable development approach. The failure of development efforts in Palestinian society was attributed to the failure to make full use of women's capacities; the persistence of legislation that discriminates against women, and in particular, the family law; values and customs that discriminate against women; the lack of attention to women's health care and family planning; and the high rates of marriage and fertility at an early age, all of which reduce women's role to that of reproduction and intensify their dependency on and subordination to men.

In this diagnosis, Khalil (1999) used an alternative discourse, based not on religious texts but on the secular notions of the public good and national interest. He focused not on the "Islamicness" (religio-cultural specificity) of Muslim societies but on the specificity of being under Occupation. Thus, "reducing fertility will weaken our demographic strength against our enemies, but this should not be at the expenses of women's health" (4). Focusing on women's individual rights "in isolation from their families and children is dangerous," he asserted, "since we have not, yet, any alternative institutions to care for them. . . . Women's work at home does not reduce their status and it should be valued, morally. . . . Women's role in society needs her education and her openness to society and her participation" (5, 6).

In criticizing the feminist calls for women's rights, seen as based on the notion of individual rights, Khalil stated that "the individual self cannot be the measure of development since that might contradict the public good of the society" (6). Using the example of a Palestinian worker employed in an Israeli settlement, he said that such a person "can gain a lot, individually, but this will be at the expense of our agricultural land [on which the settlements are built] and our economy." He added that, "in strong Western economies, the individual can be the focus of development, but not in our case where we are under Occupation and suffer from a lack of democracy. Our context necessitates the collective mobilization of people in order to resist the Occupation; this is a phase of giving to the nation and not yet taking from it" (6).

This paper manifested some awareness of the global debate on the causes of underdevelopment and whether they are related to internal factors (i.e., lack of democracy and good governance) or external ones (i.e., unequal North-South relations) (Törnquist 1999). But Khalil (1999) warned that the call for democracy and women's liberation were being used as "an ideological weapon by the neo-colonizers in the age of globalization to convince the subjugated peoples that their defeats are related to their lack of democracy and their women's status and not to the colonizer's exploitation and the drain of their wealth." In the Palestinian context, he asserted, the issues of democracy and women's rights are wielded to "disintegrate our Palestinian social structure, which always reproduces resistance, refuses Occupation, and refuses to normalize relations with our enemies" (6).

This new Islamist reading of the sustainable development discourse will likely add to the difficulties of the secularists and nationalists in general, and the secularist women's movement in particular. The latter, due to the national struggle, did not take a clear position on issues related to women's fertility or the call for sustainable development. This lack of clarity, one can predict, will give more ammunition to the articulate Islamist discourse.

The summations of the 1999 and 2000 WAD conferences, meanwhile, adopted a rather less defensive approach in addition to a more rational position vis-à-vis international conventions. The total delegitimization of the "other," in particular other feminist women's organizations, was set aside in favor of more engagement. The 1999 conference postulated a distinction between Palestinian organizations working in good faith as national actors, however different their views and their donors who "are not innocent and who work according to their own agendas." Abandoning the total rejection manifested in the workshop of 1997, the closing statement of the 1999 conference declared that "our approach to women's liberation is Islam and not the universal conventions; however, we do not refuse any of these conventions as long as they do not contradict the rules of the Islamic *shari'a* and the specificity of the Palestinian Muslim society" (WAD 1999).

The conclusions of these conferences can be encapsulated in two main points. First, Islamists should anticipate and guide Islamic reform and take the lead in women's uplifting (*nahda*), lest others lead. Secondly, there should be an emphasis on the idea that the mission to liberate women falls primarily on women themselves—women have to claim their rights and campaign for them in the light of a proper understanding of *shari'a*. The third conference was dedicated to . exploring and articulating the differences between *shari'a* and international conventions.

At the 2000 conference, a more thoughtful critique of the women's rights discourse, as figured in the international conventions, emerged. The papers presented and questioned, for the first time, the viability, not of rights discourse altogether, but its liberal, utilitarian, individualistic Western base, this time using critical feminist thought (Phillips 1993; Cornwall and Molyneux 2008). In Amira Haroun's (2000) paper, for example, we read: "The concept of rights was established (in the West) on utilitarianism, thus, utilitarian individualism supersedes rationality and engulfs all social relations. . . . [T]his conception is false since the individual was never an abstract being, the individual was always a social being" (1).

Thus, the discourse of the women's NGOs, based on liberal rights, was contested by another "Western," "feminist" discourse based on the notion of active citizenship.[16] Islamist critiques of liberalism, like the socialist feminist critiques, question the morality of narrowly defending the principle of individual rights and allowing this to take precedence over the question of social responsibility. Citizenship, as elaborated in chapter 2, is conceived of as rights alone, and in political terms is reduced to the limited practice of voting, reflecting an impoverished view of social membership. Instead it is argued that

16. The recent debate on women's rights and citizenship found its way into the Islamist women's discourse. The Islamist thinkers (al-Ghannouchi 1993; Tamimi 2002; Elmessiri 2003) follow the critiques of the Enlightenment principles of universality and individualism offered by Marxist feminists and postmodernists. These critiques suggest that, if citizenship could be refashioned in a way that divested it of abstract universalism and "false egalitarianism," it could be a more effective tool in advancing gender justice. Some authors have claimed that gender difference and the female body should be the proper basis of legal and political recognition (Phillips 1987, 1991, 1993; Lister 1997; Voet 1998).

there is a need for a more substantive version of citizenship based on participation and social responsibility, known as "social citizenship" (Molyneux 1996, 6; Cornwall and Molyneux 2008). "In our Islamic vision," writes Haroun (2000), "the notion of the individual is seen in relation to the collective; that is why the notion of individual rights, in Islam, is formed in the context of duties which help to awake in the individual the incentives to 'give' and not only to 'take'" (5).

The stress on this "give" and "take" approach in Islamic discourse is linked to the specific situation of the Palestinian people, whose significantly distinguishing traits are not so much cultural but rather national and conjunctural, a dimension that is very much missing in the feminist NGOs' discourse. The stress on "giving to the nation" should be seen in the context of the abandonment of the national agenda by the secular women's movement in Palestine. It should also be seen in a context in which the audible voice became a feminist voice claiming rights and obfuscating what should be given to the nation under the continuing Occupation.

Thus, in the absence of a clear national agenda drawn up by the nationalist, secularist women's movement, the Islamists link women's rights with the national and social needs of the Palestinian people in asking women, as did the old nationalist discourse, to serve the nation, à la Islamism this time, and to reproduce more men (Anthias and Yuval-Davis 1989).

From Words to Deeds

Islamist women have managed to build impressive, well-organized women's constituencies among highly educated and professional women, at times using relatively temporal discourses based on sustainable development and women's rights as well as new interpretations of religious texts. The question arises as to how these new readings were reflected in daily practices within the Islamic National Salvation Party. I highlight here an increasing tendency to foster gender equality, not merely complementarity, and more egalitarian social ideals.

The efforts of the Women's Action Department in the Salvation Party opened a space for common ground by mainstreaming gender issues into the dominant politics of an Islamist party. The success of the department in effecting this important change within the Islamist movement went hand in hand with demands for equal pay. In criticizing the party for privileging men's over women's work, the department was persistent in calling for equal job opportunities and equal pay for men and women doing the same work. Two members of the politburo in 2000 recalled:

> In our work with women, we need more people. We started to demand the hiring of more women, and they accepted reluctantly, but for half the pay.[17] They [the male members] thought that women didn't have the same responsibilities as men, but we refused—how did they know that women don't have the same responsibilities? It's a question of principle—if women do the same work as men, they have to get the same payment. (Youssra, interview)

> We managed to put an equal number of *motafarreghat* [full-time, paid members] in the regional administrative committees as men before the closure of the party local branches, and we were also heading toward having the same number of paid women as men in our journal before its closure by the PA. (Amira, interview)

The department's call for equal treatment by the party reached into the home. Here, the department eschewed the feminist rights discourse in favor of the pragmatic strategy of looking for solutions. In Amira's words:

> Everybody in the party claims that he supports woman's work, woman's development, but they don't put the effort into supporting her in her work. If they want her to succeed, inside and outside, then the men have to support her in the *home* [emphasis added] in order [for her] to succeed in the society. In this respect, we avoid talking

17. It was common in Gaza, where the unemployment rate was very high—39 percent in 1999—to pay women less than men in private business, and in general women were considerably less well paid (81.3 percent of average male wages in Gaza and 66 percent in the West Bank) (SIDA 1999, 26–27).

about what men "have" to do but we try to "*involve*" [emphasis added] them in finding solutions such as supporting her at home, establishing a nursery and kindergarten close to her house. In this respect, we fully support the call of the Women's Affairs [Technical] Committee[18] in their demand for an hour for working mothers to breast feed their babies, but this also requires nurseries in each workplace for women. (interview)

Inside the party, women leaders rejected the assertion by Hamas leader Mahmoud al-Zahar that women's work should be suitable for women's "capabilities and characteristics." They called for total equality in two respects: in their daily work in the party and in their rejection of the claim that women are not equal to men in military activities. As one stated:

In the daily work we have so many activities. One of the most successful events we organize each year is the political prisoners' exhibition in which we establish a big tent to host all sorts of activities: exhibiting their paintings and belongings, displaying their pictures and writings. . . . To build the tent we used to ask the help of our men, [but] this happened only in the first year. When we started to push for hiring more women with equal pay, we decided to build the tent ourselves; we wanted to show them that we are not less powerful and if we want we can do exactly what they do. Now, each year, we build the tent from A to Z by ourselves. (Youssra, interview)

It is worth noting here that the two leaders' approach contradicted not only that of some Islamist men but also of some Islamist women. Maysoon and Samira, Islamist women's leaders in the West Bank, asserted that they didn't share this vision regarding women's roles as complementary to that of men rather than equal. In sum, there were differences not only between Islamist men and women, but among the women themselves.

18. See chapter 2.

Shari'a Politics and Possible Common Ground

I have argued throughout that it is not the religious text but the political context that determines the Islamist discourse. The ever-evolving version of *shari'a* espoused by Hamas raises two issues. On the one hand, it is a challenge to the discourse used by feminist NGOs based on a liberal, individualistic notion of rights that ignores the plight the nation faces under Occupation. By putting Islam at the center of a modified notion of Palestinian nationalism, the Islamists managed to delegitimize the feminist women's discourse by portraying it as non-national and alien. On the other hand, it also poses a challenge to the ambivalent Palestinian secularism that used Islam as a source of its legitimacy. By Islamizing Palestine and nationalizing Islam, the Islamists proved successful in forging a brand of nationalism in which Islam was integral and constituted a mobilizing force for the masses.

In such a context, the secularists, while pressuring and challenging the Islamists, have nonetheless lost ground by advocating the discourse of rights in isolation from the national agenda and in the absence of a mobilizing organization. NGO activism, based on short-lived projects, does not have the potential to constitute an alternative. By becoming an opposition movement against all forms of violations of civil and human rights, the Islamists have developed a political organization. In contrast, women in NGOs have no organized constituency and the support they have, if they even get it, is derived from a decaying delegitimized authority.

I have shown how the Islamist women forged a space for a category of women who are educated, from a poorer, mainly refugee background, in which it was morally correct to be active in all spheres of public life. I have also shown how they managed to establish themselves among poorer women by providing services and defending the rights of their imprisoned men. This is an important addition to women's activism in a phase of national struggle. Meanwhile, the debate over whether *shari'a* should be understood as abrogating efforts at legal reform triggered debate within the Islamist movement itself. Islamists' search for an alternative to the secular feminist platform brought them into continuous engagement with it. I showed that the total equality approach, in their discourse, was used by highly educated and professional Islamist women to defend equal rights for women in the public sphere (at least in work and political activism) and in their daily practice.

I also showed how the top male leadership reacted swiftly to "fix" *shari'a* (Zubaida 2003, 1) in another set of laws concerning the penal code, again to silence feminist and secularist women's groups and discourage them from suggesting any reforms. The weight the top male leadership put behind *shari'a* is not only about women's rights; it is also about Islamists asserting hegemonic power in society and vis-à-vis the PA. It could also be about shaping a strategy of active citizenship for a future state, whose Palestinian or Islamic definition remains uncertain. In this respect, Molyneux (1996) warns, "social citizenship understood as community activism, participation, or moral regeneration is not always or indeed necessarily linked to projects for democratic reform or greater social cohesion. In some countries it is manipulated by 'fundamentalists' who seek to create a political community, in the furtherance of objectives which would lead to authoritarian, theocratic and highly gendered states" (6). This will not necessarily happen. My data shows that Islamists, in their quest for a platform as a national movement, were obliged to borrow and incorporate new visions to be inclusive and broaden their constituencies. Challenges from opponents pushed the Islamists to act upon notions such as pluralism, women's rights, the public good, sustainable development, and the social self versus the individual self, all borrowed, contested, and co-opted by the Islamists from their secular context. The evidence shows that certain arenas of civil society activism included women militants in a positive way, as in the students' movement, and that the party structure itself had incorporated women who were sociologically marginalized from the national leadership, in which women of the elite were overrepresented.

However, while there are moments of opening and engagement, there are also many contradictions that might lead to a potential closure and retreat into interpretations of Islam that would affect women negatively. Islamist leaders could return to insisting that women serve the role of reproducers of the nation. The leadership's stand on polygamy is not yet clear. There has been heated debate on the "suitability" of women for military actions, but what sort of Islamic state this activism might lead to depends, to a great extent, on the general context that the secularists set.

The Islamist women's discourse stems not only from the Quran but also from positive engagement with the discourses of other groups, whether secular feminists or nationalists. In my opinion, this engagement is what impels Islamist women to go back to the religious texts, to look for possible new readings in order to respond to the challenges posed by other women's groups. Further, Islamist women's discourses do not rely solely on religious texts but also on what other women's activism and discourses provoke. This engagement could also be the common ground on which Islamist and secularist women could unite by pushing for new readings of the religious texts as well as by engaging in the daily realities of women in a context of the unsolved national struggle. This mutual accommodation (Hudson 1996; Norton 1993; Salamé 2001) requires each party to maintain vigilance with regard to the changes occurring in the approaches and discourses of the other instead of taking a position of total rejection, which was exemplified by the stance of women's NGOs.

Islamists have had to build on women's modern gains such as expanded access to education and work opportunities. Thus, the kind of state they might claim will depend not on the blueprint of a religious text, but to a great extent on what form of state and society they live in, and the visions advocated and the challenges posed by other nationalist and secularist groups that maintain substantial popular support.

5

Conclusions

Islamists and the Forging of a Common Ground between Women

ONE OF THE CENTRAL AIMS of this book has been to examine the links and intersections of colonialism, nationalism, Islamism, and feminism in contemporary Palestine through a focus on three different types of women's activism and civil society organizations: the Palestinian Federation of Women's Action Committees (PFWAC), a grassroots women's group associated with the Marxist DFLP; the Women's Center for Legal Aid and Counseling (WCLAC), an NGO that exemplifies a new type of women's organization; and the Women's Action Department (WAD), representing Islamist women activists, originally as an arm of the Islamic National Salvation Party (as of 2018, WAD continues as a direct organ of Hamas). All three claim to represent women's interests and work for their emancipation. I examined the ways in which women's interests have been articulated by these three organizations, in terms of their gender ideologies and the methods employed for women's empowerment. And I have shown how the context in which each operates, and the impact of that context on their respective ideologies and methods, is affected in multiple ways by the work of the others.

Throughout, I have insisted on contextualizing the women's movements these groups represent in terms of the historical unfolding of the Palestinian entity and Palestinian nationalism. The conclusions of my primary field research, conducted through April 2004, are informed by my historical analysis, in which I undertook a rereading of the successive phases of colonialism and occupation in Palestine. Tracing the history and trajectory of Palestinian nationalism and women's activism, I noted that the foundations of class and rural-urban cleavages were created by the policies of the British Mandate between 1917 and 1948. These policies were built upon and aggravated by the Zionist settler state. The emergence of the women's movement during the Mandate period was influenced and constrained by this sociological context. Under colonial rule, modernization, and the system of national education that it introduced, enabled male elites to forge ties with their rural counterparts. While men's education was mostly in Arabic-language schools, female elites were educated in a virtually English system, and after almost three decades of British rule, the share of educated rural women never exceeded 7 percent. This was one of the main factors preventing the formation of bonds between rural and urban women.

The tensions and conflicts within Palestinian nationalism followed class, region, and gender lines. In analyzing the trajectory of Palestinian nationalism, I found that the different social layers constituting Palestinian national identity were obscured by many historians of Palestine. The specific character of Palestinian nationalism, in fact, emerged out of the discordance between the different social layers constituting the movement. Peasants, and later refugees, were always the fuel for all forms of national struggle, while the urban elites always comprised the recognized leadership. Palestinian nationalist elites were driven by the modernizing colonial discourse that depicted peasants as "traditional" and "backward." Nevertheless, the hegemony exercised by the urban elite over the Palestinian national movement was, from its inception, contested by peasants and then refugees through collective acts of resistance.

While Palestinian nationalism construed women as "auxiliary" and marginal, it also opened up a new space for women in the public sphere. Thus, regarding women's status, nationalism unleashed both repressive and emancipatory tendencies. Female elites in the successive iterations of the women's movement from the 1920s to the present often viewed rural and refugee women as unenlightened. But it was at moments when the rural-urban divide was bridged that the most important achievements of the women's movement took place. Success in mobilizing and organizing thousands of women was the ground upon which women activists built their claims to transform the gender order within their parties and in their society.

The weakening of the Palestinian economy and its integration first into the Jordanian economy and later into the Israeli market has been one of the primary causes of women's marginalization in Palestinian society. Contrary to the trends in many third world countries—and neighboring Arab states, in particular—participation by Palestinian women in the labor force, especially in agriculture, declined after the Israeli Occupation of the West Bank and Gaza began in 1967, constituting the material basis of Palestinian women's deepening dependence on men.

Despite these adverse conditions, women's activism in Palestine affected the political structures they were affiliated with and society at large. After the military defeat of 1967, the subsequent formulation of Palestinian nationalism, as in earlier instances, did not develop a gender vision. However, the leftist parties' discourse on women's emancipation provided an important platform on which women activists were able to claim much greater space in the public sphere. Women in the "revolution" succeeded in establishing constituencies among women in refugee camps in Lebanon. This constituted the basis of their claim to rights addressed to their male leaders in the national movement and their attempts to change the prevailing gender order in their communities. The uprooting of the leadership of the Palestinian national movement from Lebanon in 1982, and the dismantling of its institutions, again forced women to shift the focus of their activism from claiming equal rights to working for the survival of their communities. This shift repeats itself throughout the history of Palestinian national movements and women's activism.

The emergence of a radical and popular local national leadership in the West Bank and Gaza after 1967, unbound from the direct authoritarian practices of the PLO, was an important step toward the development of a strategy of resistance based on people's initiatives and direct participation. It was in this context that grassroots women's organizations emerged in the mid-1970s, during which activists were able, for the first time in the history of the Palestinian women's movement, to bridge the divide between urban, middle-class, and rural women. Through their activism women managed to challenge the prevailing gender order and develop a homegrown feminism that combined the national struggle with the struggle to change the prevailing gender order.

Throughout this study, I have tried to show that the demobilization of the contemporary secular women's movement in Palestine needs to be examined in the broader context of the formation of the Palestinian Authority after the signing of the Oslo Agreement in 1993, which ushered in a phase of quasi-state building that proved illusory. The continuation of the Israeli Occupation under the guise of the Oslo peace process resulted in the failure of the PA to establish Palestine as a state and caused the disintegration of the political structure of the PLO and its constituent political parties. This led to the growing influence of Islamist forces and the subsequent changes that took place in the components of Palestinian nationalism, which had thus far been led by secularists. The emergence of the PA led to radical shifts in the different forms of activism in civil society. These aimed to sustain the Palestinian communities, and to mobilize and organize them to resist the Occupation. Women were active participants in both these processes.

As demonstrated by the analysis of the three focal women's groups, the type of organization in which women's activism takes place also greatly affects the sort of feminism they develop. Both the PFWAC and the Women's Action Department were linked to a wider political project through their political parties. Women activists developed their local version of feminism within a "national" framework. This contradicted the assertion that only autonomous women's organizations can guarantee the development and articulation of their own priorities and mobilize supporters in the struggle for them (Peteet

1991, 164). Nonetheless, I reserved the term "feminism" to describe the activism of the PFWAC women as they were aware of the inequity of the prevailing gender order and were consciously working to change it, supported by the "progressive" Marxist discourse of their political leaders.

PFWAC women used the opening provided by the secular Marxist Democratic Front for the Liberation of Palestine to organize more disadvantaged rural women for the national struggle. While the DFLP and its women leaders did not have a well-articulated gender agenda, women activists managed, through direct daily contact with rural and working-class women, to articulate an agenda that combined gender equity with national concerns. The development of a feminist agenda may therefore not be contingent on the autonomy of women's organizations but, as I hope to have demonstrated, on the ability of women activists (including Islamists) to articulate their constituencies' needs and interests.

The empirical data from my study of the WCLAC as a new form of women's NGO belies the claim that NGOs are model participatory and inclusive agents of development. Furthermore, my analysis demonstrates that the emphasis on "professionalism" represented the interests of the privileged few who sought to consolidate their own power base. Thus, professionalism failed to enable the articulation and promotion of gender interests (whether practical or strategic) at the level of society or the state. Furthermore, professionalism did not lead to greater inclusion of "target groups" or broader participation in decision-making processes for any project.

Different points of view and the need for greater deliberation were seen by professional women as "difficulties" that slowed down the implementation of the set plan rather than as part of a democratic process. To overcome such difficulties, the "project logic" dictated that more restricted committees be formed to handle deliberations in a more "productive" way. Effectively, the "project logic" pushed toward vertical rather than horizontal accountability. "Project logic" places greater power in the hands of administrators, thus making NGO structures exclusive rather than inclusive. Most significantly, a shift in emphasis occurs that moves away from a focus on social change and toward a more finite project where funders, rather than participants or "target groups," are prioritized.

Given the constantly changing circumstances that character-ize Palestine, it is important to build on lessons learned from activ-ism where the growth of a mass-based, sustained social movement is required and where networking, deliberation, personal contacts, and mobilization must be maintained on a daily basis. The concentration of power and the desire to fit all activities into a "log frame"—the ubiquitous model for international development projects—neglect such requirements, and focus on painting a picture that satisfies donors (Vivian 1994, 189), magnifying the impetus to gloss over mistakes. As donors are driven by the logic of the efficient deployment of their funds, NGO leaders and staff experience pressure to prove their high level of "professionalism" and efficiency. The "project logic" and the NGO-ization of issues related to social transformation and popular participation may well preempt public deliberation and assessments vital for improvement.

NGOs in the Middle East and in Palestine have been discredited by many for being driven by the agendas of international donors and entities. But this view depicts local NGOs in relation to their donors, as mere followers with no agency. As I have shown, the link with international donors is not a one-way street, where one party imposes its will upon the other, but rather donors and local actors interact in a complex web of relationships. This is not to claim that both parties have an equal share of power, but rather to suggest that the personal interests of donors and recipients influence their decisions regarding what to take and what to leave.

I believe that the involvement of some feminist NGOs in so-called peace-building activities helped them not only to procure funding but also to support their claims to more power within the women's movement. Their involvement in peace process activism also led to the NGO-ization of the national agenda. When some donors are driven by a mission to promote "peace culture" through the "project indus-try" and place emphasis on highly professional skills, such as drawing up precise plans for project implementation, they need local partners who can deliver these requirements. Indeed, many conferences were organized by European and American donors in which the participants selected to "represent" Palestinian women were handpicked on the basis of their professional skills. Issues of vital national interest, such as the legitimacy of national resistance, the nature, size, and sovereignty of the future state, and the status of millions of Palestinian refugees were thus either ignored or nominally tackled in the form of "projects" of limited scope. Most importantly, "peace-culture" activism served to favor a globalized NGO elite over women cadres in grassroots organizations, impeding collective action in the furtherance of a national agenda.

However, links between international and local actors are of a multifold nature, with positive as well as negative consequences. In the face of the total imbalance of power in favor of Israel to the detriment of Palestinians, the latter are skeptical about the role of the international community in supporting their national rights, while at the same time, they have no other option but to rely on its sense of justice. Some international entities, in particular those belonging to the UN, play crucial roles in supporting Palestinians economically and to some extent politically to achieve their national rights. Some have also opened up spaces for Palestinian women to connect to worldwide women's networks, allowing them to gain skills and transmit knowledge.

Paradoxically, the 1998 model parliament project, which was meant to consolidate a women's front in law reform, left the participants in the different constituent groups with feelings of animosity. Rather than unifying women, the project led to further fragmentation and left clear divisions, particularly between the women's NGOs and mass organizations. As new forms of women's organization brought new discourses into the public sphere, NGOs were divorced from the socioeconomic and political situation and may have disempowered and delegitimized social actors and their movements in civil society.

Analysis of the brand of feminism developed by NGO discourse, which is based on a universal rights approach, demonstrates how discourse in such a context is not simply a matter of words, but crucially involves frames of collective action with social movements as their power structure (Snow and Benford 1988, 198; Tarrow 1994, 122). The "new" discourse used by the NGO elite might be seen to discredit old forms of organization and to co-opt popular groups. NGOs' discourse claimed that legitimacy founded on "resistance" and "sacrifice" led to the subordination and isolation of women, which had to be challenged. This was done by bringing the private—personal and family relations—into the public sphere. It is important to bear in mind that the public sphere is not a neutral arena but rather is shaped by power relations and thronged with power groups.

The NGO approach, of small projects of limited duration, proved ill-equipped to mobilize grassroots participants or to liaise with other social movements and groups on issues of national concern. NGOs might simply not be fit to tackle controversial issues for social change in which they have to face such well-mobilized groups as the Islamists. I would go so far as to suggest that the NGOs' discourse based on universal rights was so disconnected from its local context that it unwittingly aided and abetted the Islamist movement.

In my examination of the Women's Action Department, I showed how the Islamist women forged a public space for a certain category of women, those who are educated, from poorer, mainly refugee backgrounds, and who see it as morally correct to be active in all spheres of public life. In particular, they established themselves among poorer women by providing services and keeping alive the recognition of male prisoners. This was an important addition to women's activism in a phase of national struggle.

However, I also highlighted two different instances in which *shari'a*, as a guiding principle for women's rights, was used in contradictory ways. In the debate provoked by feminist women's organizations over legal reform, Islamists at first emphasized the divine and immutable nature of *shari'a* to delegitimize and silence non-Islamic women's groups. They also used it to discredit the notion of popular sovereignty advocated by the PA as the basis for the new legislation. It is still not clear whether the Islamists intend to establish a sovereignty based on the will of God rather than the will of the people. This will become apparent only in the future, as their state project remains to be spelled out.

However, the same debate on *shari'a* triggered internal soul-searching within the Islamist movement itself. Pressured by the feminist, secularist women's groups, the Islamists had to present their own alternative vision, based on *shari'a*. For this, they had to engage with the feminist, secularist position. In their discourse, they rejected and refuted the total equality approach. At the same time, highly educated and professional Islamist women were using total equality in their daily practice to defend equal rights for women in the public sphere, specifically in relation to work and political activism.

In other instances, the Islamist male leadership reacted swiftly, as Zubaida (2003) observes, to "fix" *shari'a* in place in regard to the penal code, again, to discredit feminist and secularist women's groups and thwart any of their proposed reforms. The emphasis the Islamist leadership places on *shari'a* is less about women's rights than about asserting Islamist power in society, especially vis-à-vis the Palestinian Authority. It may also aim at defining the still indeterminate nature of any future Palestinian or Islamic state through a strategy of "active citizenship." In this respect, Molyneux (1996) warns, active citizenship in some countries "is manipulated by 'fundamentalists' who seek to create a political community, in the furtherance of objectives which would lead to authoritarian, theocratic and highly gendered states" (6).

Although Islamists found refuge in the notion of "active citizenship," this might not, in the Palestinian case, necessarily lead to a more authoritarian and "gendered" state. My data show that Islamists, in their quest to define themselves as a national movement, were obliged to borrow from and incorporate new visions to broaden their constituencies. There have been some strategic moments of civil society activism when women Islamists were participants in the struggle. Certain arenas of civil society activism, such as the students' movement and the structure of the Salvation Party itself, incorporated women who were sociologically marginalized from the national leadership, where elite women were overrepresented.

However, despite moments of opening and engagement, there are threats of closure and a retreat into interpretations of Islam that might affect women negatively. Although Islamists call for women's full participation in public life, they could always fall back to an insistence on the time-honored role of women as fertile "mothers of the nation." Their stand on polygamy is not yet clear. In the case of women suicide bombers, a heated debate erupted on the suitability of women for paramilitary action. However, what sort of "Islamic" state this activism might lead to depends, I have argued, on the context that the secularists set. Numerous challenges pushed the Islamists to develop positions on secular issues such as pluralism, women's rights, the public good, sustainable development, and the social self versus the individual self, all of which are notions put on the agenda in a secular context, forcing Islamists to jump on the bandwagon.

I have problematized the term "fundamentalism" in my presentation of Hamas as a movement that "nationalized" Islam and "Islamized" nationalism, with all that this entails for women's roles. I also showed that religious ideology, in the context of the Palestinian national struggle, is evolving in a contradictory manner, affected as it is by the discourses of other political and social groups. This also calls into question what Badran (1995) calls "Islamic feminism," in which gender is assumed to derive solely from the Quran and its interpretive methodologies and *ijtihad* (independent intellectual investigation of religious texts). In the Palestinian case, as I have shown, Islamist women's discourse stems not only from the Quran but also from positive engagement with other women's discourses, whether primarily feminist or nationalist. In my opinion, it is this engagement that motivates Islamist women to turn to religious texts to seek possible new readings to respond to the challenges posed by other women's groups.

In short, Islamist women's discourses do not rely solely on religious texts but also on the discursive terrain created by other women activists. This engagement could constitute common ground for Islamist and secularist women to push together for new readings of religious texts as well as to work hand in hand in response to the daily struggles of women under Occupation. Such mutual accommodation

(Hudson 1996; Norton 1993; Salamé 2001) requires each party to maintain vigilance over the changes occurring in the discourses of the other and is preferable to the total rejection that characterizes some women's NGOs.

Critiques of the capacity of "modernization" to achieve progress and emancipation for society in general and women in particular, are, to this day, ignored in the Middle East and in Palestine. I have pointed out, for example, the ways in which the nationalist modernist elite deployed modernization to marginalize social groups such as rural women while at the same time doing little to challenge the prevailing gender order based on "Islam" and "traditions." On the other hand, both popular nationalism and Islamism have been responsive to women's activism, holding nationalists accountable to their claims to support equality between men and women. While Arab, including Palestinian, secularist nationalists criticize the aggressive political and military interventions of colonial powers, critiques of their social, economic, and cultural interventions are largely left to the Islamists. Islamist groups present themselves and are often seen by others as the only power that is challenging the failed promises of modernity.

One of the ways in which a common ground, or a "dialogic engagement" (Beinin and Stork 1997, 22), can be forged between Islamists and secularists is to interrogate colonial modernity (Massad 2015). As argued in chapter 3, the dichotomy of "authenticity" versus "modernity" (understood as Westernization) needs to be seriously challenged. Many scholars have argued that cultures and traditions are neither static nor "fixed" (al-Azmeh 1996; Chatterjee 1993) and the "tradition" that Islamists seek to revive is an invented modern construct. In endorsing Nancy Fraser's suggestion of moving beyond identity politics, I recognize the Islamists as an influential constituency representing and supported by some social groupings in civil society.

My objective has been neither to valorize nor to endorse Islamist policies but to correct their misrecognition and discursive marginalization. Fraser has argued that "misrecognition constitutes a form of institutionalized subordination, and thus a serious violation of justice" (2000, 114). Such claims for recognition seek to establish the subordinated party as a full partner in social life, able to interact with others as partners, to help in understanding, in Fraser's terms "what is impeding participatory parity in any particular instance" (119). Recognizing Islamists as equal partners in activism in civil society is important not only in the general context of the Middle East, where they are subject to brutal repression by incumbent governments, but pivotally in the case of Palestine, where the battle for national survival is ongoing. As I have argued, the violent repression to which they have been subjected has worked in their favor, if only because their prosecutors are despised by the majority of the people as corrupt and authoritarian Western cronies.

Palestinian Islamists cannot simply be confined to the private sphere along with "tradition" and "religion" (Chatterjee 1993, 26). The problem here, as Asad (2003) puts it, is that "modern citizens don't subscribe to a unitary moral system" and that "moral heterogeneity is . . . one of modern society's defining characteristics" (186). The affirmation of national solidarity does not, despite some hopes, represent a religion of the nation-state (187, 193), because the moral heterogeneity of modern society means that nothing can be identified as a collective moral sensibility.

Secularity is not the opposite of religion but may mirror it. In other words, if nationalism produces an enlightened and tolerant polity, it will also produce an enlightened and tolerant religion. If, however, nationalism is authoritarian and oppressive, it will, by the same token, produce a violent and intolerant religion. As I have shown, the Islamists "borrowed" their methods of activism and their practice of politics from the secular sphere, from which they also derived their notions and practices of democracy, citizens' rights, and gender ideology, as they also "borrowed" the use of violence in contesting the hegemony of the mainstream nationalists. The insistence on a sharp differentiation between the religious and the secular makes little sense in light of the fact that the latter continually reproduces the former.

The common invocation of modern and secular values in tandem with their misleading equation with universal rights is used to challenge the defense of the sort of "authentic" cultural "differences" usually invoked by nationalist conservatives and fundamentalist religious groups. The universal human rights approach is based on a cross-cultural framework that it uses to analyze women's oppression and subordination and suggest universal instruments for women's empowerment (Cornwall and Molyneux 2008). This was illustrated by the controversy aroused by the model parliament project through which WCLAC, as a secular feminist NGO, sought to reform existing legislation by adopting a women's human rights approach. The events following that project demonstrated that separating women's rights from collective national rights in the context of the Occupation tended to lead to the marginalization of women as a social group and subsequently to their fragmentation and demobilization. Paradoxically, the universal human rights approach, intended to be used as a tool of empowerment worldwide, weakened homegrown feminism. It also developed at the expense of understanding the historical realities created by successive waves of colonization and the subsequent roles imposed upon, or accepted by, women (Nesiah 1996, 1). The women's rights approach adopted by WCLAC, based on individual rights and international women's rights, wrongly affirmed that social power rests in the state and not in other social and political groups such as the Islamists who oppose and compete with it.

By ignoring the national context, this approach came to flagrantly contradict strongly prevailing cultural values that valorized the person who gives, sacrifices, and struggles for the sake of his or her occupied, denied, and humiliated nation. The emphasis on a rights-based approach was perceived by many, especially by Islamists, as making claims on a nation on the brink of collapse. This discredited the claimants as those who want to "take" instead of "give." By ignoring the sociopolitical context in which the "project" to change the law and to claim women's rights was implemented, the project, unwittingly, gave more ground to the Islamists to delegitimize the call to replace the gender order with an order based on universal women's rights.

In the light of both historical experience and the data emerging from my fieldwork, it would appear that the weaknesses of the Palestinian women's movement have become evident at the points where it was not able to be an inclusive mobilizing force. The greatest successes have been achieved at moments when the feminist and nationalist agendas were maximally synergistic; by contrast, the moment of imaginary state-building processes after Oslo played a crucial role in demobilizing all forms of secular political and social activism for the unintended benefit of the Islamist movement. A middle-class urban elite came to the fore, both in the PA structures (as femocrats) and in the mass organizations, at the expense of rural and refugee activists. NGO-ization served to further fragment the women's movement. I see the gains achieved by the Islamists as the result of the failure of the Palestinian political establishment, and it is thus crucial for secularists to reexamine their concepts and strategies.

Ultimately, the establishment of the Palestinian Authority in 1994 proved to be destructive both to the Palestinian national movement and to the society's women's movements. The PA failed to include the Islamist movement of Hamas, and the political system that was established under the Israeli Occupation proved to be hostile to all forms of resistance to that occupation. The prospect that all the various elements of the Palestinian women's movements could find common ground from which to pursue a unified struggle against the Occupation was unfulfilled, as detailed in the epilogue, which looks at three significant developments during the fourteen years since my primary field research concluded.

Epilogue

The Political Life of Palestinian Women since 2004

THE POLITICAL AND PUBLIC LIFE of Palestinian women has been influenced by a number of factors, most importantly successive waves of occupation of Palestine by colonizers of various sorts; the evolution and growth of the Palestinian resistance movement; the development of the national movement and, later, the Palestinian Authority; and the evolution and growth of the feminist movement. This epilogue analyzes three cases that exemplify the most important developments in and influences on the political life of women in the occupied Palestinian territory (the West Bank, including Jerusalem, and the Gaza Strip) in the years since I finished my first-hand research on Islamist women in 2004.

The aim of this chapter is to trace the effects of the fragmentation of the Palestinian national movement in the aftermath of the legislative elections of 2006 that resulted in the victory of the Islamists and the takeover of Gaza by Hamas in 2007. The ensuing political schism divided the Palestinian polity into parallel West Bank and Gaza governments, both operating in an imagined and fragmented fake sovereignty, which has altered the priorities of women in each territory and impaired their capacity to achieve mutual accommodation. I shall chart, in what follows, the transformations that the Palestinian women's movements have undergone and how global governance and transnational feminism came to displace the struggle against colonial

170

violence and the aspiration for liberation, leading to the marginalization of women's role in the national resistance.

The Palestinian legislative elections of 2006 brought the Islamists to power in Gaza in a democratic, transparent, and fair vote. A deep political schism took place after Hamas assumed power in Gaza, with the division of the Palestinian polity into two governments: the one in the West Bank fully reliant on donor funding, and the one in Gaza under siege by Israel, Egypt, and the Palestinian Authority itself. Meanwhile, across the wider region, Muslim Brothers movements supported by the communications (including media) and financial resources of Qatar, Turkey, and other supportive countries were growing in political influence in Egypt, Tunis, Libya, and Syria. Hamas was under increasing pressure to align itself with the international Muslim Brothers movement, imperiling its relations with Iran and Syria, which provided crucial backing for its resistance efforts. The removal of Mohammed Mursi from the Egyptian presidency in July 2013 placed Hamas in an even more precarious position. The military coup in Egypt deprived the movement of vital support from the Muslim Brothers and enabled Israel to intensify its siege of the Islamist government in Gaza, threatening its very survival. At the same time, Hamas's backing of anti-Assad groups in Syria angered its supporters loyal to the "resistance line" espoused by Iran, a primary sponsor of both Hamas and Assad.

The fragmentation of the Palestinian national movement has resulted in the failure to build a political system based on elections and the peaceful transfer of power in place of the "revolutionary legitimacy" of the PLO's factional quota system. The political chasm has to a great extent altered the priorities of women in the West Bank and the Gaza Strip, and impaired their capabilities, as elaborated in the following examples.

There certainly have been important achievements for women at the official political level, exemplified by the establishment of the first Ministry of Women's Affairs in 2003, the introduction of quotas for female officeholders in local elections in 2004 and in parliamentary elections in 2006, and the adoption of UN Security Council

Resolution 1325 concerning the protection of women in conflict and post-conflict situations. Nonetheless, the colonial context of the Palestinian Authority has rendered it weak and ineffectual. With no control over resources, or indeed its own fate, it has proven largely unable to satisfy the demands of women for freedom, equality, and full citizenship and has at the same time debilitated the political parties and social movements, including the feminist movement, that were organized within the PLO. Moreover, the rupture of the Palestinian political system and the establishment of two opposing governments engendered dynamics in both governance and society that have undermined women's organizational capacities, which, in turn, has weakened their ability to contribute either to their own liberation or that of the country, while jeopardizing their achievements. As seen in the following examples, some women have contributed to the perpetuation of the ruinous schism.

Case One: Official Policy after 2000

The Ministry of Women's Affairs and Gender Mainstreaming in a Situation of Conflict

With the decline of the Palestinian national movement subsequent to the Oslo Agreement and the resulting deterioration of its constituent organizations and parties, the national mechanism for gender mainstreaming—the Ministry of Women's Affairs—was founded in 2003, replacing IMCAW, amid the difficult conditions of reoccupation during the second intifada. Most national mechanisms for the integration of a gender agenda are established in stable states with full sovereignty. The first Palestinian Ministry of Women's Affairs formulated a similar agenda, ignoring the circumstances of occupation and conflict. Moreover, the later breakup of the Palestinian government led to two diametrically opposed approaches: one in the West Bank emphasizing state and democracy building, and one in the Gaza Strip giving priority to the mobilization and empowerment of women in the resistance and the defense of Palestinian rights and identity. The impact of the ongoing instability on the work of gender mainstreaming and the priorities of the Ministry of Women's Affairs falls into three basic phases.

Phase I: The Formative Stage, 2003

The Ministry of Women's Affairs based its 2004 plan on the 1997 National Strategy for the Advancement of Palestinian Women, which in turn was based on international and regional conference documents, including the 1979 Convention on the Elimination of All Forms of Discrimination against Women (CEDAW) and the resolutions of the Beijing Conference of 1995. The 1997 strategy reflected the vision of feminist activists and the General Union of Palestinian Women at the time, hence there was a focus on national liberation, the role of women in opposing occupation, and the mobilization of international cooperation and solidarity to expose the crimes of occupation against women in particular and the Palestinian people in general.

Seven years later, however, there was a clear shift in emphasis toward "construction and development of the democratic Palestinian homeland, and consolidation of an effective civil society governed by national, cultural, and humanitarian values" (MOWA-PA 2004). The three key objectives of the plan centered on a "social agenda" consisting of (1) securing a government commitment to mainstream gender, democracy, and human rights issues in the policies, plans, and programs of the various PA ministries, as well as in legislation and regulations; (2) linking lobbying activities to the development of policies and laws; and (3) building a network of relationships with governmental and international women's organizations and human rights groups to exchange experiences in applying international conventions on women and human rights, particularly CEDAW. The plan also focused heavily on the institutionalization of the ministry's work and on incorporating it within the body of government through a budget, organizational structure, and human resources.

Phase II: Political Divide, 2005–2007

The subsequent 2005–7 plan focused on educational, vocational, and technical training of young women; support for women's access to decision-making positions; and addressing endemic poverty among young women, especially heads of households. These goals were based on the Beijing Platform for Action, as well as on consultation with both governmental and nongovernmental institutions. Once again, this plan focused on development and capacity building; the emphasis on access to decision-making positions was especially popular among women working in the various ministries, promising support for their efforts to improve their job positions.

With the legislative elections in 2006, Hamas came to power in Gaza. Mariam Saleh, the first Islamist minister of women's affairs, set out to provide assurances, speaking to leaders of women's organizations that November 5.[1] However, lack of clarity regarding Hamas's position vis-à-vis the demands of the feminist movement raised doubts in the minds of some feminist activists. The Palestinian Initiative for the Promotion of Global Dialogue and Democracy (MIFTAH) coordinated several meetings for women leaders to discuss the reasons for the political "turning of the tables" and to review the work and discourse of women's organizations to extract relevant lessons. The elitism of much feminist activity and its focus on educated women in the central West Bank was criticized, and there was general agreement on the need to change the general nature of communication with Palestinian women. There was no acknowledgment, however, of the importance of opening dialogue with officials of the new governing party (MIFTAH 2006).

Saleh and her successor, Amal Siam, adjusted the vision of the Ministry of Women's Affairs, even as it became increasingly paralyzed after their efforts were rebuffed by the secular women leaders. Notwithstanding the ministry's continuing prioritization of the fight against discrimination against women and for equality, anti-violence,

1. Amal Siam, Saleh's successor in the "government of national unity" that was formed on March 17, 2007, and ended with Hamas's takeover of the Gaza Strip a month later, also called for a meeting with women's organizations and unions, but only a few responded.

and legal reform efforts, the work it was still capable of doing turned more and more to supporting women and the wives and families of detainees, prisoners, and those who had been killed—that is, emphasizing the national struggle agenda and its ramifications for women and their families (Ababneh 2014). This would become the main focus of the Ministry of Women's Affairs in Gaza after the split between Fateh and Hamas in June 2007.

Phase III: An Entrenched Divide, 2007 and Beyond

After the political split, and in a newly charged political environment, a fresh strategy for the PA Ministry of Women's Affairs in the West Bank was developed for 2008–10. The focus returned to the earlier priorities, with a new addition: combating violence, mainly domestic, against women and formulating a plan to address the issue for 2011 and beyond. The new strategy promoted government efforts to put into effect UN Security Council Resolution 1325—under which Palestinian women can file complaints concerning the violence of the Israeli Occupation to international bodies, especially the International Criminal Court—and its clauses related to the participation of women in conflict resolution and peace building. There was no explanation, however, of how the latter might be achieved.

The political division led the ministry to shift its focus away from the more "theoretical" needs of women—legal reform and a policy-making impact—toward meeting their practical needs, in particular through the implementation of relief policies. This shift was evidently made reluctantly—according to the ministry's 2009 national report, such policies were considered to be "often in conflict with 'social justice'" and with the state-building aspirations of "mainly secular" NGOs (ESCWA 2009).

However, priorities soon changed again with the 2011–13 strategy, which reverted to national issues, envisaging support for women in Jerusalem and female prisoners. The priorities, however, lacked intellectual consistency. The campaign to combat violence was understood to be directed at domestic violence rather than violence perpetrated by the Israeli Occupation, despite, for instance, the bloody war waged on the Gaza Strip in 2008–9. Furthermore, low budget allocations reflected a lack of real commitment to national issues. Out of a total ministry budget of NIS 43,813,240 (about $11 million), NIS 200,000 (2.74 percent) was allocated to family law and civil rights programming, while only NIS 128,400 (0.29 percent) was allocated to protecting the rights of women in Jerusalem and NIS 53,000 (0.12 percent) to supporting women prisoners.

The strategy statements of the Ministry of Women's Affairs were mainly based on the Declaration of Independence of 1988; the Palestinian Basic Law; the Palestinian Women's Charter of 2008; international conventions, particularly CEDAW; and UN Security Council Resolution 1325. The ministry made great efforts to raise awareness of these instruments, in particular Resolution 1325 and the Palestinian Women's Charter. It also succeeded in several other areas, the most important of which was the institutionalization of gender and women's issues in various ministries. In 2005, a Council of Ministers resolution urged ministries, particularly the larger ones, to establish units for women's affairs wherever relevant and possible. Its provisions, however, were vague and not mandatory. The ministry later worked to amend the resolution to specify clearer steps in the creation of such units and their organizational structure. On July 28, 2008, it won approval for what it saw as a crucial name change from "women's units" to "gender units" (ESCWA 2009). Nonetheless, ministries were still not required to establish such units.

As of 2014, there were twenty gender units in various ministries and official institutions. Their status varies from one ministry to the next, depending on the capacity of staff, their positions, and their influence, in addition to the overall vision of the ministry and the political will of the minister. They need more time, effort, and institutional capacity to achieve their goals. Several continue to focus on women's access to decision-making positions, which translates into placing more women in senior roles within the ministry. Some units (such as in the Ministry of Labor and the Ministry of Local

Government) have been active in forming coalitions with civil society activists in an effort to increase their influence, while others are still feeling their way.

The Ministry of Women's Affairs also supported the establishment of women's "communication" centers in key provinces (Hebron, Nablus, Bethlehem, Jenin, and Ramallah) through partnerships with local, regional, and international institutions designed to combat all forms of discrimination against women in all fields. According to documents issued by the ministry and the Palestinian Women's Charter, the aim is to empower women and enable them to participate in public life. Although this is undoubtedly an important step in mainstreaming women's issues in decentralized arenas, these centers suffer from a lack of essential human and financial resources (ESCWA 2009). In addition, women and children's departments were added to the structures of the various governorates on April 4, 2007, by presidential decree, with the aim of supporting and developing the capabilities of women and children in all spheres: political, social, and economic. However, these units were not allocated budgets that would enable them to implement the plans, programs, and activities assigned to them—a problem, indeed, facing most of the structures that have been established to institutionalize gender mainstreaming.

Thus, the Ministry of Women's Affairs in the West Bank fully abides by the state-building and gender-rights agenda based on the international conventions on women's rights. The ministry also follows the PA's political line and cannot take the initiative, either formally or informally, to bridge the gap between the women in the two Palestinian governments. The ministry is further disabled from bridging this gap by the source of its funding which, as with all Palestinian ministries, overwhelmingly derives from the so-called Madrid Quartet—the UN, the US, the EU, and Russia—and is therefore subject to the Quartet's conditions, which include no funding for any institutions run by Hamas, whether governmental or nongovernmental, before it recognizes the state of Israel and renounces "terrorism."

Case Two: The Ministry of Women's Affairs in Gaza

Different Gender Priorities

The priorities of the Ministry of Women's Affairs in the Gaza Strip differ from those of its counterpart in the West Bank. After the rupture of 2007, the mission of the Gaza ministry—formerly a division of the PA ministry—was drastically changed to reflect a clear emphasis on women's mobilization and organization, along with the implementation of projects for and the provision of services to women. In 2010, the ministry—whose budget that year was $319,000—issued a plan in which it described itself as the female arm charged with implementing the government's program to detach the Gaza economy from the Israeli economy by strengthening the government's internal capacities, achieving food security, and creating jobs for young people, while improving the legal and legislative environment for women, especially the marginalized, and providing them with needed services (MOWA-Gaza 2010). The ministry thus does not see its role as limited to planning and influencing policymaking, as does the West Bank ministry. The latter has adopted a gender and development (GAD) approach, in contrast with the former's women in development (WID) approach. Working within the WID framework, the Gaza ministry developed a plan for different categories of women, through studies presented at a conference that aimed to produce a policy paper detailing forms of intervention and transformation that would be subscribed to by all concerned government institutions (see the Ministry of Women's Affairs website, www.mowa.gov.ps).

The ministry's plans give priority to women directly affected by the Israeli Occupation: the widows and children of martyrs (Palestinians killed by Israeli forces), school and university students, and schoolteachers. The ministry provides the widows of martyrs with psychological, social, material, and legal support. For example, it succeeded in having a law passed amending the period of maternal child custody so that "the judge may authorize the continuation of custody by the mother whose husband has died and who has dedicated herself to raising and nurturing her children, for the best interest of the child, provided the mother is capable, and on the condition of continued follow-up and care by blood relations" (*Al-Waqa'i' al-Falastineyya* [Palestinian Gazette] 74, 39). Moreover, the ministry has sought to shore up the legal framework related to the rights of these women to dowry, alimony, custody, feeding and nursery fees, and inheritance (al-Sabti 2009).

The ministry has also focused on mobilizing young people to challenge Israeli occupation policies, while promoting virtuous, faith-based family values through educational institutions. The 2010 plan included numerous job-creation projects for female university graduates in civil defense, first aid, and handling unexploded ordnance. It also articulated plans to engage a large number of female university graduates in activities aimed at raising women's awareness of international treaties and conventions on women and presenting "the charter of women in Islam as a model for rights and duties" (MOWA-Gaza 2010). The plan included publication of a semi-annual newspaper covering the steadfastness of women in the siege and blockade of Gaza. It addressed what it called the "cohesive and happy family despite the blockade" and developed a "portfolio suited for a happy family"— programs to communicate the principles of proper relations between men and women that seem to address domestic violence, but within the context of Islamic culture. The plan included several schemes to improve the legal status of women through proposals for amending family law, presenting a Palestinian Women's Charter to the Legislative Council for its endorsement, and modifying terms of the 2005 Civil Service Law to ensure the equality of women in retirement. It called for studies of the social and economic situation of women that would serve as the basis for an annual conference. Programs were included to support poor families by enabling them to find permanent sources of income through training in creating income-generating projects, the granting of loans, and psychosocial training to encourage women to enter the labor market. The plan also envisaged assisting women's institutions in the provision of services through the establishment of a website—*Al-Shaqa'eq*—to provide instruction and support in writing project proposals and facilitate access to funders. Another element of the plan was the production of a series of documentary films about the struggles of widows and female heads of households, which were created in an attempt to secure funding for development projects (MOWA-Gaza 2010).

The ministry relies on extensive relationships throughout the Arab and Muslim world, facilitated by the international network of the Muslim Brothers movement, to exchange information about experiences and practices, but also to request support and funding. Ministry officials have participated in several Arab and Islamic conferences and it makes extensive use of the internet, where the ministry's activities, plans, and projects are documented. While communicating with the world, at least virtually, the two ministries in Gaza and the West Bank do not communicate with each other.

However, the appointment in 2014 of a new minister, Dr. Haifa al-Agha, to run the Women's Affairs Ministry in both the West Bank and Gaza was an important development. Al-Agha is a Gazan woman who wears hijab and is in touch with the living conditions of ordinary women. Immediately accepted and welcomed by Hamas women running the ministry in Gaza, she was greeted with suspicion by some feminists in the West Bank who saw her as having a militant background but no feminist credentials. She was immediately put to the test as to how to bridge the gap between the two separate ministries. Her initial efforts to include Hamas women in the many national teams producing the various women's plans and strategies were unsuccessful. Going forward, her ability to bridge the wide gap between the two ministries will depend on the lagging broader initiatives aimed at unifying the two territorial governments, initiatives that are blocked by regional and international players, including Israel.

In summary, the vision and methodology of the West Bank ministry are different from those of the Gaza ministry. The former focuses mainly on state building and on mainstreaming and institutionalizing issues of equality within the organs of the Palestinian Authority. In contrast, the latter, true to the modus operandi of the Islamist movement, offers support and services to the mass base of the movement, in addition to targeting women directly affected by the Occupation. This difference is also reflected in the mechanisms used by the respective ministries in their pursuit of full citizenship rights for women, for example through different versions of the Palestinian Women's Charter.

Case Three: The Palestinian Women's Charter

Between Cooperation and Conflict

The Palestinian Women's Charter proved to be a source of considerable conflict between the two ministries. The West Bank ministry sought to make the document a guiding beacon for the achievement of women's equality, while Gaza officials sought to realize some of its proposals as originally drafted, but alter others to render them compliant with the "Islamic" vision for achieving women's rights.

Background

Since its founding in 2003, the Ministry of Women's Affairs has sought to enact the provisions of the Palestinian Women's Charter, developed by the feminist movement in 1994 as a reference document for policy-making and legislation. The ministry has also proposed several related items of legislation, directed especially at combating violence against women and raising sentences for so-called honor crimes. This was in response to several homicides of women that shook public opinion.

Achievements and Obstacles

Using the Women's Charter as a guide, the West Bank Ministry of Women's Affairs and women's organizations worked together in a successful lobbying effort for various legislative and policy changes, among them quotas for women in the electoral law; an increase in the marriage age to eighteen; approval of gender-responsive government budgets; the establishment of units for women in the various ministries; and the Palestinian Authority's acceptance of UN Security Council Resolution 1325. The ministry also prompted President Abbas to adopt the Convention on the Elimination of All Forms of Discrimination against Women and in 2008 secured his blessing for the charter.

This did not, however, mean a commitment by the Palestinian Authority to abide by the charter as a reference in legislation and policymaking. Indeed, the document has faced major challenges due to a lack of community consensus. For example, clerics and the Iftaa Council (dar al-ifta') said the document was not rooted in Islam, but rather was based on secular laws and international conventions and called for ripping the Muslim family apart. They have opposed it on the grounds that it advocates rights and policies in opposition to Islamic law such as the right of women to assume any public office without condition or restriction; equality between men and women in testimony before the courts (*shahada*); denial of the right of husbands to discipline their wives; condemnation of marital rape; the increase in the marriage age to eighteen; abolition of a man's authority and the principle of wardship over his wife; the right of Muslim women to marry non-Muslims; the right of women to obtain a divorce; women's right to seek compensation in cases of arbitrary divorce; equality in laws pertaining to property and inheritance; and restrictions on polygamy. Religious conservatives saw the charter as "part of the drive to westernize Muslim women and detach them from their religion and an assault on the basic tenets of Islam; hence abiding by it or even accepting it is prohibited by *shari'a* law" (Hussein 2010, 17–18). The Iftaa Council called the document blasphemous and appealed to the president not to endorse it. These attacks ultimately led the ministry to drop its efforts to implement the charter.

Many women at the grassroots level, as became apparent in several workshops organized by women's organizations, had views similar to those of the clergy. They considered the charter a violation of Islamic law on the basis of many of the same provisions to which the clerics took exception; moreover, they criticized it on stylistic grounds, objecting to its abundant use of legalese (Hussein 2010). These observations were not much different from the views of the charter held by the Ministry of Women's Affairs in Gaza.

Palestinian Women's Charter: The Islamic Version

The two Hamas-affiliated ministers of women's affairs in the 2006–7 government and the 2007 "government of national unity" approved the adoption of the Palestinian Women's Charter, with reservations.

However, after the governing regimes split in June 2007, a revised charter was issued by the Gaza Ministry of Women's Affairs. Significant alterations notwithstanding, it is to the credit of the Gaza ministry that it has retained a version of the charter that recognizes injustice toward women and the need to develop an integrated rights and political framework, albeit in an Islamic context. Workshops were conducted to promote the contents of the altered charter. In one workshop held on June 5, 2009, the ministry official in charge of policy and planning, Amira Haroun, stated that the document serves as a legal base compatible with the special identity and culture of Palestinian society, but that the original charter promoted by the West Bank ministry is not based on Islamic law. She went on to say that "99 percent of the previous document promoted Western thought that is incompatible with Islam . . . being grounded in leftist thought based on secularism. The current ministry has modified it to bring it in line with Islamic law. Initial rewriting of the document will be accomplished through a series of workshops (26 workshops) to be held by experts to study and analyze various issues in the document" (Haroun 2009).

In the West Bank, in the course of the establishment of multiple structures and plans such as the National Committee to Combat Violence (2008), the National Strategy to Combat Violence against Women (2011–19), the Strategic National Frame for 1325 (2015), the National Action Plan for the Implementation of UNSCR 1325 on Women, Peace, and Security (2017–19), and Partners in Construction: Intersectoral National Strategic Plan to Enhance Gender Justice, Equality, and Empowerment (2017–22), there has been no significant change in the goals given top priority. The five current strategic goals set by the West Bank ministry aim at reducing violence against women by half; increasing the representation of women in decision-making government and non-government bodies by 10 percent; mainstreaming gender equality and justice in the different governmental institutions; enhancing women's participation in the economic sector; and improving the quality of life for poor and marginalized families. Most of these plans, coalitions, and strategic goals are seen by the Gaza ministry as irrelevant to their realities on the ground (MOWA-West Bank 2017, 30–36).

The West Bank ministry's strategic goals and priorities are very different from most of those that appear on the website of the Gaza ministry, which are to improve the economic standard of poor families through small-income generating projects; to consolidate the unity of the Palestinian family by raising awareness of the rights and duties of family ties; to support martyrs' families; to improve women's legal status through legal reforms; to empower women's organizations by increasing their capacity to fulfill women's societal needs; and finally, to build young women's skills, qualify them to be future leaders, and equip them to join the labor force (MOWA-Gaza 2018). Despite its very different goals, the Gaza ministry could not fully avoid the governance imposed by international entities and donors and the priorities set by these players such as the combating of domestic violence. The March 2013 final narrative report on the Millennium Development Goals Achievement Fund's Gender Equality and Women's Empowerment program in the occupied Palestinian territories—involving UNDP/PAPP, UN Women, ILO, UNESCO, UNRWA, and UNFPA—states:

> The establishment of the Hayat multipurpose center (shelter [for battered women]) in Gaza . . . initiated a breakthrough in the Gazan society in the sense that the Hamas government was forced to address GBV [gender-based violence] and VAW [violence against women] issues for the very first time at the national/policy level. However, since the negotiation process with Hamas took [so] long, the establishment of the sheltering component was delayed until January 2013[;] however, all other components, i.e., legal, psychological and social support as well as child visitation[,] were well underway. (MDG-F 2013, 10)

However, disagreement persisted on the central question of how to empower women and defend their rights. Speaking in early 2018, Amira Haroun of the Gaza ministry stated:

The [UNSC Resolution] 1325 plan refers to wars and conflicts and does not refer to our situation as colonized; it talks about peace and reconciliation and we are witnessing continuous wars and colonial expansion; it talks about protection of women and we don't see any protection. The majority of international solidarity movements go to the West Bank and not Gaza. It is sad to see women activists driven by these plans focusing on domestic violence and sexual harassment against women in Gaza who still live in trailers after the destruction of their homes by Israeli bombs in 2014, and they don't see the violence against their lives, their families, and their homes. (interview)

Haroun did see in these plans a possible means to achieve political recognition for the Islamists in the ministry: "We asked to be part of the national coalition to combat violence and the national strategic plan on violence, but our request was rejected by the cabinet in the West Bank; the same happened with our request to be part of the 1325 plan. They did not include us in forming these plans and they don't want to include us" (interview). The result is that the West Bank ministry presents these plans on its website, while the Gaza ministry does not.

Conclusion

International frames such as UN Security Council Resolution 1325, the Millennium Development Goals, and the UNDP's Sustainable Development Goals, and the sort of donor funding they promote, simply fall short of adequately addressing the particular context of Palestinian women under prolonged occupation. The one-size-fits-all campaign to save Palestinian women from patriarchy helped create a huge industry in the defense of women's rights in the Occupied Territories. But this in turn led the women's movement in the West Bank to lose its vision along with its power, even as the framing discourse was rejected to great effect by the Islamists, first as Western and then as irrelevant to women's lived realities. At the same time, however, it was not possible for them to entirely turn their backs on these frames, especially with their potential dividends in securing political legitimization for and channeling some direly needed funding to the distressed Gazans. Islamist women instrumentalized these international development frames to gain political recognition, meanwhile working to subvert them among their constituencies. By providing basic needs such as shelter, food, and job opportunities, Islamist women managed to build an impressive infrastructure for organizing women. Their agenda, still a work in progress, continuously engages with feminist frames such as women's rights and violence against women; thus the women's rights approach is not rejected altogether but used to address the needs and interests of the Islamists' constituencies, as with the legal reform of child custody and making jobs traditionally held by men accessible to women.

International development and women's rights frames heavily supported by international donors are exacerbating the weakness of the national Palestinian women's movement, which fully subscribes to them in order to emphasize its openness and "advancement." This approach meanwhile empowers the movement's Islamist counterparts, seen by the majority of Palestinians as the only organized force that stands in the face of a mighty colonial power that inflicts all forms of destruction on Palestinian men, women, and children in its effort to empty the land of its people and end Palestinian aspirations to achieve national liberation.

Appendixes

Glossary

References

Index

APPENDIX A

Chronology of Palestinian Women's Organizations

Organization	Foundation: Date/Location	Function	Affiliation
General Union of Palestinian Women (GUPW)	Founded in 1965 in Jerusalem	Umbrella organization for all Palestinian women	PLO
Palestinian Federation of Women's Action Committees (PFWAC)	Founded in 1978 in Jerusalem as the Women's Work Committee, with international branches; assumed the name by which it was subsequently known in the mid-1980s	Grassroots women's mobilization group	Democratic Front for the Liberation of Palestine (DFLP)
Women's Youth Center	Founded in 1980 in Hebron	Charitable society and training center for young women	Originally independent; in the late 1990s shifted to Islamist orientation

(Continued from previous page)

Organization	Foundation: Date/Location	Function	Affiliation
Union of Palestinian Working Women's Committees (UPWW)	Founded in 1981 in Ramallah with international branches; after splitting from the Communist Party, renamed the Palestinian Working Women's Society for Development (PWWSD)	Grassroots women's mobilization group	Palestinian Communist Party (PCP); later independent
Palestinian Women's Committees (PWC)	Founded in 1982 in Ramallah with international branches; later renamed the Union of Palestinian Women's Committees (UPWC)	Grassroots women's mobilization group	Popular Front for the Liberation of Palestine (PFLP)
Women's Social Work Committees (WSWC)	Founded in 1983 in Ramallah with international branches	Grassroots women's organization	Fateh
Women's Affairs Center (WAC)	Established in Nablus in 1988, then in Gaza in 1989	Women's study center	Independent NGO
Women's Study Center (WSC)	Founded in 1989 in Jerusalem	Women's study and training center	Established by the PFWAC; later an independent NGO

(Continued from previous page)

Organization	Foundation: Date/Location	Function	Affiliation
Muslim Women's Society	Founded in 1989 in Jerusalem	Islamic charitable society	Union of Charitable Societies
Women's Center for Legal Aid and Counseling (WCLAC)	Founded in 1991 in Jerusalem	Women's center for legal aid, counseling, advocacy, and training	Established by the PFWAC; later an independent NGO
Women's Affairs Technical Committee (WATC)	Founded in 1991 in Jerusalem; later established in Ramallah and Gaza	Women's coalition	Representing most women's grassroots organizations affiliated with political parties, as well as some independent women's groups
Palestinian Women's Action Committees (PWAC)	Founded in 1992 in Ramallah as a breakaway from the PFWAC	Grassroots organization	FIDA, a DFLP faction that officially split from the party in 1993
Jerusalem Center for Women (JCW)	Founded in 1993 in Jerusalem	Independent women's NGO	Result of a Palestinian-Israeli women's joint venture, Jerusalem Link, which also led to the founding of a corresponding Israeli women's center, Bat Shalom
Al-Huda	Founded in 1996 in Al-Bireh	Islamic charitable society	Independent; group's leaders are active in the Islamist movement

(Continued from previous page)

Organization	Foundation: Date/Location	Function	Affiliation
Al-Khansaa	Founded in 1997 in Al-Bireh	Islamic charitable society	Independent; group's leaders are active in the Islamist movement
Haneen	Founded in 1997 in Nablus	Islamic charitable society	Independent; group's leaders are active in the Islamist movement
Women's Action Department (WAD)	Founded in 1997 in Gaza City, with many branches around Gaza	Grassroots women's mobilization group	Islamic National Salvation Party
Mashraqiyat	Founded in 1998 in Gaza City	Women's center focused on reform of *shari'a* law based on new interpretations; during second intifada, shifted to provide women with emergency aid	Independent NGO

APPENDIX B

List of Interviews by Organization

Organization/ Individual	Description	Number of Interviewees	Dates
Yasser Arafat	Head of the PA and the PLO	1	Nov. 17, 1994 Oct. 2, 2000
Marwan Bargouthi	MP and secretary of the Higher Command Committee	1	Feb. 15, 2002
General Union of Palestinian Women (GUPW)	Women's union	6	Apr. 2, 2001 Apr. 8, 2001 Apr. 9, 2001 June 25, 2001
Haneen	Islamic charitable society	2	Apr. 3, 2004 Apr. 10, 2004
Amira Haroun	Deputy adjutant, Women's Affairs Ministry–Gaza	1	Jan. 28, 2018 (in addition to interviews listed above at WAD)
Al-Huda	Islamic charitable society	2	July 2, 2001

(Continued from previous page)

Organization/ Individual	Description	Number of Interviewees	Dates
Inter-Ministerial Committee for the Advancement of Women's Status (IMCAW)	Inter-ministerial gender unit	6	Oct. 3, 2000 Apr. 8, 2001 Apr. 16, 2001 May 6, 2001 Dec. 29, 2002
Islamic Bloc, Birzeit University	Activists in the Islamic students bloc	2	Dec. 18, 2002 Dec. 20, 2002
Al-Khansaa	Islamic charitable society	2	Jan. 11, 2003 Mar. 12, 2004
Ministry of Planning and International Cooperation (MOPIC)	PA ministry	2	Nov. 7, 2000 Apr. 16, 2001
Ministry of Youth and Sports	PA ministry	4	Apr. 12, 2001 Apr. 14, 2001
National Guidance	PLO-affiliated youth organization	2	Mar. 20, 2001
Palestinian Federation of Women's Action Committees (PFWAC)	Grassroots women's organization	4	Nov. 7, 2000 Apr. 28, 2001 May 6, 2001 Dec. 29, 2002
United Nations Development Fund for Women (UNIFEM)	UN women's development agency	1	June 25, 2001

(Continued from previous page)

Organization/ Individual	Description	Number of Interviewees	Dates
Women's Action Department (WAD)	Islamist women's organ in the Salvation Party	5	Oct. 1, 2000 Oct. 2, 2000 Oct. 3, 2000 Mar. 2, 2004 Apr. 30, 2004
Women's Affairs Technical Committee (WATC)	Women's coalition	4	Oct. 1, 2000 Oct. 3, 2000 Oct. 10, 2000 June 20, 2001 July 3, 2001
Women's Center for Legal Aid and Counseling (WCLAC)	Women's NGO	10	Sept. 29, 2000 Oct. 1, 2000 Apr. 2, 2001 Apr. 28, 2001 May 6, 2001 May 12, 2001 July 3, 2001 Feb. 12, 2002 Jan. 12, 2003
Women's Social Work Committees (WSWC)	Fateh women's organization	4	July 3, 2001 July 11, 2001 Dec. 22, 2002

All of the interviews were conducted and taped by the author. The actual names of some of the interviewees appear in the text, while others remain anonymous at their request. Many of the interviewees are active in more than one organization and some asked that their affiliations be kept confidential.

Glossary

I HAVE GENERALLY FOLLOWED the transliteration system of the *International Journal of Middle East Studies*, with exceptions such as the names and other transliterated words that appear as cited in Western-language sources. All translations are mine unless otherwise stated.

'abah. cloak
adab shar'eyya. religious norms
'aqa'edi. religious
'aqidat al-umma. the nation's beliefs
'assrana. modernization
awqaf. Islamic trusts or religious endowments (see *waqf*)
Ba'th Party. Renovation Party (pan-Arab secular party)
al-souwari. model parliament
al-da'wa. proselytizing
da'aya lal-fikra. publicity for the idea (i.e., the idea of the Islamization of society)
da'erat al-'amal al-nissa'i. Women's Action Department
damj. integration
dar al-fatwa. religious edict council
dawlat al-khilafa. the Islamic Caliphate that collapsed with Ottoman rule
dawrat. workshops
doross deneyya. religious courses
'eitikaf. withdrawal from societal activities to spend nights praying in mosques
fellaheen. peasants
fakk al-irtibat. disengagement
Falastine *al-Moslema.* Islamic Palestine

fatwa, fatawa. edict, edicts

al-hay'a al-idariya. local executive

halat istebdad. a state of tyranny or despotism

hamulas. leading patrilineages

hay'a 'amma. general assembly

heiba. respect

himaya. guidance and protection

i'lam. media committee

idaret sho'oun al-'asha'er. Directorate of Tribal Affairs

i'dad kader. cadre formation

ifrat. chaos

al-ijma' al-watani. the national consensus

ijtihad. independent intellectual investigation of religious texts

intilaq. flourish

al-Islam karram al-mar'a. Islam honors women

al-Isra' wal-Mi'raj. place of the ascension of the Prophet Mohammed to heaven / place of the Prophet's ascension

istikhbarat wa rad'. intelligence and preemption

al-jam'eya al-islameyya. Islamic society

jelbab. robes

jihad. holy war

kata'eb shuhada' al-aqsa. al-Aqsa Martyrs Brigades

kefah mossallah. armed struggle

al-khayr. good

kolokom ra'i wa kolokom mass'olon 'an ra'iyatehe. you are all guardians, and you are responsible for your own subjects

kotal islameyya. Islamic blocs (electoral lists)

al-kotla al-mostaqilla. independent bloc in Al-Najah University

kotlet al-'amal al-tolabi. students' work bloc (in Birzeit University)

lajnat talebat. female student committee

lejan al-islah. reconciliation committees

libass islami. Islamic dress (*jelbab* and headscarves)

al-madd al-islami. Islamic resurgence

madrassa tahfiz al-Qur'an. Quranic school

mahrajan al-mar'a al-moslema. Festival of the Muslim Woman

majlis al-shura. advisory or consultative assembly or council

makateb. offices

al-maktab al-seyassi. politburo

man'. prohibitions

maqassed al-shar'. goals of *shari'a*

markaz ta'heel al-fatat al-moslema. Center for the Rehabilitation of the Muslim Girl

modeera. director (f.)

mofawada wa daght. negotiation and lobby committee

mohram. guardian

al-mojama' al-islami. the Islamic compound

moltazema. veiled

monadel bel-haqiba. jet-setting militants

monazzamat jamahereyya. mass-based organizations

mossabaqat hifz al-Qur'an. Quranic recital competitions

mostad'afeen. oppressed

motafarreghat. full-time paid members

mujahedeen. holy fighters

al-multaqa al-nassawi. women's encounter

murshed. chairman

mythaq haraket al-moqawama al-islameyya. Hamas Charter

mythaq sharaf. covenant of honor

nafaqa. custody

nahda. uplifting

nakba. catastrophe

nassawi. feminist

al-nissa' shaqa'eq al-rijal. women are sisters to men

'ossr. hard to follow

qadi al-qudat. religious supreme judge

qanon wad'i. civil legislation

qawamat al-rajol. responsibility of man's headship

qewama. men's dominance

qodorateha wa khossosseyateha. women's capabilities and characteristics

rafiqa. comrade

ressalat al-umoma. the message of motherhood

roh al-'assr. spirit of the age

al-sahwa al-islameya. Islamic revival

saraya al-qodus. Jerusalem armies of Islamic Jihad

shahada. Islamic profession of faith

shari'a. Islamic family law

shari'a and *ossol al-din*. sources of religion

shatat. dispersal

shaykhs. local chieftains

shorakaa'. all members of the family participate in their own way as part of the family's management

al-shoura. consultation or deliberation

shuyukh al-nawahi. district tax collectors

sumud. steadfastness (policy)

sunna. the Prophet's deeds

ta'lim. education

tafsir. interpretation

al-tahrir tariq al-wehda. liberation is the path to unity

tajhil. maintaining ignorance

tarbeya wa da'awa. education and preaching

tariq al-salam. peace path

tatarrof. extremism

tathqif seyassi. political socialization

al-tawassol wal-taf'eel. linkage and mobilization

thakala. orphans' mothers

thub. traditional peasant woman's dress

ukhot. sister

'ulama'. religious clergy

umma. community of Islamic believers

uttor jamahereyya. popular mass organizations

wa-a'eddu. make ready

waqf. Islamic trust or religious endowment

wasseya, *wassaya*. testimony, testimonies

wathiqat al-mar'a. Women's Charter

al-wehda tariq al-tahrir. unity is the path to liberation

yassos. administer

yosser. easygoing

youm derassi. one-day workshop

zakat. Islamic alms

References

Primary Sources

Al-Botmeh, Reem. 2012. "A Review of Palestinian Legislation from a Women's Rights Perspective." Jerusalem: UNDP Rule of Law and Access to Justice Programme. http://www.ps.undp.org/content/dam/papp/docs /Publications/UNDP-papp-research-Legislative%20english.pdf.

ESCWA (Economic and Social Commission for Western Asia). 2009. "Palestinian National Report." Unpublished report prepared by the expert group meeting for the 15-year review of the Beijing Conference (Beijing + 15), Beirut, October 19–20.

Great Britain. Colonial Office. 1946. *The System of Education of the Jewish Community in Palestine: Report of the Commission of Enquiry Appointed by the Secretary of State for the Colonies in 1945*. London: H.M.S.O.

Great Britain. Palestine Royal Commission. 1937. *Report*. London: H.M.S.O.

GUPW (General Union of Palestinian Women). 1994. "Mossawwada Wathiqa Mabadi' Hoqoqeya Nassaweya" [Draft Document of Principles of Women's Rights], Jerusalem.

Hamas (Islamic Resistance Movement). 1988. "Charter of the Islamic Resistance Movement (Hamas) of Palestine," translated from Arabic by Muhammad Maqdsi. *Journal of Palestine Studies* 22.88: 122–34.

———. 1996. "The Practices of the Self-rule Authority against Palestinian Civil Society" [Momarasat sultat al hukm al zati ded al mojtama' al madani al falastini]. Document distributed by Hamas on May 20, 1996.

———. n.d. (ca. 1990). *Watha'eq Haraket al-Moqawama al-Islameyya* [Documents of the Islamic Resistance Movement]. N.p.: Al-Maktab al-I'lami lil-Haraka (Movement's Information Office).

Al-Haq. 1995. *Al-Mar'a wal-'Adala wal-Qanon: Nahwa Taqweyat al-Mar'a al-Falastineyya* [Woman, Justice, and Law: Toward the Empowerment of Palestinian Woman]. Ramallah: Al-Haq.

Al-Huda Association. 1998. *Al-Mar'a al-Falastineyya wa Mo'amarat al-'Almaneyyat* [Palestinian Woman and the Plot of Secular Women]. Al-Bireh: Al-Huda Association.

INSP (Islamic National Salvation Party). 1995. "Primary Statement of the Islamic National Salvation Party" [Al e'lan al awali lihizb al khalas al watani al islami], December 11.

Institute for Palestine Studies. 1993. *The Palestinian-Israeli Peace Agreement: A Documentary Record.* Washington, DC: Institute for Palestine Studies.

JMCC (Jerusalem Media and Communication Center). 2000a. "Report," February 23.

———. 2000b. "Report," May 24.

———. 2000c. "Report," June 14.

Lesch, Ann Mosley. 1992. *Transition to Palestinian Self-Government: Practical Steps toward Israeli-Palestinian Peace.* Cambridge, MA: American Academy of Arts and Sciences.

MDG-F (MDG Achievement Fund). 2013. "Final Narrative Report, Occupied Palestinian Territories. Joint Programme Title: Gender Equality—Social, Political and Economic in the oPt." MDG-F. March 2013. www .mdgfund.org/sites/default/files/Palestinian%20Territory%20-%20 Gender%20-%20Final%20Narrative%20Report.pdf.

MIFTAH (Palestinian Initiative for the Promotion of Global Dialogue and Democracy). 2006. "Women in Peace and Negotiation," Women's Political Forum, third meeting. Minutes taken by the author, MIFTAH office, Ramallah, February 26.

Ministry of Women's Affairs. 2004. "Strategic Vision and a Plan of Action" (in Arabic). Ramallah, March.

———. 2010. "Action Plan" (in Arabic). Gaza.

———. 2017. "Partners in Construction: Intersectoral National Strategic Plan to Enhance Gender Justice, Equality, and Empowerment" (in Arabic). Ramallah.

———. 2018. "Goals" (in Arabic). Gaza. Accessed February 20, 2018. www.mowa.gov.ps/mowa1/gov/index.php. Gaza.

MOPIC (Ministry of Planning and International Cooperation). 1995. "Palestinian Development Plan for 1996–1998." Ramallah: MOPIC.

———. 1998. "Palestinian Development Plan for 1998–2000." Ramallah: MOPIC.

———. 1999. "Palestinian Development Plan for 1999–2003." Ramallah: MOPIC.

Nass'a (Women for Peace and Justice in Palestine). 2002a. Nass'a Documents, Jerusalem, January.

———. 2002b. Statement. Nass'a Documents, Jerusalem, February.

Palestine. [1946] 1991. *A Survey of Palestine Prepared in December 1945 and January 1946 for the Information of the Anglo-American Committee of Inquiry.* Vol. 2. Reprinted in full for the Institute for Palestine Studies, Washington, DC.

PASSIA (Palestine Academic Society for the Study of International Affairs). 1990. "The West Bank and Gaza Strip, Jerusalem" (in Arabic), Jerusalem.

PCBS (Palestinian Central Bureau of Statistics). 1996. "Census" (in Arabic). Ramallah: PCBS.

———. 1997a. "Census" (in Arabic). Ramallah: PCBS.

———. 1997b. "The Demographic Survey in the West Bank and Gaza: Final Report." Ramallah: PCBS.

———. 1997c. "Labour Force Survey: Main Findings (October 1996–January 1997 Round)." Ramallah: PCBS.

———. 1998. "Demographic Survey." Ramallah: PCBS.

PCBS (Gender Unit). 1998. "Women and Men in Palestine: Trends and Statistics." Ramallah: PCBS.

PCRD (Palestinian Center for Research and Dialogue). 2004. "Opinion Poll," April 22, 2004.

PECDAR (Palestinian Economic Council for Development and Reconstruction). 1997. "UNESCO Report." Jerusalem: PECDAR.

———. 1998. "UNESCO Report." Jerusalem: PECDAR.

———. 1999. "UNESCO Report." Jerusalem: PECDAR.

PENGON (Palestinian Environmental NGOs Network). 2003. *Stop the Wall in Palestine: Facts, Testimonies, Analysis and Call to Action.* Jerusalem: PENGON.

PFWAC (Palestinian Federation of Women's Action Committees). 1988. "The Program and Internal Platform of the Palestinian Federation of Women's Action Committees in the Occupied Territories" (in Arabic), Jerusalem.

PNGD (Political and National Guidance Directorate, Palestinian National Authority). 1988. "Al-Walaa wal-Iltizam" (Belonging and Commitment). Internal document.

PUWAC (Palestinian Union of Women's Action Committees). 1992. "Dawrat al-Demoqrateya wal-Bina'i" [Workshop on Democracy and Construction]. Jerusalem: PUWAC.

PWWC (Palestinian Women's Work Committees). 1985. "Nidal al-Mar'a" [Woman's Struggle]. Jerusalem: PWWC, March.

Qafisha, Moataz. 2000. "A Report on Palestinian Citizenship: Reality, Legal Status and Universal Conventions." Legal Reports Series, no. 15. Ramallah: Palestinian Independent Commission for Citizens' Rights.

Said, Nader Izzat. 2000. "Palestine, Human Development Report 1998–1999." Ramallah: Birzeit University Development Studies Programme.

Sayigh, Yezid, and Khalil Shikaki. 1999. "Strengthening Palestinian Public Institutions." Independent Task Force Report sponsored by the Council on Foreign Relations. Last updated June 25, 1999. https://www.pcpsr.org/sites/default/files/strengtheningpalinstfull.pdf.

Al-Seyassa al-Falastineyya [Palestine Policy] (Nablus). 1996. "Election Day Exit Poll" (in Arabic). Vol. 3, no. 10.

SIDA (Swedish International Development Cooperation Agency). 1999. "Towards Gender Equality in the Palestinian Territories: A Profile on Gender Relations." Prepared by the Women's Studies Center, Birzeit University. Stockholm: SIDA. Accessed July 13, 2018. https://www.sida.se/contentassets/ed5ae8b4b9a64cc2b909f71191b03fb1/13960.pdf.

UNDP (United Nations Development Programme). 1995. Human Development Report 1995. New York: Oxford University Press.

WAD (Women's Action Department). 1997. "Al-Mar'a al-Falastineyya ila Ayna [Palestinian Woman: Where Next]." Proceedings of the workshop and conference sponsored by the Islamic National Salvation Party, Gaza, April 27.

———. 1999. Closing Statement. In Documents of the Second Women's Conference, "Al-Mar'a al-Falastineyya bayna Tahaddeyat al-Waqe' wa Tomohat al-Mostaqbal" [Palestinian Woman between Actual Challenges and Future Aspirations], Gaza, August 16.

WCLAC (Women's Center for Legal Aid and Counseling). 1995. Towards Equality: An Examination of the Status of Palestinian Women in Existing Law. Jerusalem: WCLAC.

————. 1998. Model Parliament Brochure. Jerusalem: WCLAC.

————. 1999. "Annual Report" (in Arabic). Jerusalem: WCLAC.

————. 2000. "Annual Report" (in Arabic). Jerusalem: WCLAC.

————. 2001. "Annual Report" (in Arabic). Jerusalem: WCLAC.

————. n.d. *Al-Barlman al-Falastini al-Souwari, al-Marah wal-Tashri'* [Palestinian Model Parliament, Woman and Legislation]. Jerusalem: WCLAC.

World Bank. 1992. *Governance and Development.* Washington, DC: World Bank.

Arabic-Language Sources*

Abdel-Jawad, Saleh. 1986. "Derassa fi Haraka Fateh" [A Study of the Fateh Movement]. Unpublished ms.

'Abdul Hadi, Maha. 1999. *Waqi'a al-Mar'a fi Falastine: Wejhat Nazar Islameyya* [The Status of Palestinian Women: An Islamic View]. Nablus: Markaz al-Bohoth wal-Derassat al-Falastineyya.

Abu 'Ali, Khadija. 1975. *Moqaddema hawla Waki' al-Mar'a wa Tajrobateha fi al-Thawra al-Falastineyya* [Introduction to Women's Reality and Their Experience in the Palestinian Revolution]. Beirut: General Union of Palestinian Women (GUPW).

Abu 'Amr, Zeyad. 1989. *Al-Haraka al-Islameya fil-Dhaffa al-Gharbiya wa Qita' Ghazza* [The Islamic Movement in the West Bank and the Gaza Strip]. Acre: Dar al-Aswar.

Abul-Omrein, Khaled. 2000. *Hamas: Haraket al-Moqawama al-Islamiya fi Falastine* [Hamas: The Islamic Resistance Movement in Palestine]. Cairo: Marqaz al-Hadara al-'Arabeyya.

Abu Serdana, Mahmoud. n.d. *Al-Qada' al-Shar'i fi 'Ahd al-Sulta al-Wataneyya al-Falastineyya* [The *Shari'a* Judiciary under the Palestinian Authority]. Gaza: Palestinian Authority.

Al-'Amad, Salwa. 1981. "Molahathat hawla Waqi'a al-Mar'a fil-Thawra al-Falastineyya" [Observations on Women's Status in the Palestinian Revolution]. *Sho'oun Falastineyya* [Palestine Affairs] 113: 9–20.

Amin, Samir. 1989. "Al-Ijtihad wal-Ibda' fil-Thakafa al-'Arabeyya, wa amam Tahaddeyat al-'Assr" [Interpretation and Creativity in the Arabic Culture

* All translations from Arabic are my own, unless otherwise stated.

in the Face of Contemporary Challenges]. In *Al-Din fil-Mojtama' al-'Arabi* [Religion in Arab Society]. Beirut: Markaz Derassat al-Wehda al-'Arabeyya.

'Awwad, Saleh. 1989. *Al-Intifada, al-Thawra, Derassat al-Dakhel* [The Intifada, the Revolution: Study of the Interior]. Tunis: Al-Zaytouna.

Al-Azem, Sadeq Jalal. 2004. "Hamlet wal-Hadatha" [Hamlet and Modernity]. Paper presented at the conference on "Al-Hadatha wal-Hadatha al-'Arabeyya" [Modernity and Arab Modernity], held at the Markaz al-Derassat wal-Abhath al-'Almaneyya fil-'Alam al-'Arabi [Secular Studies and Research Center in the Arabic World].

Al-Azmeh, Aziz. 1992. *Al-Ilmaniyya min Manzur Mukhtalif* [Secularism from a Different Perspective]. Beirut: Markaz Derassat al-Wehda al-'Arabeyya.

Al-Bargouthi, Iyad. 2000. *Al-Islam al-Seyassi fi Falastine: Ma wara al-Seyassa* [Political Islam in Palestine: Beyond Politics]. Jerusalem: Jerusalem Media and Communication Center (JMCC).

Al-Ghounimi, Zeinab. 1981. "Halaqa Derasseya hawla Awda' al-Mar'a al-Falastineyya" [Workshop on the Status of Palestinian Women]. *Sho'oun Falastineyya* [Palestine Affairs] 114: 123–28.

Al-Khalili, Ghazi. 1977. *Al-Mar'a al-Falastineyya wal-Thawra* [Palestinian Women and the Revolution]. Beirut: Markaz al-Abhath wal-Derassat al-Falastineyya.

Al-Madhoun, Rib'ie. 1987. "The Islamic Movement in Palestine, 1928–1987." *Sho'oun Falastineyya* [Palestine Affairs] 178.

Al-Salehi, Bassam. 1993. *Al-Za'ama al-Seyasseyya wal-Deneyya fil-Ard al-Mohtalla: Waqe'ha wa Tatawworha* [The Political and Religious Elite in the Occupied Territories: Reality and Evolution]. Jerusalem: Dar al-Quds lil-Nashr.

Al-Taher, Labib. 1992. "Hal al-Dimoqrateya Matlab Ijtima'i?" [Is Democracy a Social Demand?]. In *Al-Mojtama' al-Madani wa Dawruh fi Tahqiq al-Dimoqrateya* [Civil Society and Its Role in Realizing Democracy], edited by S. al-Alwai. Beirut: Markaz Derassat al-Wehda al-'Arabeyya.

Al-Taheri, Nur al-Din. 1995. *Hamas: Haraket al-Moqawama al-Islameyya fi Falastine* [Hamas: The Islamic Resistance Movement in Palestine]. Casablanca: Dar al-Itissam.

Bardaweel, Salah. 1997. "Al-Mar'a al-Falastineyya ila Ayna" [Palestinian Woman: Where Next?]. Paper presented at the workshop on Al-Mar'a al-Falastineyya ila Ayna, organized by the Women's Action Department of the Islamic National Salvation Party, Gaza, April 24.

Barghouti, Mustafa. 2000. "Mostaqbal al-Harakat al-Ijtima'iya wal-Siyasseya fi Falastine" [The Future of Social and Political Movements in Palestine]. *Al-Ayyam* (Ramallah), April 8, 2000.

Beydoun, Aza S. 2002. *Nissa' wa Jam'eyat: Libnaneyat bayna Insaf al-That wa Khedmat al-Ghayr* [Women and Societies: Lebanese Women between Self-assertion and Caring for Others]. Beirut: Dar al-Nahar.

Bishara, Azmi. 1996. *Mossahama fi-Naqd al-Mojtama' al-Madani* [A Contribution to the Critique of Civil Society]. Ramallah: Muwatin.

Budeiri, Musa. 1995. "Al falastinioun bayn al haweya al watania wal haweya al diniya" [Palestinians between National Identity and Religious Identity]. *Majallat al-Derassat al-Falastineyya* 21, no. 6: 3–26.

Elmessiri, Abdel-Wahab. 1997. "Ma'alim al-Khittab al-Islami al-Jadid" [Features of the New Islamic Discourse]. In *Al-Shar'ia al-Seyasseya fil-Islam* [Political Legitimacy in Islam], edited by Azzam Tamimi. London: Liberty for Muslim World Publications.

Al-Hamad, Jawad, and Iyad al-Bargouthi. 1997. *Derassa fi Fikr al-Seyassi li-Haraket al-Moqawama al-Islameyya (Hamas), 1987–1996* [A Study in the Political Ideology of the Islamic Resistance Movement (Hamas)]. Amman: Middle East Study Center.

Hilal, Jamil. 1998. *Al-Nezam al-Seyassi al-Falastini ba'd Oslo* [The Palestinian Political System after Oslo]. Ramallah: Muwatin (Palestinian Institute for the Study of Democracy).

———. 1999. *Al-Mojtama' al-Falastini wa Ishkaleyat al-Dimoqrateya* [Palestinian Society and Democracy Problems). Nablus: Center for Palestine Research and Studies.

Hilal, Jamil, and Majdi al-Malki. 1997. *Nezam al-Takaful al-Ijtima'i Ghayr al-Rasmi. Ghayr al-Mum'assas. Fil-Daffa al-Gharbiya wa Qita' Ghazza* [Informal Social Support System (Non-institutionalized) in the West Bank and Gaza Strip]. Ramallah: Palestine Economic Policy Research Institute (MAS).

Hroub, Khaled. 1996. *Hamas: Al-Fekr wal-Momarassa al-Seyasseya* [Hamas: Ideology and Political Practice]. Beirut: Institute for Palestine Studies.

Ibrahim, Fathi. 1989. *Al-Manhaj, Moqaddema hawla Markazeyat Falastine* [The Approach: An Introduction to the Centrality of Palestine]. Beirut: Dar al-Fikr al-Arabi.

Ibrahim, Sa'd al-Din, or Saad Eddin, ed. 1993. *Al-Mojtama' al-Madani wal-Tahawwol al-Dimoqrati fil-Watan al-'Arabi* [Civil Society and Democratic Transformation in the Arab World]. Cairo: Markaz Ibn Khaldoun.

Jad, Islah. 1991. "Tatawwur al-Dawr al-Seyassi lil-Mar'a al-Falastineyya hatta al-Intifada" [Evolution of the Political Role of Palestinian Woman in the Intifada]. Parts 1 and 2. *Sho'oun al-Mar'a*, May 1991: 94–107; January 1992: 75–83.

———. 1996. "Al-Haraka al-Nassaweya al-Falastineyya wal-Intikhabat al- Tashri'eya" [The Palestinian Women's Movement and the Legislative Elections]. *Al-Seyassa al-Falastineyya* [Palestinian Policy] 3.10: 19–40.

———. 2000. *Palestinian Women: A Status Report-Women and Politics.* Birzeit: Birzeit University, Women's Studies Institute.

Jad, Islah, George Giacaman, Hadeel Qazaz, and Ahmed al-Khalidi. 2003. "Qira'a Nassaweya le-Mosswaddat al-Dosstor al-Falastini" [A Feminist Reading of the Draft of the Palestinian Constitution]. *Review of Women's Studies* (Birzeit University) 1.1: 8–12.

Kanafani, Ghassan. 1972. *The 1936–1939 Revolt in Palestine: Background and Details.* New York: Committee for a Democratic Palestine.

Kayed, Aziz. 1999. *Taqrir hawl Tadakhol al-Salaheyat fi Mo'assassat al-Solta al-Wataneyya al-Falastineyya* [A Report on the Overlapping of Authority in the Palestinian National Authority]. Ramallah: Palestinian Independent Commission for Citizens' Rights.

———. 2000. *Taqrir hawla Ishkaleyat al-'Ilaqa bayna al-Soltatayen al-Tashri'eya wal-Tanfizeya fil-Solta al-Wataneya al-Falastineyya* [Report on the Problematic Relationship between the Legislative and the Executive in the Palestinian Authority]. Ramallah: Palestinian Independent Commission for Citizens' Rights.

Khartabil, Wadi'a. 1995. *Bahthan 'an al-Amal wal-Watan* [In Search of Hope and Homeland]. Beirut: Bissan.

'Othman, Zeyad. 1998. "Al-Barlman al-Souwari, al-Mar'a wal-Tashri' bayna al-Tajdeed wal-Qawlaba" [The Model Parliament: Women and Legislation between Renewal and Preservation]. *Al-Seyassa al-Falastineyya* [Palestinian Policy] 19: 57–85.

Sayigh, Yezid. 1987. *Al-Urdon wal-Falastiniyon* [Jordan and the Palestinians]. London: Riad El-Rayyes Books.

Shafiq, Mounir. 1977. "Mawdo'at hawla Nidal al-Mar'a" [Issues of Women's Struggle]. *Sho'oun Falastineyya* [Palestine Affairs] 62: 200–227.

Shalabi, Yasser. 2001. "Al-Ta'thirat al-Dawleya 'ala Tahdid Ro'aa al-Monazzamat Ghayr al-Hokomeyya al-Falastineyya wa-Adwareha" [International and Local Impacts on the Visions and Roles of Palestinian NGOs]. MA thesis, Birzeit University, Palestine.

Al-Shu'aibi, 'Issa. 1986. *Al-Kayaneyya al-Falastineyya: Al-Wa'i al-Dhati wal-Tatawwor al-Mo'assassati, 1947–1977* [Palestinian Statism: Entity, Consciousness, and Institutional Development, 1947–1977]. Beirut: Palestine Liberation Organization Research Center.

Zu'aytir, Akram. 1980. *Yawmiyyat Akram Zu'aytir: Al-Haraka al-Wataneyya al-Falastineyya 1935–1939* [Diary of Akram Zu'aytir: The Palestinian National Movement, 1935–1939]. Beirut: Palestine Studies Association.

Secondary Sources

Ababneh, Sara. 2014. "The Palestinian Women's Movements versus Hamas: Attempting to Understand Women's Empowerment outside a Feminist Frame." *Journal of International Women's Studies* 15, no. 1: 35–53.

'Abd al-Hadi, Mahdi. 1988. "The Jordanian Disengagement: Causes and Effects" (in Arabic and English). Jerusalem: Palestinian Academic Society for the Study of International Affairs (PASSIA).

Abdel-Jawad, Saleh. 1998. "Sociocide: War by Other Means." *Al-Ahram Weekly* (Cairo), December 31, 1998. http://weekly.ahram.org.eg/Archive /1998/1948/359_salh.htm.

———. 2003. "The Role of Foreign Forces in Formulating and Promoting Palestinian Elites" (in French). Paper presented to post-graduate students in the History Department, University of Paris II, April 29.

———. 2006. "The Arab and Palestinian Narratives of the 1948 War." In *Israeli and Palestinian Narratives of Conflict: History's Double Helix*, edited by Robert I. Rotberg, 72–114. Bloomington: Indiana Univ. Press.

———. n.d. "Roots of the Civil Resistance Movement in the West Bank." Unpublished paper.

Abu Amr, Ziad. 1994. *Islamic Fundamentalism in the West Bank and Gaza*. Bloomington: Indiana Univ. Press.

Abu Farha, 'Abdel Rahman. 2004. "On Women Suicide Bombers" (in Arabic). Palestine-Info Gaza, January 28, 2004.

Abu-Ghayth, Gayth. 2004. "Al-Qanon al-Falastini wal-Qada bel-'Orf" [Palestinian Law and Customary Rules]. Paper presented at "Nahwa Qanon Falastini Muwahhad" [Toward a Palestinian Unified Law], a workshop organized by the Palestinian Information Center, Gaza, January 15.

Abul-Haija, Ibrahim. 2000. "Al-Mar'a al-Falastineyya—Waqa'a wa 'Afaq: Al-Mashrou' al-Tahriri al-Islami" [The Palestinian Woman—Facts and Prospects: The Islamic Liberation Project]. Paper presented at the Third Women's Conference, "Al-Mar'a al-Falastineyya wal-Tahawlat al-Ijtima'iya" [Palestinian Woman and Social Change], Gaza, August 8–9.

Abu-Lughod, Janet. 1987. "The Demographic Transformation of Palestine." In *The Transformation of Palestine*, edited by Ibrahim Abu-Lughod, 139–64. Evanston, IL: Northwestern Univ. Press.

Abu-Lughod, Lila. 1998. *Remaking Women: Feminism and Modernity in the Middle East*. Princeton, NJ: Princeton Univ. Press.

———. 2013. *Do Muslim Women Need Saving?* Cambridge: Harvard Univ. Press.

Abu Musa, Khitam. 1997. "Al-Mar'a fil-Tasawwour al-Islami" [Women in Islamic Thought]. Paper presented at the workshop on Al-Mar'a al-Falastineyya ila Ayna [Palestinian Woman: Where Next?], organized by the Women's Action Department of the Islamic National Salvation Party, Gaza, April 24.

Afkhami, Mahnaz. 1994. "Women in Post-Revolutionary Iran: A Feminist Perspective." In *In the Eye of the Storm: Women in Post-Revolutionary Iran*, edited by Mahnaz Afkhami and Erika Friedle, 131–50. Syracuse, NY: Syracuse Univ. Press.

———. 1995. "Introduction." In *Faith and Freedom: Women's Human Rights in the Muslim World*, edited by Mahnaz Afkhami, 1–16. London: I. B. Tauris.

Afkhami, Mahnaz, and Erika Friedl, eds. 1997. *Muslim Women and the Politics of Participation: Implementing the Beijing Platform*. Syracuse, NY: Syracuse Univ. Press.

Afshar, Haleh. 1985. "Women, State and Ideology in Iran." *Third World Quarterly* 7.2: 256–78.

———. 1994. "Why Fundamentalism? Iranian Women and Their Support for Islam." University of York Department of Politics Working Paper no. 2.

———. 1998. *Islam and Feminisms: An Iranian Case-Study.* Basingstoke: Macmillan.

Afshar, Haleh, and Carolyne Dennis, eds. 1992. *Women and Adjustment Policies in the Third World.* Basingstoke: Macmillan.

Agarwal, Bina. 1994. *A Field of One's Own: Gender and Land Rights in South Asia.* Cambridge: Cambridge Univ. Press.

———. 1997. "Bargaining and Gender Relations: Within and Beyond the Household." *Feminist Economics* 2.1: 1–50.

Ahmed, Leila. 1982. "Feminism and Feminist Movements in the Middle East, a Preliminary Exploration: Turkey, Egypt, Algeria, People's Democratic Republic of Yemen." Women's Studies International Forum 5, no. 2 (1982): pp. 153–68.

———. 1992. *Women and Gender in Islam: Historical Roots of a Modern Debate.* New Haven, CT: Yale Univ. Press.

Alexander, Jacqui. 1991. "Redrafting Morality: The Postcolonial State and the Sexual Offences Bill of Trinidad and Tobago." In *Third World Women and the Politics of Feminism*, edited by Chandra T. Mohanty, Ann Russo, and Lourdes Torres, 133–52. Bloomington: Indiana Univ. Press.

Al-Ali, Nadje Sadig. 1998. *Standing on Shifting Ground: Women's Activism in Contemporary Egypt.* PhD diss., University of London.

Alvarez, Sonia. 1989. "Women's Movements and Gender Politics in the Brazilian Transition." In *The Women's Movement in Latin America: Feminism and the Transition to Democracy*, edited by Jane S. Jaquette, 13–64. Boston: Unwin Hyman.

———. 1990. *Engendering Democracy in Brazil: Women's Movements in Transition Politics.* Princeton, NJ: Princeton Univ. Press.

Amawi, Abla. 2000. "Gender and Citizenship in Jordan." In *Gender and Citizenship in the Middle East*, edited by Suad Joseph, 158–84. Syracuse, NY: Syracuse Univ. Press.

Anderson, Benedict. 1983. *Imagined Communities: Reflections on the Origin and Spread of Nationalism.* London: Verso.

Anthias, Floya, and Nira Yuval-Davis. 1989. "Introduction." In *Woman-Nation-State*, edited by Floya Anthias and Nira Yuval-Davis, 1–15. Basingstoke and London: Macmillan.

Antonius, George. 1946. *The Arab Awakening: The Story of the Arab National Movement.* New York: Capricorn Books.

Anwar, Zainah. 2009. *Wanted: Equality and Justice in the Muslim Family*. Selangor: Musawah.

Aruri, Naseer, ed. 1989. *Occupation: Israel over Palestine*. 2d ed. Belmont, MA: AAUG Press.

Asad, Talal. 2003. *Formation of the Secular: Christianity, Islam, Modernity*. Stanford, CA: Stanford Univ. Press.

Ayubi, Nazih. 1991. *Political Islam: Religion and Politics in the Arab World*. London: Routledge.

——. 1995. *Over-Stating the Arab State: Politics and Society in the Middle East*. London: I. B. Tauris.

Al-Azem, Sadeq Jalal. 1995. "Dimensions of Palestinian Politics." *Journal of Palestine Studies* 27.1: 23–36.

Al-Azmeh, Aziz. 1988. "Arab Nationalism and Islamism." *Review of Middle East Studies* 4: 33–51.

——. 1993. "Islamism and the Arabs." Chapter 1 in *Islams and Modernities*. London and New York: Verso.

——. 1996. *Islams and Modernities*. 2d ed. London and New York: Verso.

Baden, Sally, and Anne Marie Goetz. 1998. "Who Needs [Sex] When You Can Have [Gender]? Conflicting Discourses on Gender at Beijing." In *Feminist Visions of Development: Gender, Analysis and Policy*, edited by Cecile Jackson and Ruth Pearson, 18–37. London: Routledge.

Badie, Bertrand. 1986. "'State,' Legitimacy and Protest in Islamic Culture." In *The State in Global Perspective*, edited by Ali Kazancigil, 250–65. Aldershot, UK and VT/Paris: Gower/Unesco.

Badran, Margot. 1994. "Gender Activism: Feminists and Islamists in Egypt." In *Identity Politics and Women: Cultural Reassertions and Feminisms in International Perspective*, edited by Valentine M. Moghadam, 202–27. Boulder, CO: Westview Press.

——. 1995. *Feminists, Islam, and Nation: Gender and the Making of Modern Egypt*. Princeton, NJ: Princeton Univ. Press.

Barghouti, Mustafa. 1994. "Monazzamat al-Mojtama' al-Madani wa Dawreha fil-Marhala al-Moqbela" [Civil Society Organizations and Their Role in the Coming Era]. Paper presented at the Conference on The Future of Palestinian Civil Society, Birzeit University, May 13–15.

——. 2002. "Istratejeya Bina' al-Dawla al-Falastineyya al-Mostaqilla" [A Strategy for Building the Independent Palestinian State]. Paper presented at the Civil Society Coalition Conference on Reform and Reconstruction, Ramallah, November 26.

Baron, Beth. 1994. *The Women's Awakening in Egypt: Culture, Society and the Press*. New Haven, CT: Yale Univ. Press.

———. 1996. "Silence on Attacks on Women by Fundamentalists." *Contention* 5.3: 99–117.

Beck, Lois, and Nikki Keddie, eds. 1978. *Women in the Muslim World*. Cambridge: Harvard Univ. Press.

Beckman, Bjorn. 1998. "The Liberation of Civil Society: Neo-liberal Ideology and Political Theory in an African Context." In *People's Rights: Social Movements and the State in the Third World*, edited by Manoranjan Mohanty and Partha N. Mukherji. New Delhi and London: Sage.

Be'er, Yizhar, and Saleh Abdel-Jawad. 1994. *Collaborators in the Occupied Territories: Human Rights Abuses and Violations*. Jerusalem: B'tselem (Israeli Information Center for Human Rights in the Occupied Territories).

Beinin, Joel, and Joe Stork, eds. 1997. *Political Islam: Essays from Middle East Report*. Berkeley: University of California Press.

Beinin, Joel, and Frédéric Vairel, eds. 2011. *Social Movements, Mobilization, and Contestation in the Middle East and North Africa*. Stanford, CA: Stanford Univ. Press.

Benhabib, Seyla. 1999. "'Nous' et 'les Autres.'" In *Multicultural Questions*, edited by Christian Joppke and Steven Lukes. Oxford: Oxford Univ. Press. https://global.oup.com/academic/product/multicultural-questions -9780198296102?cc=us&lang=en&#.

Benvenisti, Meron. 1986. *Report: Demographic, Economic, Legal, Social and Political Development in the West Bank*. Jerusalem: West Bank Data Base Project.

———. 2000. *Sacred Landscape: The Buried History of the Holy Land since 1948*. Berkeley: University of California Press.

Bhabha, Homi. 1990. *Nation and Narration*. New York: Routledge.

Bill, James A., and Robert Springborg. 1990. *Politics in the Middle East*. 3d ed. New York: HarperCollins.

Binder, Leonard. 1988. *Islamic Liberalism: A Critique of Development Ideologies*. Chicago: University of Chicago Press.

Bobbio, Norberto. 1987. "Gramsci and the Concept of Civil Society." In *Which Socialism?*, translated by Roger Griffin, edited and introduced by Richard Bellamy. Cambridge, UK: Polity Press.

Bodman, Herbert, and Nayereh Tohidi, eds. 1998. *Women in Muslim Societies: Diversity within Unity.* Boulder, CO: Lynne Rienner Publishers.

Boggs, Carl. 1976. *Gramsci's Marxism.* London: Pluto Press.

Bourdieu, Pierre. 1977. *Outline of a Theory of Practice.* Translated by Richard Nice. Cambridge: Cambridge Univ. Press.

Brand, Laurie. 1988. *Palestinians in the Arab World: Institution Building and the Search for State.* New York: Columbia Univ. Press.

———. 1998. "Women and the State in Jordan: Inclusion or Exclusion?" In *Islam, Gender, and Social Change*, edited by Yvonne Haddad and John Esposito, 100–123. Oxford: Oxford Univ. Press.

Bratton, Michael, and Nicolas van de Walle. 1997. *Democratic Experiments in Africa: Regime Transitions in Comparative Perspective.* Cambridge: Cambridge Univ. Press.

Brown, Karen MacCarthy. 1994. "Fundamentalism and the Control of Women." In *Fundamentalism and Gender*, edited by John Stratton Hawley, 175–202. Oxford: Oxford Univ. Press.

Brynen, Rex. 1995. "The Neopatrimonial Dimension of Palestinian Politics." *Journal of Palestine Studies* 25.1: 23–36.

———. 2000. *A Very Political Economy: Peacebuilding and Foreign Aid in the West Bank and Gaza.* Washington, DC: United States Institute of Peace Press.

Budeiri, Musa. 1979. *The Palestine Communist Party, 1919–1948: Arab and Jew in the Struggle for Internationalism.* London: Ithaca Press.

———. 1994. "The Palestinians: Tensions between Nationalist and Religious Identities: An Attempt at Interpretation." Paper prepared for the workshop on Rethinking Nationalism in the Arab World, University of Colorado, Boulder, September 21–24.

———. 1995. "The Nationalist Dimension of Islamic Movements in Palestinian Politics." *Journal of Palestine Studies* 24.3: 194–208.

———. 2001. "A Chronicle of a Defeat Foretold: The Battle for Jerusalem in the Memoirs of Anwar Nusseibeh." *Jerusalem Quarterly File* 11/12: 40–51.

Burke, Edmund, III. 1988. "Islam and Social Movements: Methodological Reflections." In *Islam, Politics, and Social Movements*, edited by Edmund Burke, III, and Ira Lapidus, 17–36. Berkeley: University of California Press.

Burke, Edmund, III, and Ira Lapidus, eds. 1988. *Islam, Politics, and Social Movements*. Berkeley: University of California Press.

Caldeira, Teresa. 1998. "Justice and Individual Rights: Challenges for Women's Movements and Democratization in Brazil." In *Women and Democracy: Latin America and Central and Eastern Europe*, edited by Jane Jaquette and Sharon Wolchik, 75–103. Baltimore: Johns Hopkins Univ. Press.

Calhoun, Craig. 1993. "Nationalism and Ethnicity." *Annual Review of Sociology* 19: 211–39.

Campo, Juan Eduardo. 1995. "The Ends of Islamic Fundamentalism: Hegemonic Discourse and the Islamic Question in Egypt." *Contention* 4.3: 167–94.

Carapico, Sheila. 2000. "NGOs, INGOs, Go-NGOs and Do-NGOs: Making Sense of Non-Governmental Organizations." *Middle East Report* 30.214: 12–15.

———. 2002. "Foreign Aid and Democratization." *Middle East Journal* 56.3: 379–95.

Carroll, Thomas F. 1992. *Intermediary NGOs: The Supporting Link in Grassroots Development*. West Hartford, CT: Kumarian Press.

Castells, Manuel. 1996–98. *The Information Age: Economy, Society and Culture*. 3 vols. Malden, MA, and Oxford, UK: Blackwell.

Chabbott, Colette. 1999. "Development INGOs." In *Constructing World Culture: International Nongovernmental Organizations since 1875*, edited by John Boli and George Thomas, 222–26. Stanford, CA: Stanford Univ. Press.

Charlesworth, Hilary. 1994. "What Are 'Women's International Human Rights'?" In *Human Rights of Women: National and International Perspectives*, edited by Rebecca J. Cook, 58–84. Philadelphia: University of Pennsylvania Press.

Charlesworth, Hilary, and Christine Chinkin. 2000. *The Boundaries of International Law: A Feminist Analysis*. Manchester: Juris Publishing/ Manchester Univ. Press.

Charlton, Sue Ellen M., Jana Everett, and Kathleen Staudt, eds. 1989. *Women, the State, and Development*. Albany: State University of New York Press.

Charrad, Mounira. 2000. "Lineage versus Individual in Tunisia and Morocco." In *Gender and Citizenship in the Middle East*, edited by Suad Joseph, 70–87. Syracuse, NY: Syracuse Univ. Press.

————. 2001. *States and Women's Rights: The Making of Postcolonial Tunisia, Algeria and Morocco.* Berkeley: University of California Press.

Chatterjee, Partha. 1989. "Colonialism, Nationalism, and Colonized Women: The Contest in India." *American Ethnologist* 16.4: 622–33.

————. 1990. "The Nationalist Resolution of the Women's Question." In *Recasting Women: Essays in Indian Colonial History,* edited by Kumkum Sangari and Sudesh Vaid, 233–53. New Brunswick, NJ: Rutgers Univ. Press.

————. 1993. *The Nation and Its Fragments: Colonial and Postcolonial Histories.* Princeton, NJ: Princeton Univ. Press.

Chatty, Dawn, and Annika Rabo, eds. 1997. *Organizing Women: Formal and Informal Women's Groups in the Middle East.* Oxford and New York: Berg.

Chinchilla, Norma S. 1992. "Marxism, Feminism, and the Struggle for Democracy in Latin America." In *The Making of Social Movements in Latin America: Identity, Strategy and Democracy,* edited by Arturo Escobar and Sonia Alvarez, 37–51. Boulder, CO: Westview Press.

Chowdhry, Prem. 1989. "Customs in a Peasant Economy: Women in Colonial Haryana." In *Recasting Women: Essays in Colonial History,* edited by Kumkum Sangari and Sudesh Vaid, 302–36. New Delhi: Kali for Women.

Clancy-Smith, Julia. 1999. "A Woman without Her Distaff: Gender, Work, and Handicraft Production in Colonial North Africa." In *Social History of Women and Gender in the Modern Middle East,* edited by Margaret Meriwether and Judith Tucker, 25–53. Boulder, CO: Westview Press.

Clapham, Christopher. 1985. *Third World Politics: An Introduction.* Madison: University of Wisconsin Press.

Clarke, Gerard. 1998. *The Politics of NGOs in South-East Asia.* London: Routledge.

Cobban, Helena. 1984. *The Palestinian Liberation Organisation: People, Power, and Politics.* Cambridge: Cambridge Univ. Press.

Cock, Jacklyn. 1989. "Keep the Fires Burning: Militarisation and the Politics of Gender in South Africa." *Review of African Political Economy* 45/46: 50–64.

Cohen, Abner. 1965. *Arab Border-Villages in Israel.* Manchester: University of Manchester Press.

Cohen, Amnon. 1982. *Political Parties in the West Bank under the Jordanian Regime, 1949–1967.* Ithaca, NY: Cornell Univ. Press.

Cole, Juan, and Deniz Kandiyoti. 2002. "Nationalism and the Colonial Legacy in the Middle East and Central Asia: Introduction." *International Journal of Middle East Studies* 34: 189–203.

Coomaraswamy, Radhika. 1994. "To Bellow Like a Cow: Women, Ethnicity, and the Discourse of Rights." In *Human Rights of Women: National and International Perspective*, edited by Rebecca Cook, 39–57. Philadelphia: University of Pennsylvania Press.

Cornwall, Andrea, and Maxine Molyneux, eds. 2008. *The Politics of Rights: Dilemmas for Feminist Praxis.* London and New York: Routledge.

Crone, Patricia. 1980. *Slaves on Horses: The Evolution of the Islamic Polity.* Cambridge: Cambridge Univ. Press.

Dakkak, Ibrahim. 1983. "Back to Square One: A Study in the Re-Emergence of the Palestinian Identity in the West Bank, 1967–1980." In *Palestinians over the Green Line*, edited by Alexander Scholch, 64–101. London: Ithaca Press.

Darwish, Mahmoud. 2002. "A State of Siege," translated by Ramsis Amun. *Arab World Books*, January. http://www.arabworldbooks.com/Literature /poetry4.html.

Davis, Eric. 1987. "The Concept of Revival and the Study of Islam and Politics." In *The Islamic Impulse*, edited by Barbara Stowasser, 37–58. Washington, DC, London, and Sydney: Croom Helm in association with the Center for Contemporary Arab Studies, Georgetown University.

Deen, Thalif. 2003. "Report," *IPS.com*, November 12.

Dekmejian, Hrair. 1988. "Islamic Revival: Catalysts, Categories, and Consequences." In *The Politics of Islamic Revivalism: Diversity and Unity*, edited by Shireen Hunter, 3–22. Bloomington: Indiana Univ. Press.

Diani, Mario. 1992. "The Concept of Social Movement." *Sociological Review* 40: 1–25.

———. 2000. "Networks and Social Movements: From Metaphor to Theory?" Paper presented at the Conference on Social Movement Analysis: The Network Perspective. University of Strathclyde, Glasgow, June 23–25. https://www.scribd.com/document/127624819/Diani-Networks -and-Social-Movements-from-Metaphor-o-Theory.

Diwan, Ishac. 1995. "Will Arab Workers Prosper or Be Left Out in the Twenty-First Century?" Regional Perspectives on World Development Report 1995 Series. Washington, DC: World Bank.

Donohue, John, and John Esposito, eds. 1982. *Islam in Transition: Muslim Perspectives*. New York and Oxford: Oxford Univ. Press.

Eagleton, Terry, and Pierre Bourdieu. 1992. "Doxa and Common Life." *New Left Review* 191 (January–February): 111–21.

Edwards, Michael. 1999. "Legitimacy and Values in NGOs and Voluntary Organisations: Some Sceptical Thoughts." In *Voluntary Action: Reshaping the Third Sector*, edited by David Lewis, 258–67. London: Earthscan Publications.

Edwards, Michael, and Alan Fowler, eds. 2002. *The Earthscan Reader on NGO Management*. London: Earthscan.

Edwards, Michael, and David Hulme. 2002. "Making a Difference: Scaling-up the Developmental Impact of NGOs—Concepts and Experiences." In *The Earthscan Reader on NGO Management*, edited by Michael Edwards and Alan Fowler, 211–16. London: Earthscan.

———, eds. 1992. *Making a Difference: NGOs and Development in a Changing World*. London: Earthscan Publications.

———. 1995. *Non-Governmental Organisations: Performance and Accountability beyond the Magic Bullet*. London: Earthscan.

Eickelman, Dale, and James Piscatori. 1996. *Muslim Politics*. Princeton, NJ: Princeton Univ. Press.

Eisenstadt, Samuel N. 1972. *Traditional Patrimonialism and Modern Neopatrimonialism*. London: Sage.

Eisenstein, Zillah. 1981. *The Radical Future of Liberal Feminism*. New York: Longman.

———. 1988. *The Female Body and the Law*. Berkeley: University of California Press.

———, ed. 1978. *Capitalist Patriarchy and the Case for Socialist Feminism*. New York: Monthly Review Press.

Elmessiri, Abdel-Wahab. 2003. "Towards a New Islamic Discourse: Re-Capturing the Islamic Paradigm." *Islam Online*, July 17. https://archive.islamonline.net/english/Contemporary/2003/07/article04c.shtm.

Enloe, Cynthia. 1988. *Does Khaki Become You? The Militarisation of Women's Lives*. London: Pandora Press.

Escobar, Arturo. 1992. "Culture, Economics, and Politics in Latin American Social Movements Theory and Research." In *The Making of Social Movements in Latin America: Identity, Strategy, and Democracy*, edited by Arturo Escobar and Sonia Alvarez, 62–88. Boulder, CO: Westview Press.

Escobar, Arturo, and Sonia E. Alvarez. 1992. *The Making of Social Movements in Latin America: Identity, Strategy, and Democracy*. Boulder, CO: Westview Press.

Esman, Milton, and Norman Uphoff. 1984. *Local Organizations: Intermediaries in Rural Development*. Ithaca, NY: Cornell Univ. Press.

Esposito, John. 1992. *The Islamic Threat: Myth or Reality?* New York: Oxford Univ. Press.

———, ed. 1983. *Voices of Resurgent Islam*. New York: Oxford Univ. Press.

Etienne, Mona, and Eleanor Leacock, eds. 1980. *Women and Colonization*. New York: Praeger.

Evans, Peter, Dietrich Rueschemeyer, and Theda Skocpol, eds. 1985. *Bringing the State Back*. Cambridge: Cambridge Univ. Press.

Farrington, John, and Anthony Bebbington. 1993. *Reluctant Partners? Non-Governmental Organisations, the State and Sustainable Agricultural Development*. London and New York: Routledge.

Fernea, Elizabeth Warnock. 1998. *In Search of Islamic Feminism*. New York: Doubleday.

———, ed. 1985. *Women and the Family in the Middle East: New Voices of Change*. Austin: University of Texas Press.

Fleischmann, Ellen. 2003. *The Nation and Its "New" Women: The Palestinian Women's Movement, 1920–1948*. Berkeley: University of California Press.

Foucault, Michel. 1980. *Power/Knowledge: Selected Interviews and Other Writings, 1972–1977*, edited by Colin Gordon. New York: Pantheon.

Fowler, Alan, ed. 1997. *Striking a Balance: A Guide to Enhance the Effectiveness of Non-Governmental Organisations in International Development*. London: Earthscan.

Fowler, Alan, with Piers Campbell and Brian Pratt. 1992. *Institutional Development and NGOs in Africa: Policy Perspectives for European Development Agencies*. Oxford, UK: INTRAC.

Fox, Diana Joyce. 1998. *An Ethnography of Four Non-Governmental Development Organizations*. Lewiston, NY: Edwin Mellen Press.

Franzway, Suzanne, Dianne Court, and R. W. Connell. 1989. *Staking a Claim: Feminism, Bureaucracy and the State.* London: Paladin/Allen & Unwin.

Fraser, Nancy. 2000. "Rethinking Recognition." *New Left Review* 3 (May–June): 107–20.

Friedman, Gil. 1999. *The Palestinian Draft Basic Law: Prospects and Potentials.* Jerusalem: Palestinian Independent Commission for Citizens' Rights.

Friedman, John. 1992. *Empowerment: The Politics of Alternative Development.* Oxford: Blackwell.

Geertz, Clifford. 1983. *Local Knowledge: Further Essays in Interpretive Anthropology.* New York: Basic Books.

Gellner, Ernest. 1983. *Nations and Nationalism.* Oxford: Basil Blackwell.

———. 1991. "Civil Society in Historical Context." *International Social Science Journal* 129: 495–510.

———. 1992. *Postmodernism, Reason and Religion.* London: Routledge.

Gershoni, Israel, and James P. Jankowski. 1995. *Redefining the Egyptian Nation: 1930–1945.* Cambridge: Cambridge Univ. Press.

Ghali, Mona. 1997. *Palestinian Women: A Status Report. 6, Education.* Birzeit: Women's Studies Program, Birzeit University.

Al-Ghannouchi, Rachid. 1993. *Muslim Women in Tunisia between Quran Rulings and the Reality of the Tunisian Society* [Al mara' al muslima fi tunis bayna tawjihat al quran wa waqi'a al mojtama' al tunsi]. Dar Al Qalam: Kuwait.

Giacaman, George. 2000. "Popular Movements and Democratic Transformation in Palestine." In *The Palestinian Women's Movement: Problematics of Democratic Transformation and Future Strategies,* edited by Institute of Women's Studies, 45–53. Proceedings of the Fifth Annual Conference, organized by Muwatin, the Palestinian Institute for the Study of Democracy, December 1999. Ramallah: Muwatin Publications.

Giacaman, Rita, Islah Jad, and Penny Johnson. 2000. "Transit Citizens: Gender and Citizenship under the Palestinian Authority." In *Gender and Citizenship in the Middle East,* edited by Suad Joseph, 137–57. Syracuse, NY: Syracuse Univ. Press.

Giacaman, Rita, and Penny Johnson. 1994. "Searching for Strategies: The Palestinian Women's Movement in the New Era." *Middle East Report* 24, no. 186: 22–26.

————. 2001. "Searching for Strategies: The Palestinian Women's Movement in the New Era." In *Women and Power in the Middle East*, edited by Suad Joseph and Susan Slyomovics, 150–58. Philadelphia: University of Pennsylvania Press.

Gibbon, Peter. 1998. "Some Reflections on 'Civil Society' and Political Change." In *Democratization in the Third World*, edited by Lars Rudebeck and Olle Törnquist, with Virgilio Rojas, 23–56. New York: St. Martin's Press.

Giddens, Anthony. 1984. *The Constitution of Society*. Berkeley: University of California Press.

Göçek, Fatma Müge, and Shiva Balaghi, eds. 1994. *Reconstructing Gender in the Middle East*. New York: Columbia Univ. Press.

Goetz, Anne Marie. 1991. "Feminism and the Claim to Know: Contradictions in Feminist Approaches to Women in Development." In *Gender and International Relations*, edited by Rebecca Gran and Kathleen Newland, 134–57. Celtic Court, Buckingham: Open Univ. Press.

————. 1995. "The Politics of Integrating Gender to State Development Processes: Trends, Opportunities and Constraints in Bangladesh, Chile, Jamaica, Mali, Morocco and Uganda." UNRISD/UNDP World Conference on Women (Beijing) Occasional Paper no. 2. Geneva: United Nations Research Institute for Social Development.

————. 1996. "Dis/organising Gender: Women Development Agents in State and NGO Poverty-Reduction Programmes in Bangladesh." In *Women and the State: International Perspectives*, edited by Shirin Rai and Geraldine Lievesley, 118–42. London: Taylor & Francis.

————. 2003. "Women's Political Effectiveness: A Conceptual Framework." In *No Shortcuts to Power: African Women in Politics and Policy Making*, edited by Anne Marie Goetz and Shireen Hassim, 29–80. London and New York: Zed Books.

————, ed. 1997. *Getting Institutions Right for Women in Development*. London and New York: Zed Books.

Goetz, Anne Marie, and Shireen Hassim. 2003. *No Shortcuts to Power: African Women in Politics and Policy Making*. London and New York: Zed Books.

Granqvist, Hilma. 1931–35. *Marriage Conditions in a Palestinian Village*, 2 vols. Helsingfors: Akademische Buchhandlung.

Gresh, Alain. 1988. *The PLO: The Struggle Within*. London: Zed Books.

Habermas, Jurgen. 1993. "Further Reflection on the Public Discourse." In *Habermas and the Public Sphere*, edited by Craig Calhoun, 421–61. Cambridge: MIT Press.

Haddad, Toufic. 2018. *Palestine Ltd.: Neoliberalism and Nationalism in the Occupied Territory*. London: I. B. Tauris.

Haddad, Yvonne. 1980. "Palestinian Women: Patterns of Legitimation and Domination." In *The Sociology of the Palestinians*, edited by Khalil Nakhleh and Elia Zureik, 147–75. London: Croom Helm.

———. 1985. "Islam, Women and Revolution." In *Women, Religion, and Social Change*, edited by Yvonne Yazbeck Haddad and Ellison Banks Findly, 275–306. Albany: State University of New York Press.

Haddad, Yvonne, and John Esposito, eds. 1998. *Islam, Gender, and Social Change*. Oxford: Oxford Univ. Press.

Haeri, Shahla. 1993. "Obedience versus Autonomy: Women and Fundamentalism in Iran and Pakistan." In *Fundamentalisms and Society: Reclaiming the Sciences, the Family, and Education*, vol. 2 of *The Fundamentalism Project*, edited by Martin E. Marty and R. Scott Appleby, 181–213. Chicago: University of Chicago Press.

Haim, Sylvia G., ed. 1962. *Arab Nationalism: An Anthology*. Berkeley: University of California Press.

Al-Haj, Majid. 1987. *Social Change and Family Processes: Arab Communities in Shefar-A'm*. Boulder, CO: Westview Press.

Hale, Sondra. 1993. "Transforming Culture or Fostering Second-Hand Consciousness? Women's Front Organizations and Revolutionary Parties: The Sudan Case." In *Arab Women: Old Boundaries, New Frontiers*, edited by Judith Tucker, 149–74. Bloomington: Indiana Univ. Press.

———. 1994. "Gender, Religious Identity, and Political Mobilizations in Sudan." In *Identity Politics and Women: Cultural Reassertions and Feminism in International Perspective*, edited by Valentine M. Moghadam, 125–46. Boulder, CO: Westview Press.

———. 1997. "The Women of Sudan's National Islamic Front." In *Political Islam: Essays from Middle East Report*, edited by Joel Beinin and Joe Stork, 234–52. Berkeley: University of California Press.

———. 2000. "The Islamic State and Gendered Citizenship in Sudan." In *Gender and Citizenship in the Middle East*, edited by Suad Joseph, 88–106. Syracuse, NY: Syracuse Univ. Press.

Hammami, Rema. 1990. "Women, the Hijab and the Intifada." *Middle East Report* 20.3/4: 24–28.

———. 1991. "Women's Political Participation in the Intifada: A Critical Overview." In *Mo'tamar al-Intifada wa Ba'd Qadaya al-Mar'a al-Ejtima'ia* [Conference on the Intifada and Some Women's Social Issues], edited by the Women's Studies Committee of the Bisan Center for Research and Development, 73–84. Proceedings of a conference held in Jerusalem on December 14, 1990. Ramallah: Markaz Bisan lil-Buhuth wal-Inma'.

———. 1995. "NGOs: The Professionalization of Politics." *Race and Class* 37.2: 51–64.

———. 1997. "Palestinian Women: A Status Report—Labor and Economy: Gender Segmentation in Palestinian Economic Life." Palestine: Women's Studies Program, Birzeit University.

Hammami, Rema, and Penny Johnson. 1999. "Equality with a Difference: Gender and Citizenship in Transitional Palestine." *Social Politics* 6.3: 314–43.

Hammami, Rema, and Martina Rieker. 1988. "Feminist Orientalism and Orientalist Marxism." *New Left Review* 170: 93–106.

Hanafi, Sari, and Linda Tabar. 2002. "NGOs, Elite Formation and the Second Intifada." *Between the Lines* (Jerusalem) 2.18 (October): 31–37. http://www.ism-italia.org/wp-content/uploads/ngos-elite-formation -and-the-second-intifada.pdf.

Hann, Chris. 1996. "Introduction: Political Society and Civil Anthropology." In *Civil Society: Challenging Western Models*, edited by Chris Hann and Elizabeth Dunn, 1–26. London and New York: Routledge.

Hann, Chris, and Elizabeth Dunn, eds. 1996. *Civil Society: Challenging Western Models*. London and New York: Routledge.

Al-Haq. 1990. *A nation under siege: al-Haq annual report on human rights in the occupied Palestinian territories, 1989*. Ramallah, Palestine: al-Haq.

Haroun, Amira. 2000. "Introduction." Paper presented at the Third Women's Conference, "Al-Mar'a al-Falastineyya wal-Tahawlat al-Ijtema'iyya" [Palestinian Woman and Social Change], Gaza, August 8–9.

———. 2009. "The Palestinian Women's Bill of Rights." Paper presented at the workshop on the Palestinian Women's Bill of Rights, Gaza, June 5.

Harris, Colette. 2000. "The Changing Identity of Women in Tajikistan in the Post-Soviet Period." In *Gender and Identity Construction: Women of*

Central Asia, the Caucasus and Turkey, edited by Feride Acar and Ayse Günes-Ayata, 205–28. Leiden: E. J. Brill.

Hasso, Frances Susan. 1997. *Paradoxes of Gender/Politics: Nationalism, Feminism and Modernity in Contemporary Palestine*. PhD diss., University of Michigan.

Hatem, Mervat F. 1986. "The Enduring Alliance of Nationalism and Patriarchy in Muslim Personal Status Laws: The Case of Modern Egypt." *Feminist Issues* 6.1: 19–43.

———. 1993. "Toward the Development of Post-Islamist and Post-Nationalist Feminist Discourses in the Middle East." In *Arab Women: Old Boundaries, New Frontiers*, edited by Judith Tucker, 29–48. Bloomington: Indiana Univ. Press.

———. 1994. "Egyptian Discourses on Gender and Political Liberalization: Do Secularist and Islamist Views Really Differ?" *Middle East Journal* 48.4: 661–76.

———. 2000. "The Pitfalls of the National Discourses on Citizenship in Egypt." In *Gender and Citizenship in the Middle East*, edited by Suad Joseph, 33–57. Syracuse, NY: Syracuse Univ. Press.

Hawley, John Stratton, ed. 1994. *Fundamentalism and Gender*. Oxford and New York: Oxford Univ. Press.

Hawley, John Stratton, and Wayne Proudfoot. 1994. "Introduction." In *Fundamentalism and Gender*, edited by John Stratton Hawley, 3–46. Oxford and New York: Oxford Univ. Press.

Heiberg, Marianne, and Geir Øvensen. 1993. *Palestinian Society in Gaza, West Bank and Arab Jerusalem: A Survey of Living Conditions*. Oslo: FAFO Research Foundation.

Hélie-Lucas, Marie-Aimée. 1994. "The Preferential Symbol for Islamic Identity: Women in Muslim Personal Laws." In *Identity Politics and Women: Cultural Reassertions and Feminisms in International Perspective*, edited by Valentine M. Moghadam, 391–407. Boulder, CO: Westview Press.

Hilal, Jamil. 1977. "Class Transformation in the West Bank and Gaza." *Journal of Palestine Studies* 6: 167–75.

———. 2002. "Secularism in Palestinian Political Culture: A Tentative Discourse." *International Social Science Review* 3.1: 1–27.

Hilal, Jamil, and Mushtaq H. Khan. 2004. "State-Society Relationships, Rent-Seeking and the Nature of the PNA Quasi-State." In *State*

Formation in Palestine, edited by Mushtaq Khan, George Giacaman, and Inge Amundsen. London: Routledge.

Hilhorst, Dorothea. 2003. *The Real World of NGOs: Discourses, Diversity and Development*. London: Zed Books.

Hillel, Frisch. 1998. *Countdown to Statehood: Palestinian State Formation in the West Bank and Gaza*. Albany: State University of New York Press.

Hiltermann, Joost. 1990. "Work and Action: The Role of the Working Class in the Uprising." In *Intifada: Palestine at the Crossroads*, edited by Jamal Nassar and Roger Heacock, 143–58. New York: Praeger.

Hirst, David. 1977. *The Gun and the Olive Branch*, vol. 2. New York: D. Appleton.

Hobsbawm, Eric. 1983. "Introduction: Inventing Traditions." In *The Invention of Tradition*, edited by Eric Hobsbawm and Terence Ranger, 1–14. Cambridge, UK: Cambridge Univ. Press.

Hoodfar, Homa. 1995a. "State Policy and Gender Equity in Post-Revolutionary Iran." In *Family, Gender and Population Policy in the Middle East*, edited by Carla Makhlouf Obermeyer. Cairo: American Univ. Press.

———. 1995b. "The Veil in Their Minds and on Our Heads: The Persistence of Colonial Images of Muslim Women." *Resources for Feminist Research* 22.3/4: 5–18.

Hourani, Albert. 1981. *The Emergence of the Modern Middle East*. London: Macmillan.

———. 1983. *Arabic Thought in the Liberal Age, 1798–1939*. 2d ed. Cambridge: Cambridge Univ. Press.

Hroub, Khalid. 1996. "Obstacles to Democratisation in the Middle East." *Contention* 14: 81–106.

———. 2000. *Hamas: Political Thought and Practice*. Washington, DC: Institute for Palestine Studies.

Hudson, Michael (1996) "Obstacles to Democratisation in the Middle East" *Contention* 14: 81–106.

Hunter, Shireen, ed. 1988. *The Politics of Islamic Revivalism: Diversity and Unity*. Bloomington: Indiana Univ. Press.

Hussein, Khadija. 2010. "Rereading the Palestinian Women's Bill of Rights" (in Arabic). Unpublished report, Women's Affairs Committee, Ramallah.

Ibrahim, S. E. 1995. "Civil Society and Prospects of Democratisation in the Arab World." In *Civil Society in the Middle East*, vol. 1, edited by Augustus R. Norton. Leiden: E. J. Brill.

El Jack, Amani. 2003. "Gender and Armed Conflict: Overview Report." *IDS BRIDGE Bulletin* (Institute of Development Studies, University of Sussex) 13 (August). http://www.bridge.ids.ac.uk/sites/bridge.ids.ac .uk/files/reports/CEP-Conflict-Report.pdf.

Jackson, Cecile, and Ruth Pearson, eds. 1998. *Feminist Visions of Development.* New York: Routledge.

Jad, Islah. 1990. "From Salons to the Popular Committees: Palestinian Women, 1919–1989." In *Intifada: Palestine at the Crossroads*, edited by Jamal Nassar and Roger Heacock, 125–42. New York: Praeger.

———. 1995. "Claiming Feminism, Claiming Nationalism: Women's Activism in the Occupied Territories." In *The Challenge of Local Feminisms: Women's Movements in Global Perspective*, edited by Amrita Basue, 226–50. Boulder, CO: Westview Press.

Jad, Islah, Penny Johnson, and Rita Giacaman. 2000. "Gender and Citizenship under the Palestinian Authority." In *Gender and Citizenship in the Middle East*, edited by Suad Joseph, 137–57. Syracuse, NY: Syracuse Univ. Press.

Jaggar, Allison. 1983. *Feminist Politics and Human Nature.* Totowa, NJ: Rowman and Allenheld.

Jamal, Amal. 2001. "Engendering State-Building: The Women's Movement and Gender-Regime in Palestine." *Middle East Journal* 55.2: 256–57.

Jamison, Andrew. 1995. "The Shaping of the Global Environmental Agenda: The Role of Non-Governmental Organisations." In *Risk, Environment and Modernity*, edited by Scott Lash, Bronislaw Szerszynsky, and Brian Wynne, 224–45. London: Sage.

Jammal, Laila. 1985. *Contributions by Palestinian Women to the National Struggle for Liberation.* Washington, DC: Middle East Public Relations.

Jankowski, James, and Israel Gershoni, eds. 1997. *Rethinking Nationalism in the Arab Middle East.* New York: Columbia Univ. Press.

Jarbawi, Ali. 1990. "Palestinian Elites in the Occupied Territories: Stability and Change through the Intifada." In *Intifada: Palestine at the Crossroads*, edited by Jamal Nassar and Roger Heacock, 287–305. New York: Praeger.

Jayawardena, Kumari. 1986. *Feminism and Nationalism in the Third World.* New Delhi: Kali for Women.

Johnson, Cheryl. 1986. "Class and Gender: A Consideration of Yoruba Women during the Colonial Period." In *Women and Class in Africa*, edited by Claire Robertson and Iris Berger, 237–54. New York: Holmes and Meier.

Jones, Kathleen, and Anna Jónasdóttir, eds. 1988. *The Political Interests of Gender: Developing Theory and Research with a Feminist Face.* London: Sage.

Jorgensen, Lars. 1996. "What Are NGOs Doing in Civil Society?" In *NGOs, Civil Society and the State: Building Democracy in Transitional Societies,* edited by Andrew Clayton, 36–55. Oxford, UK: INTRAC.

Joseph, Suad. 1986. "Women and Politics in the Middle East." *Middle East Report* 16.1: 3–8.

———. 1994. "Problematizing Gender and Relational Rights: Experiences from Lebanon." *Social Politics* 1.3: 271–85.

———. 1997. "The Reproduction of Political Process among Women Activists in Lebanon: 'Shopkeepers' and 'Feminists.'" In *Organizing Women: Formal and Informal Women's Groups in the Middle East,* edited by Dawn Chatty and Annika Rabo, 57–80. Oxford and New York: Berg.

———, ed. 2000. *Gender and Citizenship in the Middle East.* Syracuse, NY: Syracuse Univ. Press.

Joseph, Suad, and Susan Sylomovics. 2001. "Introduction." *Women and Power in the Middle East.* Philadelphia: Univ. of Pennsylvania Press, 1–19.

Juergensmeyer, Mark. 1993. "Why Religious Nationalists Are Not Fundamentalists." *Religion* 23: 85–92.

———. 1996. "Response to Munson: Fundaphobia: The Irrational Fear of Fundamentalism." *Contention* 5.3: 127–32.

Kabeer, Naila. 1989. "The Quest for National Identity: Women, Islam, and the State in Bangladesh." Institute of Development Studies Discussion Paper no. 268. Brighton: IDS at the University of Sussex.

———. 1992. "Triple Roles, Gender Roles, Social Relations: The Political Subtext of Gender Training." Institute of Development Studies Discussion Paper no. 313. Brighton: IDS at the University of Sussex.

———. 1999. "The Conditions and Consequences of Choice: Reflections on the Measurement of Women's Empowerment." United Nations Research Institute for Social Development Discussion Paper no. 108. Geneva: UNRISD.

Kandil, Amani. 1995. *Civil Society in the Arab World.* Washington, DC: Civicus.

Kandiyoti, Deniz. 1988. "Bargaining with Patriarchy." *Gender and Society* 2.3: 271–90.

———. 1991a. "Identity and Its Discontents: Women and the Nation." *Millennium Journal of International Studies* 20.3: 429–43.

———. 1996. "Contemporary Feminist Scholarship and Middle East Studies." In *Gendering the Middle East:* Emerging Perspectives, edited by Deniz Kandiyoti, 1–27. London: IB Tauris.

———. 1998. "Some Awkward Questions on Women and Modernity in Turkey." In *Remaking Women: Feminism and Modernity in the Middle East*, edited by Lila Abu-Lughod, 270–87. Princeton, NJ: Princeton Univ. Press.

———. 2000. "Foreword." In *Gender and Citizenship in the Middle East*, edited by Suad Joseph, xiii-xvii. Syracuse, NY: Syracuse Univ. Press.

———. 2001. "The Politics of Gender and the Conundrums of Citizenship." In *Women and Power in the Middle East*, edited by Suad Joseph and Susan Slyomovics, 52–58. Philadelphia: University of Pennsylvania Press.

———, ed. 1991b. *Women, Islam and the State*. London: Macmillan.

Karam, Azza. 1998. *Women, Islamisms and the State: Contemporary Feminisms in Egypt*. London and New York: Macmillan/St. Martin's Press.

Katz, Sheila H. 1996. "Political Conflict and Identity." In *Gendering the Middle East: Emerging Perspectives*, edited by Deniz Kandiyoti, 85–107. London: IB Tauris.

———. 2003. *Women and Gender in Early Jewish and Palestinian Nationalism*. Gainesville: University Press of Florida.

Kayyali, Abdel-Wahab. 1979. *Palestine: A Modern History*. London: Croom Helm.

Keane, John. 1988. *Democracy and Civil Society*. London and New York: Verso.

Keddie, Nikki. 1979. "Problems in the Study of Middle Eastern Women." *International Journal of Middle East Studies* 10: 225–40.

———. 1998. "The New Religious Politics: Where, When, and Why Do 'Fundamentalisms' Appear?" *Comparative Studies in Society and History* 40.4: 696–723.

———. 1999. "The New Religious Politics and Women Worldwide: A Comparative Study." *Journal of Women's History* 10.4: 11–34.

Kedourie, Elie. 1960. *Nationalism*. London: Hutchinson & Co.

———. 1992. *Democracy and Arab Political Culture*. Washington, DC: Washington Institute for Near East Policy.

Kerkvliet, Benedict. 1991. *Everyday Politics in the Philippines: Class and Status Relations in a Central Luzon Village*. Quezon City: New Day Publishers.

Khalidi, Rashid. 1997. *Palestinian Identity: The Construction of Modern National Consciousness*. New York: Columbia Univ. Press.

Khalidi, Walid, ed. 1971. *From Haven to Conquest: Readings in Zionism and the Palestine Problem until 1948*. Beirut: Institute for Palestine Studies.

———. 1992. *All That Remains: The Palestinian Villages Occupied and Depopulated by Israel in 1948*. Washington, DC: Institute for Palestine Studies.

Khalil, Nehad. 1997. "Waqi' al-Mar'a al-Falastineyya fi Seyaq al-Taghayyor al-Ijtima'i" [Status of Palestinian Women in the Context of Social Change]. Paper presented at "Al-Mar'a al-Falastineyya ila Ayna [Palestinian Woman: Where Next?]," a workshop organized by the Women's Action Department of the Islamic National Salvation Party, Gaza, April.

———. 1999. "Dawr al-Mar'a fi 'Amaleyat al-Tanmeya" [Women's Role in the Development Process]. Paper presented at the Second Women's Conference, "Al-Mar'a al-Falastineyya bayna Tahaddeyat al-Waqe' wa Tomohat al-Mostaqbal" [Palestinian Woman between Actual Challenges and Future Aspirations], Gaza, August 16.

Khan, Mushtaq, George Giacaman, and Inge Amundsen, eds. 2004. *State Formation in Palestine*. London: Routledge.

Kimmerling, Baruch, and Joel S. Migdal. 1993. *Palestinians: The Making of a People*. New York: Free Press.

———. 2003. *The Palestinian People: A History*. Cambridge: Harvard Univ. Press.

Klein, Naomi. 2002. *Fences and Windows: Dispatches from the Frontlines of the Globalization Debate*. New York: Picador.

Koonz, Claudia. 1988. *Mothers in the Fatherland: Women, the Family, and Nazi Politics*. London: Methuen.

Korten, David C. 1987. "Third-Generation NGO Strategies: A Key to People-Centered Development." *World Development* 15, suppl.: 145–60.

Kramer, Gudrun. 1992. "Islam et Pluralisme." In *Démocratie et démocratisations dans le monde arabe* [Democracy and Democratizations in the Arab World], edited by Colloque franco-égyptien de politologie, 339–51. Cairo: CEDEJ.

Kuttab, Eileen. 1993. "Palestinian Women in the Intifada: Fighting on Two Fronts." *Arab Studies Quarterly* 15.2: 69–85.

Al-Labadi, Fadwa. 1992. "On Women's Day: The Palestinian Women's Movement on Trial," *News From Within* 8, no. 5: 8–11. Jerusalem.

Laclau, Ernesto. 1985. "New Social Movements and the Plurality of the Social." In *New Social Movements and the State in Latin America*, edited by David Slater, 27–42. Amsterdam: CEDLA.

Laclau, Ernesto, and Chantal Mouffe. 1985. *Hegemony and Socialist Strategy: Towards a Radical Democratic Politics*, translated by Winston Moore and Paul Cammack. London: Verso.

———. 1987. "Post-Marxism without Apologies." *New Left Review* 166 (November–December): 79–106.

Lapidus, Ira M. 1988. "Islamic Political Movements: Patterns of Historical Change." In *Islam, Politics and Social Movements*, edited by Edmund Burke, III, and Ira Lapidus, 3–17. Berkeley and London: University of California Press.

Laqueur, Walter, and Barry Rubin, eds. 1984. *The Israel-Arab Reader: A Documentary History of the Middle East Conflict*. New York: Penguin.

Lavine, Avraham. 1982. "Social Services in the Administered Territories." In *Judea, Samaria, and Gaza: Views on the Present and Future*, edited by Daniel Judah Elazar, 145–67. Washington, DC: American Enterprise Institute.

Lawrence, Bruce. 1987. "Muslim Fundamentalist Movements: Reflections toward a New Approach." In *The Islamic Impulse*, edited by Barbara Stowasser, 15–36. Washington, DC, London, and Sydney: Croom Helm in association with the Center for Contemporary Arab Studies, Georgetown University.

Lazreg, Marnia. 1988. "Feminism and Difference: The Perils of Writing as a Woman on Women in Algeria." *Feminist Studies* 14.1: 81–107.

———. 1994. *The Eloquence of Silence: Algerian Women in Question*. New York: Routledge.

Leonard, David K. 1982. "Choosing among Forms of Decentralization and Linkage." In *Institutions of Rural Development for the Poor*, edited by

David K. Leonard and Dale Rogers Marshall, 193–226. Berkeley: Institute of International Studies, University of California.

Lesch, Ann Mosely. 1979. *Arab Politics in Palestine, 1917–1939: The Frustration of a National Movement.* Ithaca, NY: Cornell Univ. Press.

———. 1984. "Palestine: Land and People." In *Occupation: Israel over Palestine,* edited by Naseer Aruri, 29–54. London: Zed Books.

Levi, Sasson. 1982. "Local Government in the Administered Territories." In *Judea, Samaria, and Gaza: Views on the Present and Future,* edited by Daniel Judah Elazar, 103–22. Washington, DC: American Enterprise Institute.

Levy, Caren. 1996. "The Process of Institutionalising Gender in Policy and Planning." University College, London, Development Planning Unit Working Paper no. 7. London: UC Development Planning Unit.

Lewis, Bernard. 1964. *The Middle East and the West.* New York: Harper Torchbooks.

———. 1988. *The Political Language of Islam.* Chicago: University of Chicago Press.

———. 1990. "The Roots of Islamic Rage." *Atlantic Monthly* 266 (September): 47–58.

Lindberg, Staffan, and Árni Sverrisson, eds. 1997. *Social Movements in Development: The Challenge of Globalization and Democratization.* New York: St. Martin's Press.

Lister, Ruth. 1997. *Citizenship: Feminist Perspectives.* New York: New York Univ. Press.

Litvak, Meir. 1996. *The Islamization of Palestinian Identity: The Case of Hamas.* Tel Aviv: Moshe Dayan Center for Middle Eastern and African Studies, Tel Aviv University.

Longo, Patrizia. 2001. "Revisiting the Equality/Difference Debate: Redefining Citizenship for the New Millennium." *Citizenship Studies* 5.3: 269–84. https://doi.org/10.1080/13621020120085243.

MacKinnon, Catharine. 1989. *Toward a Feminist Theory of the State.* Cambridge: Harvard Univ. Press.

Mahmood, Saba. 1996. "Feminism and Religious Difference." Paper presented at the Women, Culture and Modernity Conference, Carsten Niebuhr Institute of Near Eastern Studies, Copenhagen, February 18–21.

———. 2005. *Politics of Piety: The Islamic Revival and the Feminist Subject.* Princeton, NJ: Princeton Univ. Press.

Mama, Amina. 1995. "Feminism or Femocracy? State Feminism and Democratisation in Nigeria." *Africa Development/Afrique et développement* (Dakar) 20: 37–58.

Mandel, Neville. 1975. *The Arabs and Zionism before World War I*. Berkeley: University of California Press.

Manoranjan, Mohanty, and Partha Nath Mukherji, with Olle Tronquist, eds. 1998. *People's Rights: Social Movements and the State in the Third World*. New Delhi and London: Sage.

Ma'oz, Moshe. 1984. *Palestinian Leadership on the West Bank: The Changing Role of the Arab Mayors under Jordan and Israel*. London: Frank Cass & Co.

Marshall, T. H. 1950. *Citizenship and Social Class, and Other Essays*. Cambridge: Cambridge Univ. Press.

Marshall, T. H., and Tom Bottomore. 1992. *Citizenship and Social Class*. London: Pluto.

Marty, Martin E., and R. Scott Appleby, eds. 1991. *Fundamentalisms Observed*. Vol. 1 of *The Fundamentalism Project*. Chicago: Chicago Univ. Press.

———. 1994. *Accounting for Fundamentalisms*. Vol. 4 of *The Fundamentalism Project*. Chicago: Chicago Univ. Press.

Masalha, Nur. 1992. *Expulsion of the Palestinians: The Concept of "Transfer" in Zionist Political Thought, 1882–1948*. Washington, DC: Institute for Palestine Studies.

———. 1997. *A Land without a People: Israel, Transfer and the Palestinians, 1949–96*. London: Faber and Faber.

Massad, Joseph. 1995. "Conceiving the Masculine: Gender and Palestinian Nationalism." *Middle East Journal* 49.3 (summer): 467–83.

———. 2000. "The 'Post-Colonial' Colony: Time, Space, and Bodies in Palestine/Israel." In *The Pre-Occupation of Postcolonial Studies*, edited by Fawzia Afzal-Khan and Kalpana Seshadri-Crooks, 311–46. Durham, NC, and London: Duke Univ. Press.

———. 2001. *Colonial Effects: The Making of National Identity in Jordan*. New York: Columbia Univ. Press.

———. 2015. *Islam in Liberalism*. Chicago: University of Chicago Press.

McClintock, Anne. 1993. "Family Feuds: Gender, Nationalism and the Family." *Feminist Review* 44: 61–80.

Melucci, Alberto. 1985. "The Symbolic Challenge of Contemporary Social Movements." *Social Research* 52.4: 789–816.

Middle East Research and Information Project (MERIP). 2000. "Critiquing NGOs: Assessing the Last Decade" (Special Issue). *MERIP* 30.214 (spring). https://www.merip.org/mer/mer214.

Milton-Edwards, Beverley. 1996. *Islamic Politics in Palestine*. London: Tauris Academic Studies.

Minow, Martha. 1987. "Interpreting Rights: An Essay for Robert Cover." *Yale Law Journal* 96: 1860–910.

Mir-Hosseini, Ziba. 1996. "Divorce, Veiling and Feminism in Post-Khomeini Iran." In *Women and Politics in the Third World*, edited by Haleh Afshar, 142–70. London: Routledge.

———. 1999. *Islam and Gender: The Religious Debate in Contemporary Iran*. London: I. B. Tauris.

———. 2003. "Stretching the Limits: A Feminist Reading of the Shari'a in Post-Khomeini Iran." In *Islam, Gender and Family*, vol. 3 of *Islam: Critical Concepts in Sociology*, edited by Bryan S. Turner, 284–320. London: Routledge.

Mogannam, Matiel. 1937. *The Arab Woman and the Palestine Problem*. London: Herbert Joseph Limited.

Moghadam, Valentine M. 1988. "Women, Work and Ideology in the Islamic Republic." *International Journal of Middle East Studies* 20.2: 221–43.

———. 1992. "Revolution, Islam and Women: Sexual Politics in Iran and Afghanistan." In *Nationalisms and Sexualities*, edited by Andrew Parker, Mary Russo, Doris Sommer, and Patricia Yaeger, 424–46. New York and London: Routledge.

———. 1993. "Islamist Movements and Women's Responses." In *Modernizing Women: Gender and Social Change in the Middle East*, edited by Valentine M. Moghadam, 151–92. Boulder, CO: Lynne Rienner.

———. 1994a. "Introduction: Women and Identity Politics in Theoretical and Comparative Perspective." In *Identity Politics and Women: Cultural Reassertions, Gender and Feminisms in International Perspective*, edited by Valentine M. Moghadam, 76–97. Boulder, CO: Westview Press.

———. 1997. *Women, Work and Economic Reform in the Middle East and North Africa*. Boulder: Lynne Rienner.

————, ed. 1994b. *Gender and National Identity: Women and Politics in Muslim Societies*. London and Karachi: Zed Books and Oxford Univ. Press.

Moghissi, Haideh. 1993. "Women in the Resistance Movement in Iran." In *Women in the Middle East: Perceptions, Realities and Struggles for Liberation*, edited by Haleh Afshar, 158–71. London: Macmillan.

————. 1994. *Populism and Feminism in Iran: Women's Struggles in a Male-Dominated Revolutionary Movement*. London: Macmillan.

————. 1995. "Public Life and Women's Resistance." In *Iran after the Revolution*, edited by Saeed Rahnema and Sohrab Behdad, 251–67. London: I. B. Tauris.

Mohanty, Chandra Talpade. 1988. "Under Western Eyes: Feminist Scholarship and Colonial Discourses." *Feminist Review* 30: 61–88.

————. 1991. "Cartographies of Struggle: Third World Women and the Politics of Feminism." In *Third World Women and the Politics of Feminism*, edited by Chandra Talpade Mohanty, Ann Russo, and Lourdes Torres, 1–50. Bloomington: Indiana Univ. Press.

Molyneux, Maxine. 1985. "Mobilization without Emancipation? Women's Interests, State and Revolution in Nicaragua." *Feminist Studies* 11.2: 227–54.

————. 1991. "The Law, the State and Socialist Policies with Regard to Women: The Case of the People's Democratic Republic of Yemen, 1967–1990." In *Women, Islam and the State*, edited by Deniz Kandiyoti, 237–71. London: Macmillan.

————. 1996. "Women's Rights and the International Context in the Post-Communist States." In *Mapping the Women's Movement: Feminist Politics and Social Transformation in the North*, edited by Mónica Threlfall, 232–59. London: Verso.

————. 2001. *Women's Movements in International Perspective: Latin America and Beyond*. Basingstoke and New York: Macmillan.

Moore, Henrietta. 1988. *Feminism and Anthropology*. Cambridge, UK: Polity Press.

Moser, Caroline O. N. 1989. "Gender Planning in the Third World: Meeting Practical and Strategic Needs." *World Development* 17.11: 1799–825.

Munson, Henry. 1988. *Islam and Revolution in the Middle East*. New Haven, CT: Yale Univ. Press.

————. 2003. "Islam, Nationalism and Resentment of Foreign Domination." *Middle East Policy* 10.2: 40–53.

Muslih, Muhammad Y. 1988. *The Origins of Palestinian Nationalism*. New York: Columbia Univ. Press.

———. 1995. "Palestinian Civil Society." In *Civil Society in the Middle East*, vol. 1, edited by Augustus R. Norton, 243–68. Leiden: E.J. Brill.

Muwatin (Palestinian Institute for the Study of Democracy). 2000. *The Palestinian Women's Movement: Problematics of Democratic Transformation and Future Strategies*. Proceedings of the Fifth Annual Muwatin Conference, December 17–18, 1999. Ramallah: Muwatin Publications.

Najmabadi, Afsaneh. 1991. "Hazards of Modernity and Morality: Women, State, and Ideology in Contemporary Iran." In *Women, Islam and the State*, edited by Deniz Kandiyoti, 48–76. London: Macmillan.

———. 1998. "Feminism in an Islamic Republic: Years of Hardship, Years of Growth." In *Islam, Gender, and Social Change*, edited by Yvonne Haddad and John Esposito, 59–84. Oxford: Oxford Univ. Press.

Nakhleh, Khalil. 1977. "Anthropological and Sociological Studies on the Arabs in Israel: A Critique." *Journal of Palestine Studies* 6.4: 41–70.

Nelson, Barbara, and Najma Chowdhury, eds. 1994. *Women and Politics Worldwide*. New Haven, CT: Yale Univ. Press.

Nesiah, Vasuki. 1996. "Towards a Feminist Internationality: A Critique of US Feminist Legal Scholarship." In *Feminist Terrains in Legal Domains: Interdisciplinary Essays on Woman and Law in India*, edited by Ratna Kapur, 11–35. New Delhi: Kali for Women.

Norton, Augustus Richard. 1993. "The Future of Civil Society in the Middle East." *Middle East Journal* 47.2: 205–16.

———, ed. 1995. *Civil Society in the Middle East*, 2 vols. Leiden: E. J. Brill.

Nussbaum, Martha. 2002. "Women's Capabilities and Social Justice." In *Gender Justice, Development, and Rights*, edited by Maxine Molyneux and Shahra Razavi, 45–77. Oxford: Oxford Univ. Press.

Omvedt, Gail. 1980. *We Smash This Prison*. London: Zed Press.

———. 1994. "Peasants, Dalits and Women: Democracy and India's New Social Movements." *Journal of Contemporary Asia* 24.1: 35–48.

Ong, Aihwa, and Michael Peletz, eds. 1995. *Bewitching Women, Pious Men: Gender and Body Politics in Southeast Asia*. Berkeley: University of California Press.

Palestine-Info. 2004. "Ayyat al-Akhras Killed on March 29, 2002" (in Arabic). Palestine-Info Gaza, January 22, 2004.

———. 2004. "Special File on Ahmad Yassine after His Assassination" (in Arabic). March 20.

Papanek, Hanna. 1994. "The Ideal Woman and the Ideal Society: Control and Autonomy in the Construction of Identity." In *Identity Politics and Women: Cultural Reassertions and Feminisms in International Perspective,* edited by Valentine M. Moghadam, 42–75. Boulder, CO: Westview Press.

Parker, Christopher. 1999. *Resignation or Revolt? Socio-Political Development and the Challenges of Peace in Palestine.* London: I. B. Tauris.

Parpart, Jane, and Kathleen Staudt, eds. 1989. *Women and the State in Africa.* Boulder, CO: Lynne Rienner.

Pateman, Carole. 1988. *The Sexual Contract.* Cambridge, UK: Polity Press.

Pavlowsky, Agnès. 1998. *Hamas, ou, Le miroir des frustrations palestiniennes* [Hamas, or, The Mirror of Palestinian Frustrations]. Paris and Montreal: L'Harmattan.

Peteet, Julie. 1991. *Gender in Crisis: Women and the Palestinian Resistance Movement.* New York: Columbia Univ. Press.

———. 1998. "Post-Partition Palestinian Identities and the Moral Community." *Social Analysis* 42.1: 63–87.

Peterson, V. Spike, and Anne Sisson Runyan. 1993. *Global Gender Issues.* Boulder, CO: Westview.

Petras, James. 1990. "The Redemocratization Process." In *Democracy in Latin America: Visions and Realities,* edited by Susanne Jonas and Nancy Stein, 85–100. New York: Bergin and Gravey.

———. 1997. "Imperialism and NGOs in Latin America." *Monthly Review* 47.7: 10–27.

———. 2000. "The Third Way: Myth and Reality." *Monthly Review* 51.10 (March). https://monthlyreview.org/2000/03/01/the-third-way/.

Phillips, Anne. 1991. *Engendering Democracy.* Cambridge, UK: Polity Press.

———. 1993. *Democracy and Difference.* Cambridge, UK: Polity Press.

———. 2002. "Multiculturalism, Universalism, and the Claims of Democracy." In *Gender Justice, Development, and Rights,* edited by Maxine Molyneux and Shahra Razavi, 115–40. Oxford: Oxford Univ. Press.

———, ed. 1987. *Feminism and Equality.* New York: New York Univ. Press.

Pinto-Duschinsky, Michael. 1991. "Foreign Political Aid: The German Political Foundations and Their US Counterparts." *International Affairs* 67.1: 33–66.

Pipes, Daniel. 1983. *In the Path of God: Islam and Political Power.* New York: Basic Books.

———. 1990. "The Muslims Are Coming! The Muslims Are Coming!" *National Review* 42 (November 19): 29.

———. 1992. "Fundamental Questions about Muslims." *Wall Street Journal,* October 30, 1992.

Porath, Yehoshuah. 1974. *The Emergence of the Palestinian Arab National Movement, 1918–1929.* London: Frank Cass & Co.

Pringle, Rosemary, and Sophie Watson. 1992. "Women's Interests and the Post-Structuralist State." In *Destabilizing Theory: Contemporary Feminist Debates,* edited by Michele Barrett and Anne Phillips, 53–73. Stanford, CA: Stanford Univ. Press.

Purushothaman, Sangeetha. 1997. *The Empowerment of Women in India: Grassroots Women's Networks and the State.* Thousand Oaks, CA: Sage.

PUWWC (Palestinian Union of Women's Work Committees). 1987a. *The Development of the Palestinian Women Movement.* Jerusalem: PUWWC.

Qassoum, Mufid. 2002. "Aborting the Revolution: Imperial Agendas, 'Civil Society' and Global Manipulation." *Between the Lines* (Jerusalem) 3.19 (December). http://www.ism-italia.org/wp-content/uploads/Aborting -the-Revolution-Imperial-Agendas-Civil-Society-and-Global-Manipula tion-Mufid-Qassoum-December-2002-Between-the-Lines.pdf.

Radhakrishnan, R. 1992. "Nationalism, Gender and the Narrative of Identity." In *Nationalisms and Sexualities,* edited by Andrew Parker, Mary Russo, Doris Sommer, and Patricia Yaeger, 77–95. New York: Routledge.

Radtke, H. Lorraine, and Henderikus J. Stam, eds. 1994. "Introduction." In *Power/Gender: Social Relations in Theory and Practice,* 1–14. London: Sage.

Raffer, Kunibert, and H. W. Singer. 1996. *The Foreign Aid Business: Economic Assistance and Development Co-Operation.* Cheltenham, UK and Brookfield, VT: Edward Elgar.

Rai, Shirin. 1996. "Women and the State in the Third World." In *Women and the State: International Perspectives,* edited by Shirin Rai and Geraldine Lievesley, 5–22. London: Taylor & Francis.

Rai, Shirin, and Geraldine Lievesley, eds. 1996. *Women and the State: International Perspectives.* London: Taylor & Francis.

Raphaeli, Nimrod. 1968. "Military Government in the Occupied Territories: An Israeli View." *Middle East Journal* 23.2: 177–90.

Razavi, Shahra, and Carol Miller. 1995. "Gender Mainstreaming: A Study of Efforts by the UNDP, the World Bank and the ILO to Institutionalize Gender Issues." United Nations Research Institute for Social Development Occasional Paper no. 4. Geneva: UNRISD.

Reiss, Nira. 1996. "British Public Health Policy in Palestine, 1918–1947." In *Health and Disease in the Holy Land: Studies in the History and Sociology of Medicine from Ancient Times to the Present*, edited by Manfred Waserman and Samuel Kottek, 301–27. Lewiston, NY: Edwin Mellen Press.

Rhode, Deborah. 1989. *Justice and Gender*. Cambridge: Harvard Univ. Press.

Robinson, Glenn E. 1997. *Building a Palestinian State: The Incomplete Revolution*. Bloomington: Indiana Univ. Press.

Rodinson, Maxime. 1973. *Israel: A Colonial Settler State?* New York: Monad Press.

Rosaldo, Renato. 1989. *Culture and Truth: The Remaking of Social Analysis*. Boston: Beacon Press.

Rosenfeld, Henry. 1964. "From Peasantry to Wage Labor and Residual Peasantry: The Transformation of an Arab Village." In *Process and Pattern in Culture*, edited by Robert A. Manners, 211–36. Chicago: Aldine.

———. 1992. *Women in Movement: Feminism and Social Action*. London: Routledge.

Rothenberg, Celia E. 1998–99. "A Review of the Anthropological Literature in English on the Palestinian *Hamula* and the Status of Women." *Journal of Arabic and Islamic Studies* 2 (December): 24–48. https://www.journals.uio.no/index.php/JAIS/article/view/4549.

Rowbotham, Sheila. 1992. *Women in Movement: Feminism and Social Action*. New York: Routledge.

Rowlands, Jo. 1998. "A Word of the Times, But What Does It Mean? Empowerment in the Discourse and Practice of Development." In *Women and Empowerment: Illustrations from the Third World*, edited by Haleh Afshar. London: Macmillan.

Roy, Arundhati. 2003. "Confronting Empire," speech delivered at Porto Alegre, Brazil, January 27. http://www.sterneck.net/politik/roy-empire/index.php.

Roy, Olivier. 1999. *The Failure of Political Islam*. 2d ed. Translated by Carol Volk. London: I. B. Tauris.

Roy, Sara. 1986. *The Gaza Strip Survey.* Jerusalem: West Bank Data Base Project.

———. 1993. "Gaza: New Dynamics of Civic Disintegration." *Journal of Palestine Studies* 22.4: 20–31.

———. 1995. *The Gaza Strip: The Political Economy of De-Development.* Washington, DC: Institute for Palestine Studies.

———. 1996. "Economic Deterioration in the Gaza Strip." *Middle East Research and Information Project* 26.200: 36–39.

———. 1998. "The Palestinian Economy after Oslo." *Current History* (January): 19–25.

———. 2000. "The Transformation of Islamist NGOs in Palestine." *Middle East Report* 30.214: 24–27.

Rubenberg, Cheryl A. 2001. *Palestinian Women: Patriarchy and Resistance in the West Bank.* Boulder, CO: Lynne Rienner.

Al-Sabti, Randa. 2009. "The Most Important Pillars and Themes of the Women's Bill of Rights" (in Arabic). Paper presented at the workshop on the Palestinian Women's Bill of Rights, Gaza, June 5.

Sadowski, Yahya. 1997. "The New Orientalism and the Democracy Debate." In *Political Islam: Essays from Middle East Report,* edited by Joel Beinin and Joe Stork, 33–50. Berkeley: University of California Press.

Sahliyeh, Emile. 1988. *In Search of Leadership: West Bank Politics since 1967.* Washington, DC: Brookings Institution.

Said, Edward W. 1979. *Orientalism.* London: Routledge and Kegan Paul.

———. 1994. *Culture and Imperialism.* London: Vintage.

Salamé, Ghassan, ed. 2001. *Democracy without Democrats? The Renewal of Politics in the Muslim World.* Reprint, London: Tauris.

Salamon, Lester. 1993. "The Global Associational Revolution: The Rise of the Third Sector on the World Scene." Institute of Policy Studies Occasional Paper no. 15. Baltimore: Johns Hopkins Univ. Press.

Saleh, Samir Abdallah. 1990. "The Effects of Israeli Occupation on the Economy of the West Bank and Gaza Strip." In *Intifada: Palestine at the Crossroads,* edited by Jamal Nassar and Roger Heacock, 37–52. New York: Praeger.

Sampson, Steven. 1996. "The Social Life of Projects: Importing Civil Society to Albania." In *Civil Society: Challenging Western Models,* edited by Chris Hann and Elizabeth Dunn, 121–42. London: Routledge.

Sandler, Shmuel, and Hillel Frisch. 1982. "The Political Economy of the Administered Territories." In *Judea, Samaria, and Gaza: Views on the Present and Future*, edited by Daniel Judah Elazar. Washington, DC: American Enterprise Institute.

Sangari, Kumkum, and Sudesh Valid, eds. 1989. *Recasting Women: Essays in Colonial History*. New Delhi: Kali Press.

Sayigh, Rosemary. 1979. *Palestinians: From Peasants to Revolutionaries. A People's History*. London: Zed Press.

———. 1987. "Femmes palestiniennes: Une histoire en quête d'historiens" [Palestinian Women: A History in Search of Historians]. *Revue d'études Palestiniennes* 23 (spring): 13–33.

———. 1988. "Palestinian Women: Triple Burden, Single Struggle." *Peuples Méditerranées* 44/45: 247–68.

———. 1993. "Palestinian Women and Politics in Lebanon." In *Arab Women: Old Boundaries, New Frontiers*, edited by Judith Tucker, 175–94. Bloomington: Indiana Univ. Press.

Sayigh, Yezid. 1997. *Armed Struggle and the Search for State: The Palestinian National Movement, 1949–1993*. Oxford: Clarendon Press.

Al-Sayyid, Mustapha K. 1993. "A 'Civil Society' in Egypt?" *Middle East Journal* 47.2: 228–42.

Schiff, Ze'ev, and Ehud Ya'ari. 1989. *Intifada: The Inside Story of the Palestinian Uprising That Changed the Middle East Equation*. New York: Simon & Schuster.

Schlesinger, Philip. 1987. "On National Identity: Some Conceptions and Misconceptions Criticized." *Social Science Information* 26.2: 219–64.

Scholch, Alexander. 1982. "European Penetration and the Economic Development of Palestine, 1856–82." In *Studies in the Economic and Social History of Palestine in the Nineteenth and Twentieth Centuries*, edited by Roger Owen, 10–87. Carbondale: Southern Illinois Univ. Press.

Schulz, Helena Lindholm. 1985. *Weapons of the Weak: Everyday Forms of Peasant Resistance*. New Haven, CT: Yale Univ. Press.

———. 1999. *The Reconstruction of Palestinian Nationalism: Between Revolution and Statehood*. Manchester: Manchester Univ. Press.

Scott, James C. 1990. *Domination and the Arts of Resistance*. New Haven, CT: Yale Univ. Press.

Scott, Joan W. 1988. *Gender and the Politics of History*. New York: Columbia Univ. Press.

———. 1990. "Deconstructing Equality-versus-Difference: Or, the Uses of Poststructuralist Theory for Feminism." In *Conflicts in Feminism*, edited by Marianne Hirsch and Evelyn F. Keller, 134–48. New York: Routledge.

Sedgwick, Eva Kosofsky. 1992. "Nationalisms and Sexualities in the Age of Wilde." In *Nationalisms and Sexualities*, edited by Andrew Parker, Mary Russo, Doris Sommer, and Patricia Yaeger, 235–45. New York: Routledge.

Semyonov, Moshe. 1994. "Trends in Labor Market Participation and Gender-Linked Occupational Differentiation." In *Women and the Israeli Occupation: The Politics of Change*, edited by Tamar Mayer, 123–30. New York: Routledge.

Shahid, Serene Husseini. 1999. *Jerusalem Memories*, edited by Jean Said Makdisi. Beirut: Naufal.

Al-Shanti, 'Aisha. 2002. "Lil-Nissa' Fakat" [For Women Only]. *Al-Jazeera* (Doha), February 6.

Sharabi, Hisham. 1988. *Neopatriarchy: A Theory of Distorted Change in Arab Society*. Oxford: Oxford Univ. Press.

Sharkey, Heather J. 2003. *Living with Colonialism: Nationalism and Culture in the Anglo-Egyptian Sudan*. Berkeley: University of California Press.

Shavit, Ari. 2004. "Survival of the Fittest," interview with Benny Morris. *Haaretz*, January 8, 2004. https://www.haaretz.com/1.5262454.

Shohat, Ella. 1989. *Israeli Cinema: East/West and the Politics of Representation*. Austin: University of Texas Press.

Siniora, Randa. 2000. "Lobbying for a Palestinian Family Law: The Experience of the Palestinian Model Parliament: Women and Legislation." Paper presented at the International Conference on Islamic Family Law in the Middle East and North Africa: Theory, Practice and the Chances of Reform, Amman, Jordan, June 24–25.

Slevin, Peter. 2002. "Preparing for Democracy: State Dept. Connects Arab Women, Political Consultants." *Washington Post*, November 4, 2002, sec. A, p. 3.

Smith, Anthony. 1971. *Theories of Nationalism*. London: Harper.

———. 1976. *Nationalist Movements*. London and Basingstoke: Macmillan.

———. 1991. *National Identity*. London: Penguin.

Smith, Pamela Ann. 1984. *Palestine and the Palestinians*. London: Croom Helm.

Snow, David, and Robert Benford. 1988. "Ideology, Frame, Resonance, and Participant Mobilisation." In *International Social Movement Research*, vol. 1, *From Structure to Action: Comparative Social Movement Research across Cultures*, edited by Bert Klandermans, Hanspeter Kriesi, and Sidney Tarrow, 197–217. London: JAI Press.

Sonbol, Amira. 1988. "Egypt." In *The Politics of Islamic Revivalism: Diversity and Unity*, edited by Shireen Hunter, 23–38. Bloomington: Indiana Univ. Press.

———. 1990. *The Postcolonial Critic: Interview, Strategies, Dialogues.* New York: Routledge.

Staudt, Kathleen. 1989. "Gender Politics in the Bureaucracy: Theoretical Issues in Comparative Perspective." In *Women, International Development and Politics*, edited by Kathleen Staudt, 3–36. Philadelphia: Temple Univ. Press.

Stowasser, Barbara. 1987. "Introduction." In *The Islamic Impulse*, edited by Barbara Stowasser, 1–14. Washington, DC: Croom Helm in association with the Center for Contemporary Arab Studies, Georgetown University.

Suzuki, Naoki. 1998. *Inside NGOs: Managing Conflicts between Headquarters and the Field Offices in Non-Governmental Organisations.* London: Intermediate Technology Publications.

Swedenburg, Ted. 1988. "The Role of the Palestinian Peasantry in the Great Revolt (1936–1939)." In *Islam, Politics and Social Movements*, edited by Edmund Burke, III, and Ira Lapidus, 169–206. Berkeley, Los Angeles, and London: University of California Press.

———. 1995. *Memories of Revolt: The 1936–1939 Rebellion and the Palestinian National Past.* Minneapolis: University of Minnesota Press.

Swirski, Barbara. 2000. "Citizenship of Jewish and Palestinian Arab Women in Israel." In *Gender and Citizenship in the Middle East*, edited by Suad Joseph, 314–46. Syracuse, NY: Syracuse Univ. Press.

Takatka, Andalib. 2004. "Wasseya" [Testament]. Palestine-Info Gaza, January 22.

Tamari, Salim. 1981. "Building Other People's Homes." *Journal of Palestine Studies* 11.1: 31–66.

———. 1989. "What the Uprising Means." In *Intifada: The Palestinian Uprising against Israeli Occupation*, edited by Zachary Lockman and Joel Beinin, 127–41. Boston: South End Press.

———. 1990. "The Revolt of the Petite Bourgeoisie: Urban Merchants and the Palestinian Uprising." In *Intifada: Palestine at the Crossroads*, edited by Jamal Nassar and Roger Heacock, 159–74. New York: Praeger.

———. 2004. "Ishaq al-Shami and the Predicament of the Arab Jew in Palestine." *Jerusalem Quarterly File* 21.2: 10–26.

Tamimi, Azzam. 1998. "Human Rights in Islam." Institute of Islamic Political Thought: London, March 4.

———. 2002. "Can Islam Be Secularized." Institute of Islamic Political Thought: London, November.

Tamimi, Azzam, and John Esposito, eds. 2000. *Islam and Secularism in the Middle East*. London: C. Hurst.

Tandon, Rajesh. 1996. "An African Perspective." In *Compassion and Calculation: The Business of Private Foreign Aid*, edited by David Sogge, 179–84. London and Chicago: Pluto Press with Transnational Institute.

Taraki, Lisa. 1989. "Mass Organizations in the West Bank." In *Occupation: Israel over Palestine*. 2d ed. Edited by Naseer Aruri, 431–63. Belmont, MA: AAUG Press.

———. 1990. "The Development of Political Consciousness among Palestinians in the Occupied Territories, 1967–1987." In *Intifada: Palestine at the Crossroads*, edited by Jamal Nassar and Roger Heacock, 53–72. New York: Praeger.

———. 2003. "Islam Is the Solution: Jordanian Islamists and the Dilemma of the 'Modern Woman.'" In *Islam: Critical Concepts in Sociology*, vol. 3, *Islam, Gender and the Family*, edited by Bryan Turner, 643–61. London: Routledge.

Tarrow, Sidney. 1994. *Power in Movement: Social Movements, Collective Action, and Politics*. Cambridge: Cambridge University Press.

———. 2000. *Colonial Citizens: Republican Rights, Paternal Privilege and Gender in French Syria and Lebanon*. New York: Columbia Univ. Press.

Al-Tibawi, Abdel-Latif. 1956. *Arab Education in Mandatory Palestine: A Study of Three Decades of British Administration*. London: Luzac.

Tibi, Bassam. 1987. "Islam and Arab Nationalism." In *The Islamic Impulse*, edited by Barbara Stowasser, 59–75. Washington, DC, London, and Sydney: Croom Helm, in association with the Center for Contemporary Arab Studies, Georgetown University.

Tilly, Charles, ed. 1975. *The Formation of National States in Western Europe*. Princeton, NJ: Princeton Univ. Press.

————. 1984. "Social Movements and National Politics." In *Statemaking and Social Movements: Essays in History and Theory*, edited by Charles Bright and Susan Harding, 297–317. Ann Arbor: University of Michigan Press.

Al-Torki, Soraya. 2000. "The Concept and Practice of Citizenship in Saudi Arabia." In *Gender and Citizenship in the Middle East*, edited by Suad Joseph, 215–36. Syracuse, NY: Syracuse Univ. Press.

Törnquist, Olle. 1999. *Politics and Development: A Critical Introduction*. London and New Delhi: Sage.

Touraine, Alain. 1981. *The Voice and the Eye: An Analysis of Social Movements*, translated by Alan Duff. Cambridge: Cambridge Univ. Press.

————. 1983. "Problems in the Historiography of Women in the Middle East: The Case of Nineteenth-Century Egypt." *International Journal of Middle East Studies* 15: 321–36.

————. 1988. *Return of the Actor: Social Theory in Postindustrial Society*, translated by Myrna Godzich. Minneapolis: University of Minnesota Press.

Tucker, Judith. 1993. "Introduction" and "The Arab Family in History: 'Otherness' and the Study of the Family." In *Arab Women: Old Boundaries, New Frontiers*, edited by Judith Tucker, 175–207. Bloomington: Indiana Univ. Press.

Tucker, Judith, ed. 1993. *Arab Women: Old Boundaries, New Frontiers*. Bloomington: Indiana Univ. Press.

Turner, Bryan S. 1984. "Orientalism and the Problem of Civil Society." In *Orientalism, Islam and Islamists*, edited by Assaf Hussein, 23–42. Brattleboro, VT: Amana Press.

————. 2003. "Politics and Culture in Islamic Globalism." In *Islam: Critical Concepts in Sociology*, edited by Bryan S. Turner, 1–41. London: Routledge.

Tvedt, Terje. 1998. *Angels of Mercy or Development Diplomats? NGOs and Foreign Aid*. Trenton, NJ: Africa World Press.

Uphoff, Norman. 1986. *Local Institutional Development: An Analytical Sourcebook with Cases*. West Hartford, CT: Kumarian Press.

————. 1993. "Grassroots Organizations and NGOs in Rural Development: Opportunities with Diminishing States and Expanding Markets." *World Development* 21.4: 607–22.

Usher, Graham. 1994. "The Islamist Movement and the Palestinian Authority: Graham Usher Speaks with Bassam Jarrar." *Middle East Report* 24.189: 28–29.

————. 1997. "What Kind of Nation? The Rise of Hamas in the Occupied Territories." In *Political Islam: Essays from Middle East Report*, edited by Joel Beinin and Joe Stork, 339–54. Berkeley: University of California Press.

————. 1999. *Dispatches from Palestine: The Rise and Fall of the Oslo Peace Process*. London: Pluto Press.

Van Dijk, Jan A. G. M. 1999. "The One-Dimensional Network Society of Manuel Castells." *New Media & Society* 1, no. 1 (April 1): 127–38. https://doi.org/10.1177/1461444899001001015.

Vatikiotis, P. J. 1983. "Religion and the State." In *Islam, Nationalism and Radicalism in Egypt and the Sudan*, edited by Gabriel R. Warburg and Uri M. Kupferschmidt, 55–72. New York: Praeger.

————. 1987. *Islam and the State*. London: Croom Helm.

Victor, Barbara. 2002. *Shahidas: Les femmes kamikazes de Palestine* [Army of Roses: Inside the World of Palestinian Women Suicide Bombers], translated by Robert Macia and Florence Bouzinac. Paris: Flammarion.

Vivian, Jessica. 1994. "NGOs and Sustainable Development in Zimbabwe: No Magic Bullets." *Development and Change* 25, no. 1: 167–93.

Voet, Rian. 1998. *Feminism and Citizenship*. London: Sage.

Vogel, Ursula. 1988. "Under Permanent Guardianship: Women's Condition under Modern Civil Law." In *The Political Interests of Gender: Developing Theory and Research with a Feminist Face*, edited by Kathleen Jones and Anna Jónasdóttir, 135–59. London: Sage.

Al-Waqa'i' al-Falastineyya. (Palestinian Gazette). 74, 39.

Waterbury, John. 2001. "Democracy without Democrats? The Potential for Political Liberalisation in the Middle East." In *Democracy without Democrats? The Renewal of Politics in the Muslim World*, edited by Ghassan Salamé. London: I. B. Tauris.

Waylen, Georgina. 1996. *Gender in Third World Politics*. Buckingham: Open Univ. Press.

WCLAC (Women's Center for Legal Aid and Counseling). 2003. "Internal Platform, Article 3: Hopes and Challenges," November 20.

Welchman, Lynn. 1999. *Islamic Family Law: Text and Practice in Palestine*. Jerusalem: Women's Center for Legal Aid and Counseling (WCLAC).

————. 2003. "In the Interim: Civil Society, the Shari'a Judiciary and Palestinian Personal Status Law in the Transitional Period." *Islamic Law and Society* 10.1: 34–69.

White, Jenny. 2002. *Islamist Mobilization in Turkey: A Study in Vernacular Politics.* Seattle: University of Washington Press.

Wieringa, Saskia, ed. 1995. *Subversive Women: Women's Movements in Africa, Asia, Latin America and the Caribbean.* London: Zed Books.

Williams, Raymond. 1977. *Marxism and Literature.* Oxford: Oxford Univ. Press.

Wils, Frits. 1995. "NGOs in Latin America: Past Strategies, Current Dilemmas, Future Challenges." International NGO Training and Research Centre (INTRAC) Occasional Paper no. 8. Oxford, UK: INTRAC.

Wilson, Elizabeth. 1977. *Women and the Welfare State.* London: Tavistock.

Yeatman, Anna. 1990. *Bureaucrats, Technocrats, Femocrats: Essays on the Contemporary Australian State.* Sydney: Allen & Unwin.

Young, Kate. 1993. *Planning Development with Women.* Basingstoke: Macmillan.

Yuval-Davis, Nira. 1991. "The Citizenship Debate: Women, Ethnic Processes, and the State." *Feminist Review* 2.39: 58–68.

———. 1993. "Gender and Nation." *Ethnic and Racial Studies* 16.4: 621–32.

———. 1997. "Citizenship and Difference." In *Gender and Nation,* 68–92. London and Thousand Oaks, CA: Sage.

Al-Zahar, Mahmoud. 1999. "Al-Mar'a wal-Mosharaka al-Seyasseya" [Women and Political Participation]. Paper presented at the Second Women's Conference, "Al-Mar'a al-Falastineyya bayna Tahaddeyat al-Waqe' wa Tomohat al-Mostaqbal" [Palestinian Woman between Actual Challenges and Future Aspirations], Gaza, August 16.

Zaki, Moheb. 1995. *Civil Society and Democratization in Egypt, 1981–1994.* Cairo: Dar al-Kutub.

Zerubavel, Yael. 1995. *Recovered Roots: The Collective Memory and the Making of Israeli National Tradition.* Chicago: University of Chicago Press.

Zionism. 2018. *Wikipedia,* July 3. http://en.wikipedia.org/wiki/Zionism.

Zubaida, Sami. 1988. "Islam, Cultural Nationalism and the Left." *Review of Middle East Studies* 4: 1–33.

———. 1992. "Islam, the State and Democracy: Contrasting Conceptions of Society in Egypt." *Middle East Report* 179: 2–10.

———. 1993. *Islam, the People and the State: Political Ideas and Movements in the Middle East.* Rev. ed. London: I. B. Tauris.

———. 1995. "Is There a Muslim Society? Ernest Gellner's Sociology of Islam." *Economy and Society* 24.2: 151–88.

———. 1997. "Religion, the State, and Democracy: Contrasting Conceptions of Society in Egypt." In *Political Islam: Essays from Middle East Report*, edited by Joel Beinin and Joe Stork, 51–63. Berkeley and Los Angeles: University of California Press.

———. 2000. "The Trajectories of Political Islam: Egypt, Iran and Turkey." *Political Quarterly* 71, suppl. 1: 60–78.

———. 2003. *Law and Power in the Islamic World*. London and New York: I. B. Tauris.

Index

Page numbers in italics denote illustrations.

Islah Jad is a lecturer on gender issues and politics in the Cultural Studies Department and the Women's Studies Institute of Birzeit University. She is a senior researcher on gender issues in the Arab region and Palestine, and a consultant for Palestinian ministries, international organizations, and NGOs. She is the author of numerous articles on Palestinian and Arab women's political participation and development, and a lead author of the United Nations Development Program's *Arab Human Development Report 2005: Towards the Rise of Women in the Arab World*. She is a founder and former director of the Women's Studies Institute at Birzeit University.